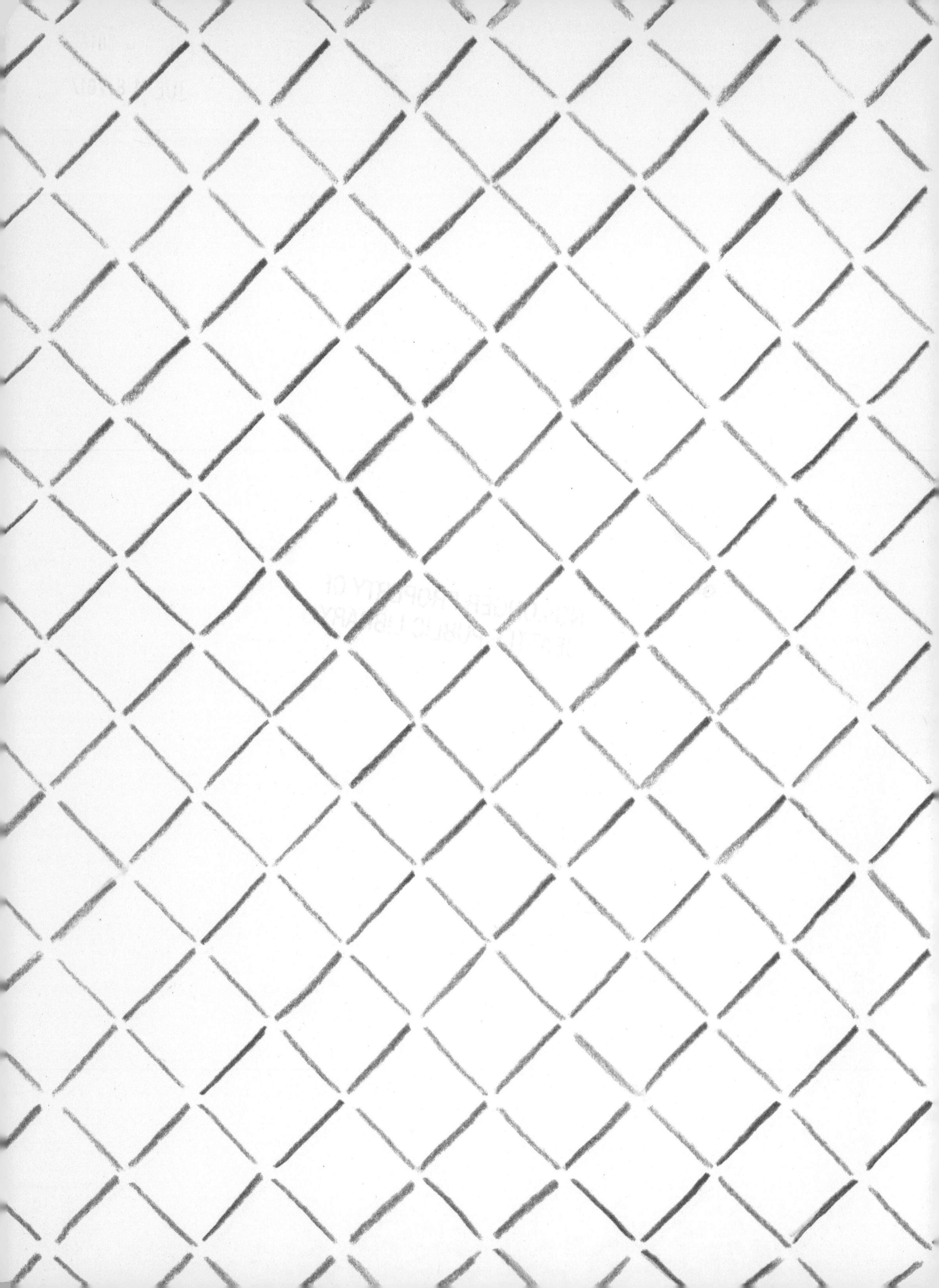

POMPEII

FRANK SANTORO

PICTVREBOX,INC

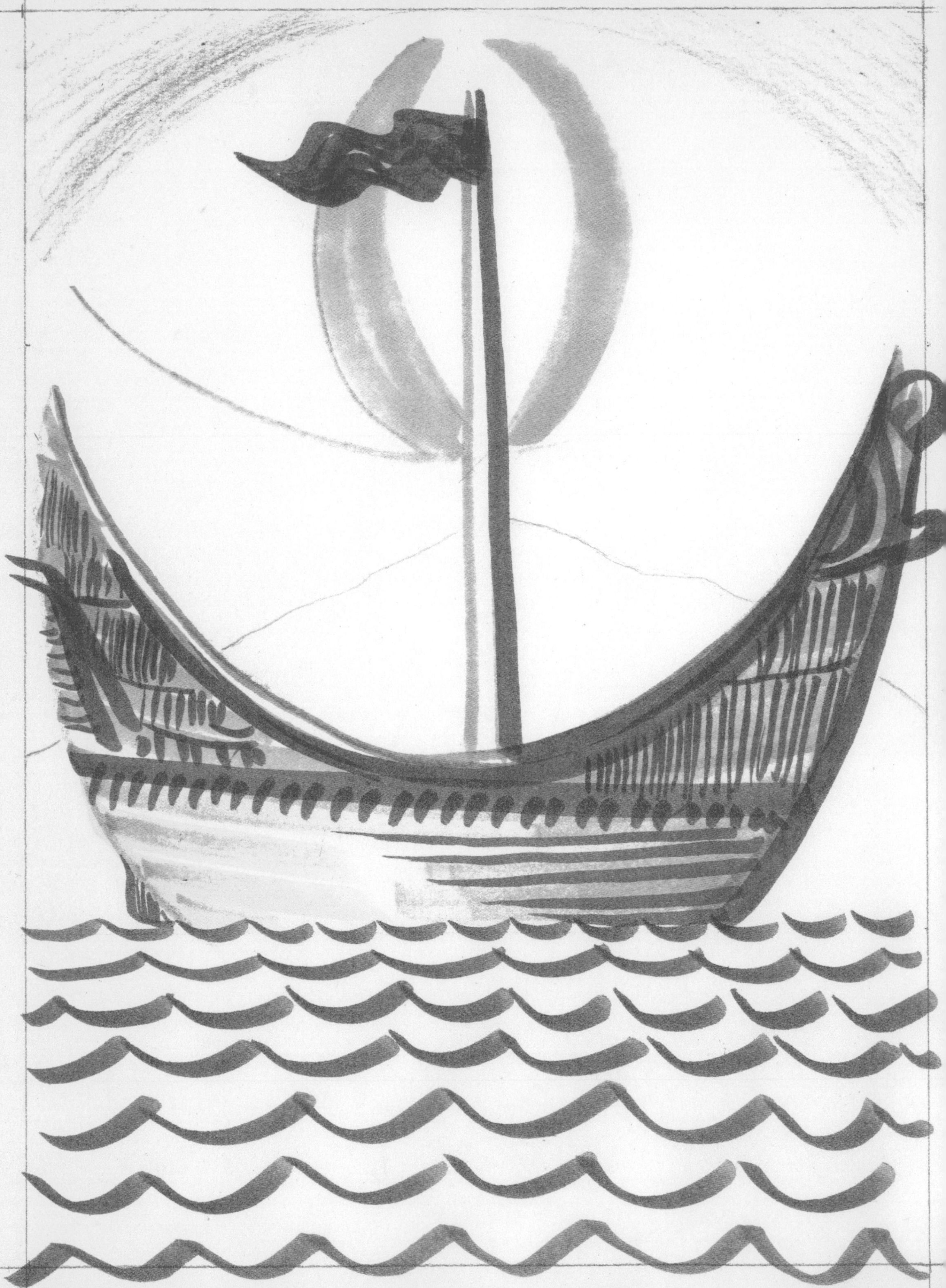

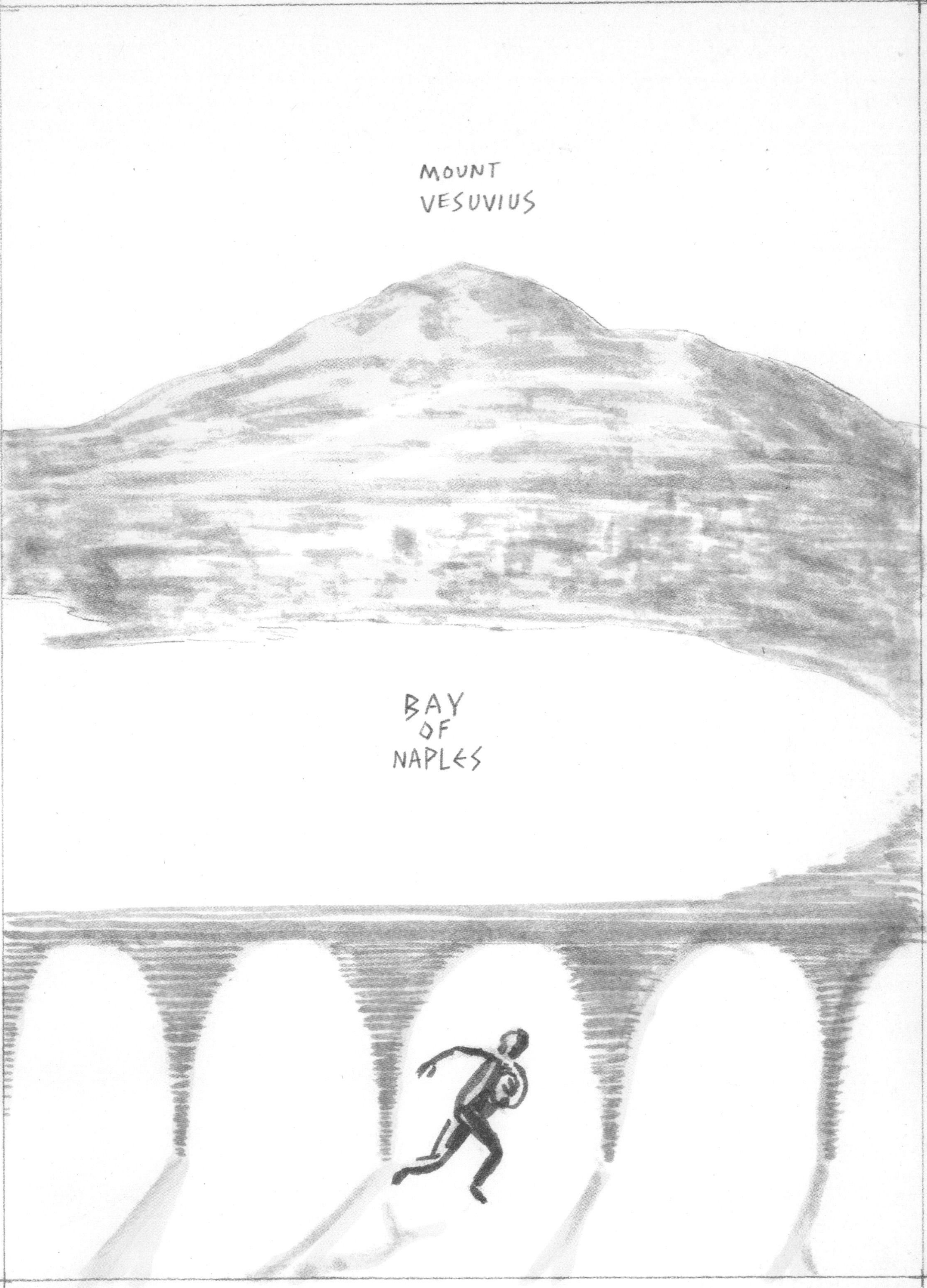
MOUNT
VESUVIUS
BAY
OF
NAPLES

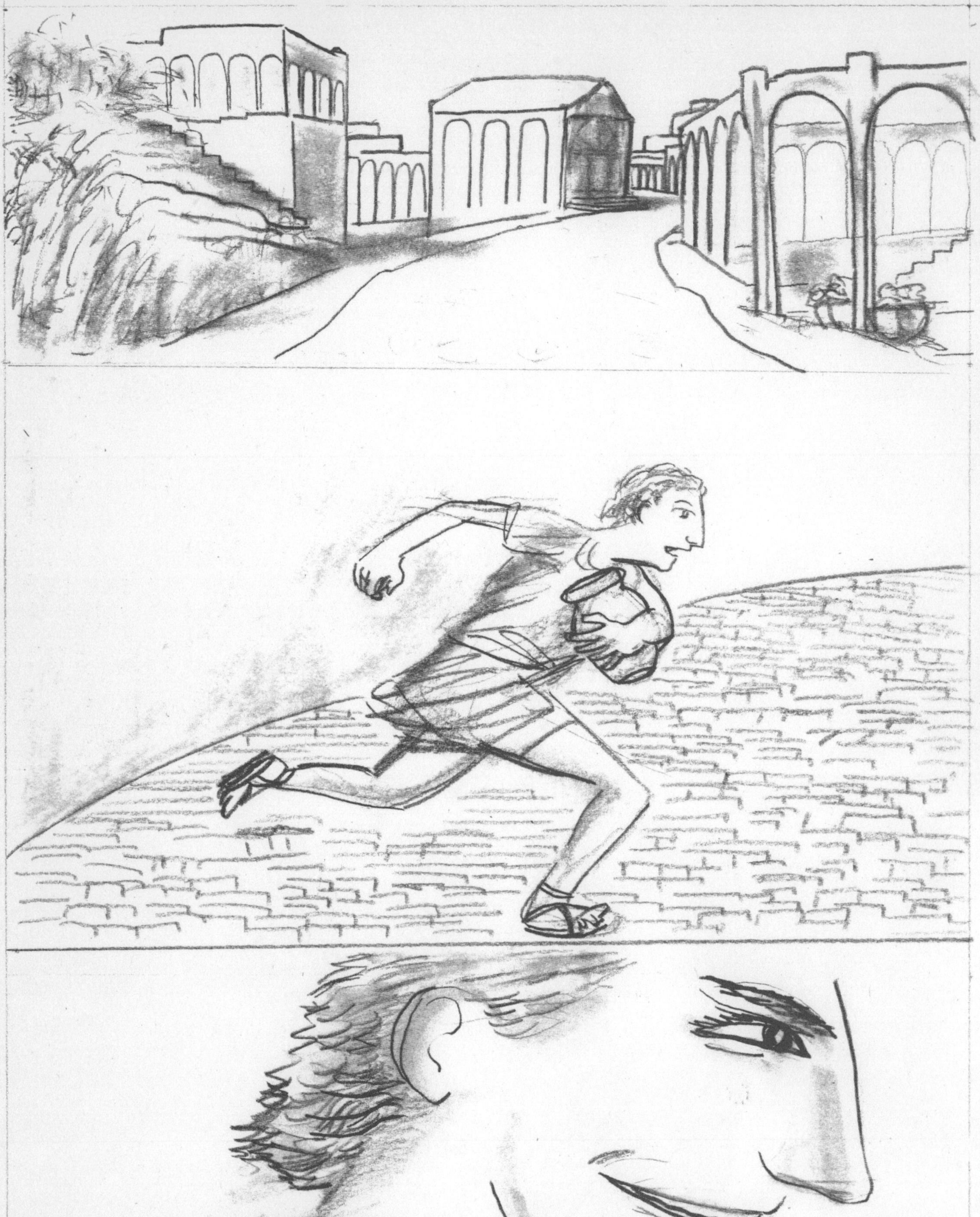

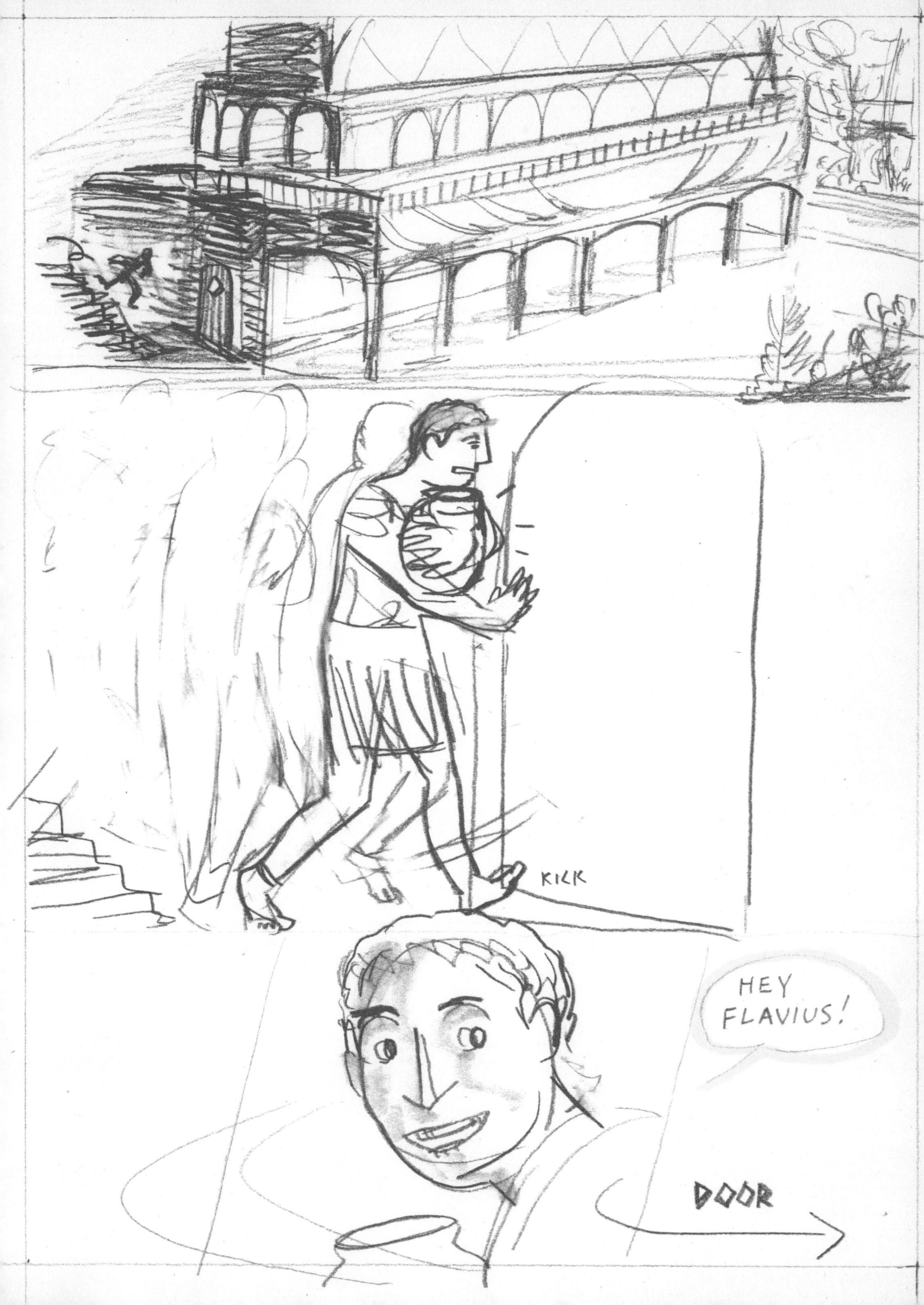
KICK
HEY FLAVIUS!
DOOR

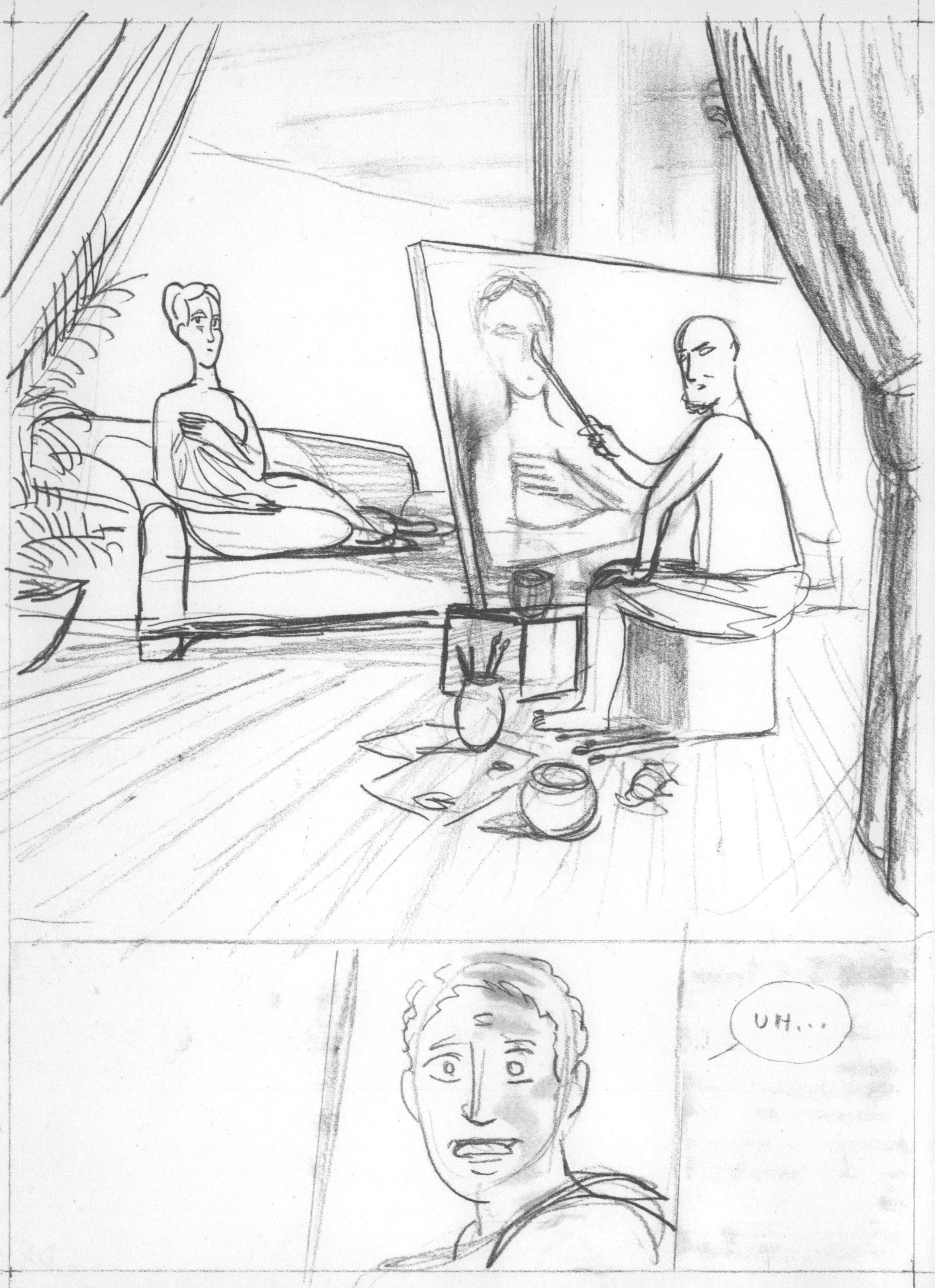
UH...

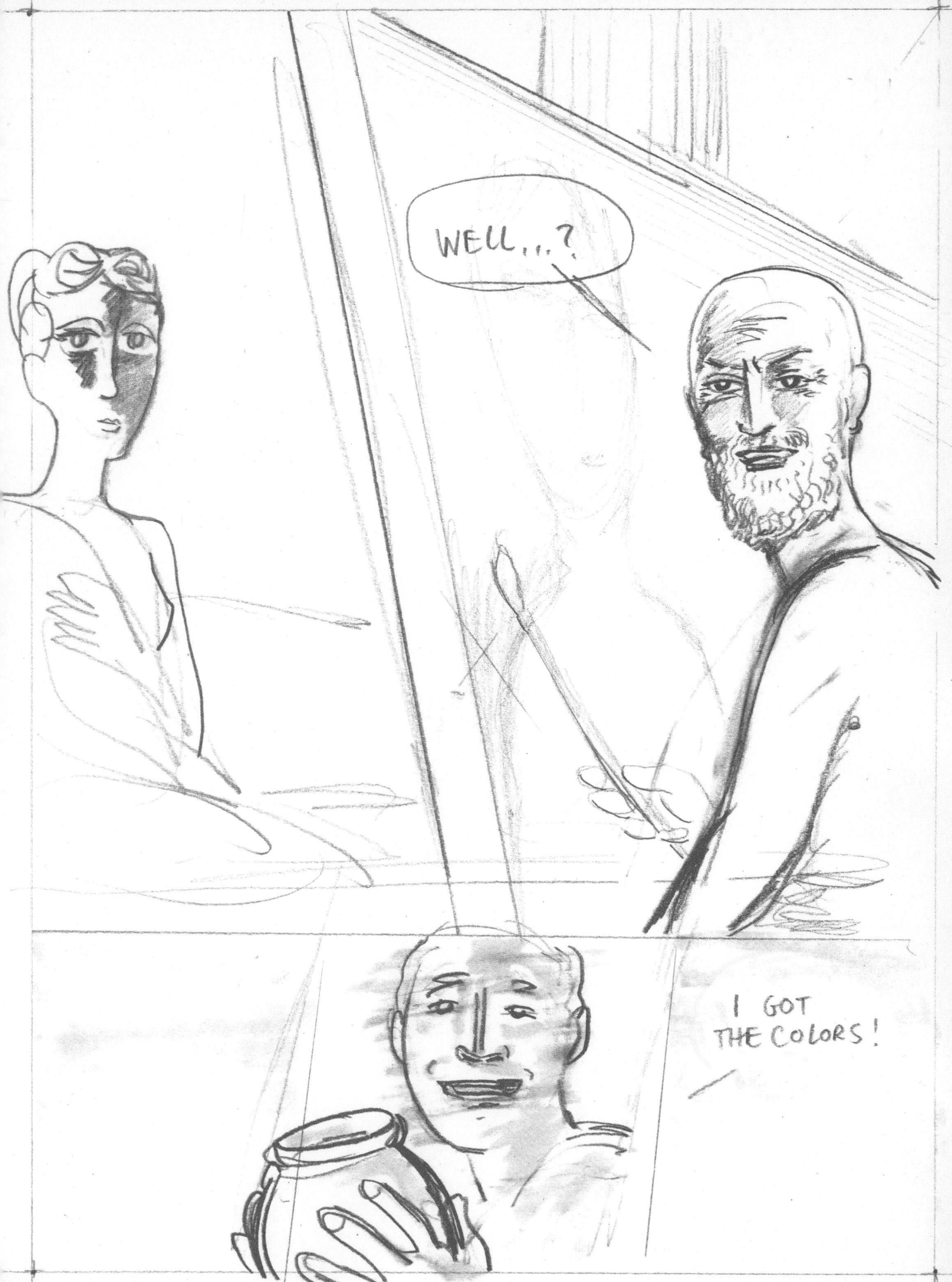
WELL...?
I GOT THE COLORS!

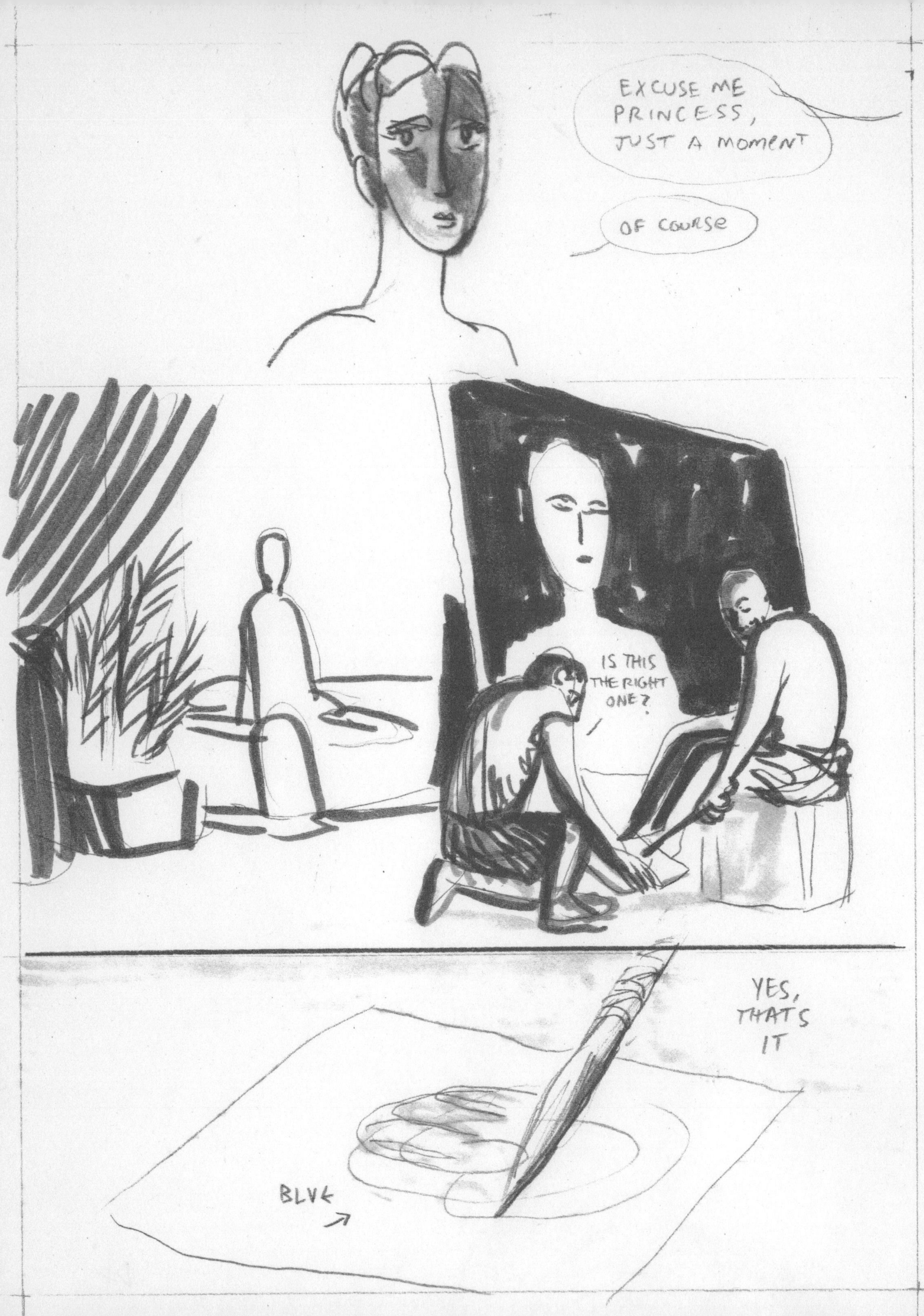
EXCUSE ME PRINCESS, JUST A MOMENT
OF COURSE
IS THIS THE RIGHT ONE?
YES, THATS IT
BLUE

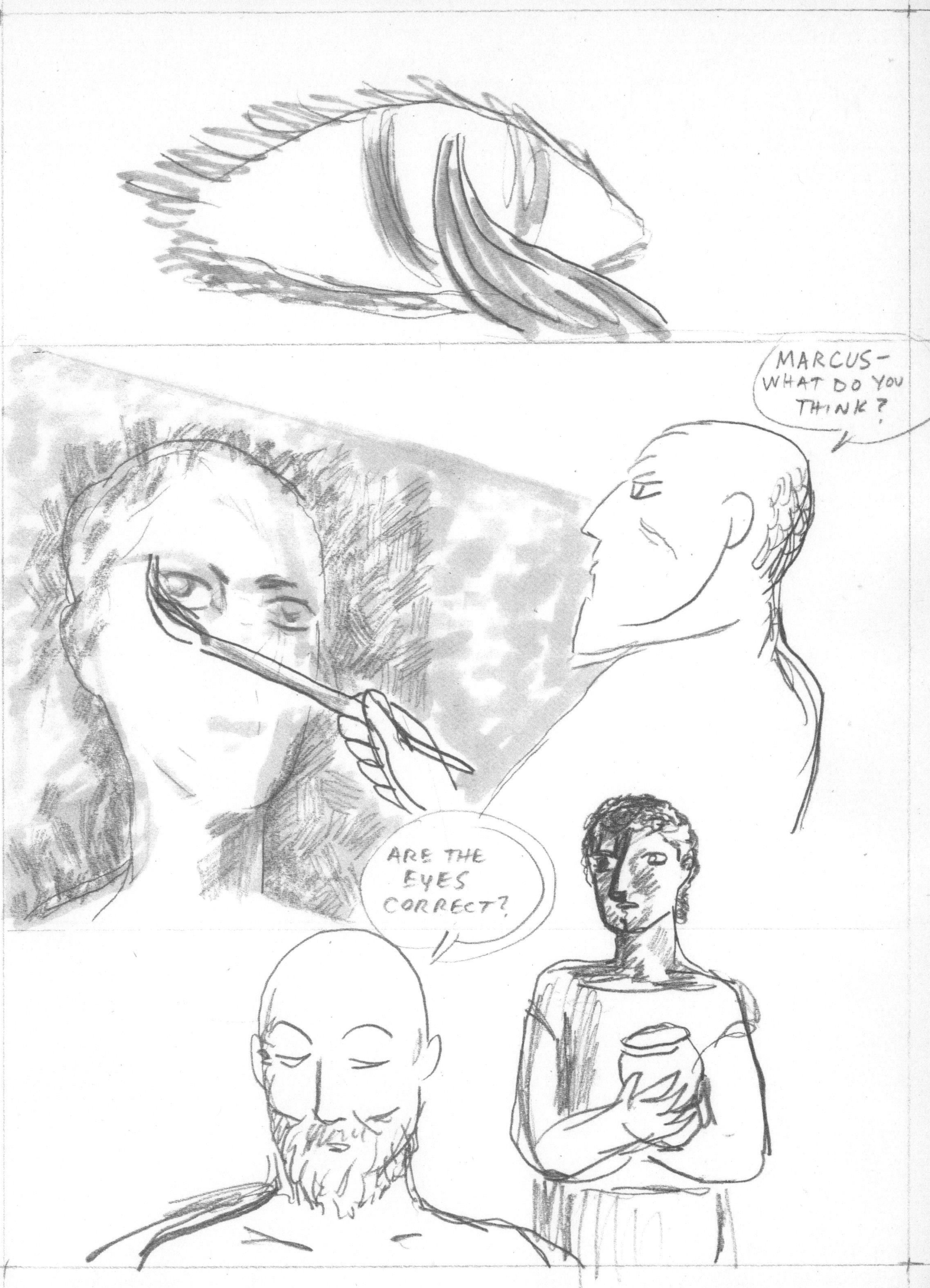
MARCUS-
WHAT DO YOU
THINK?
ARE THE
EYES
CORRECT?

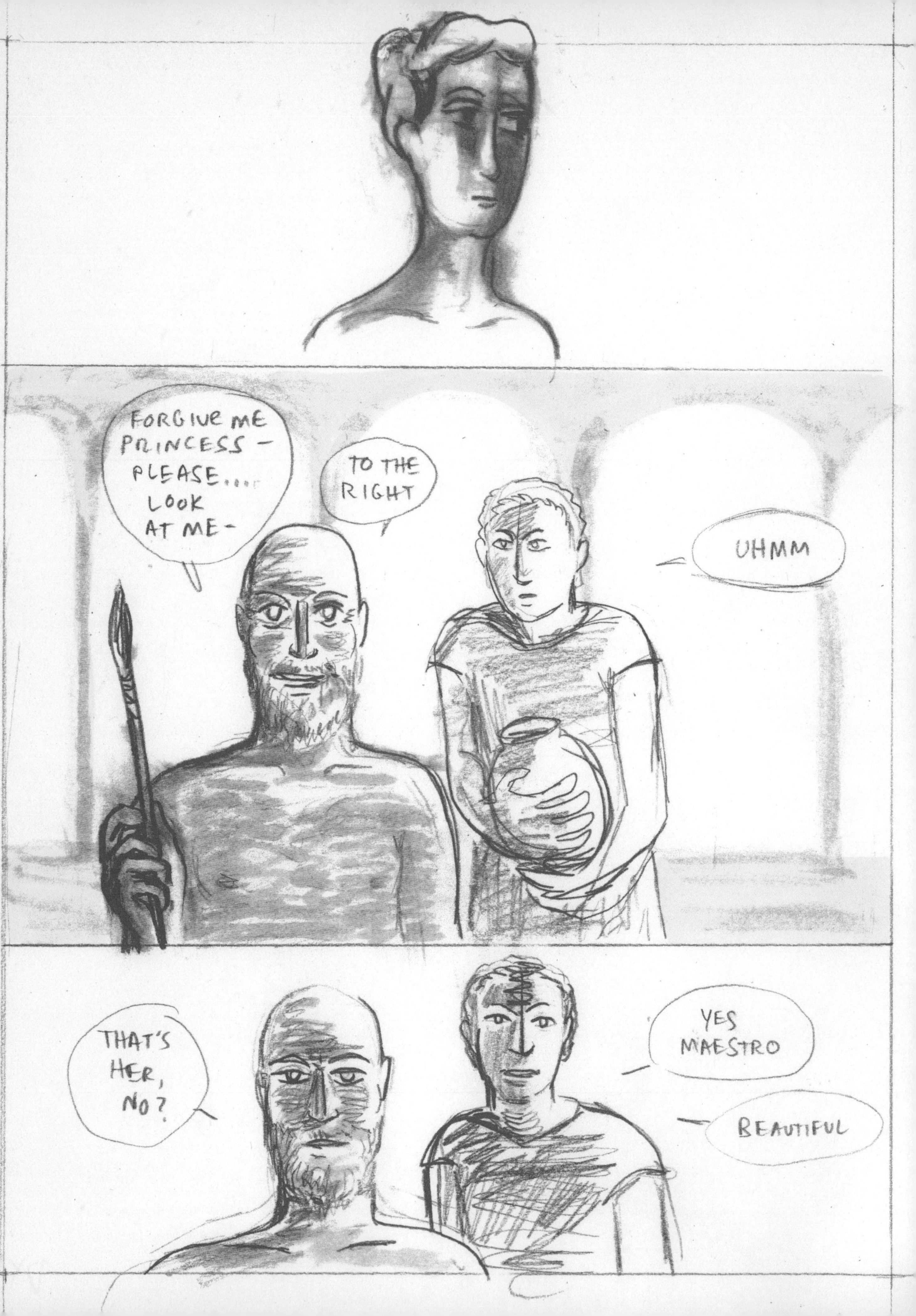
FORGIVE ME PRINCESS - PLEASE.... LOOK AT ME -
TO THE RIGHT
UHMM
THAT'S HER, NO?
YES MAESTRO
BEAUTIFUL

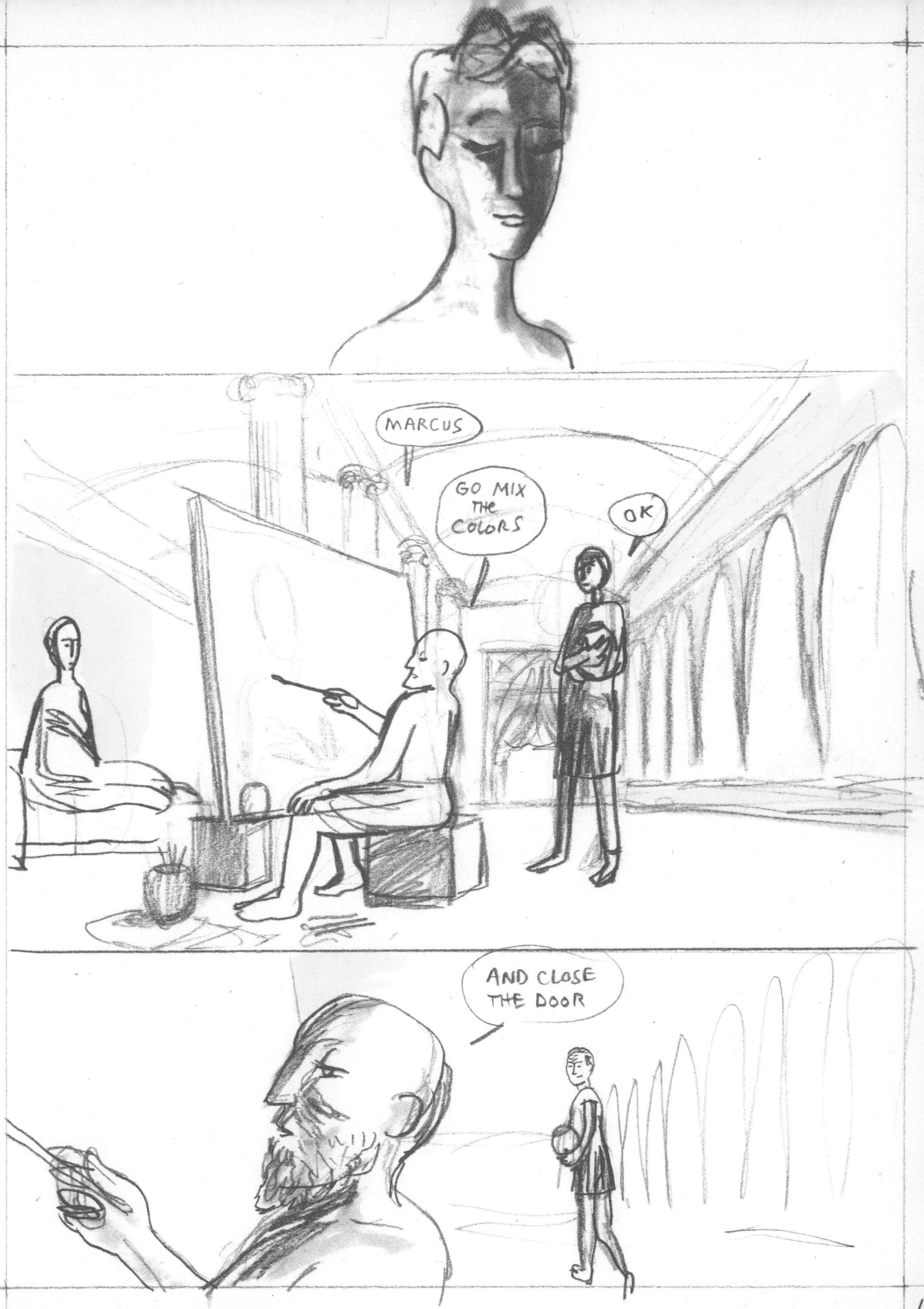
MARCUS
GO MIX THE COLORS
OK
AND CLOSE THE DOOR

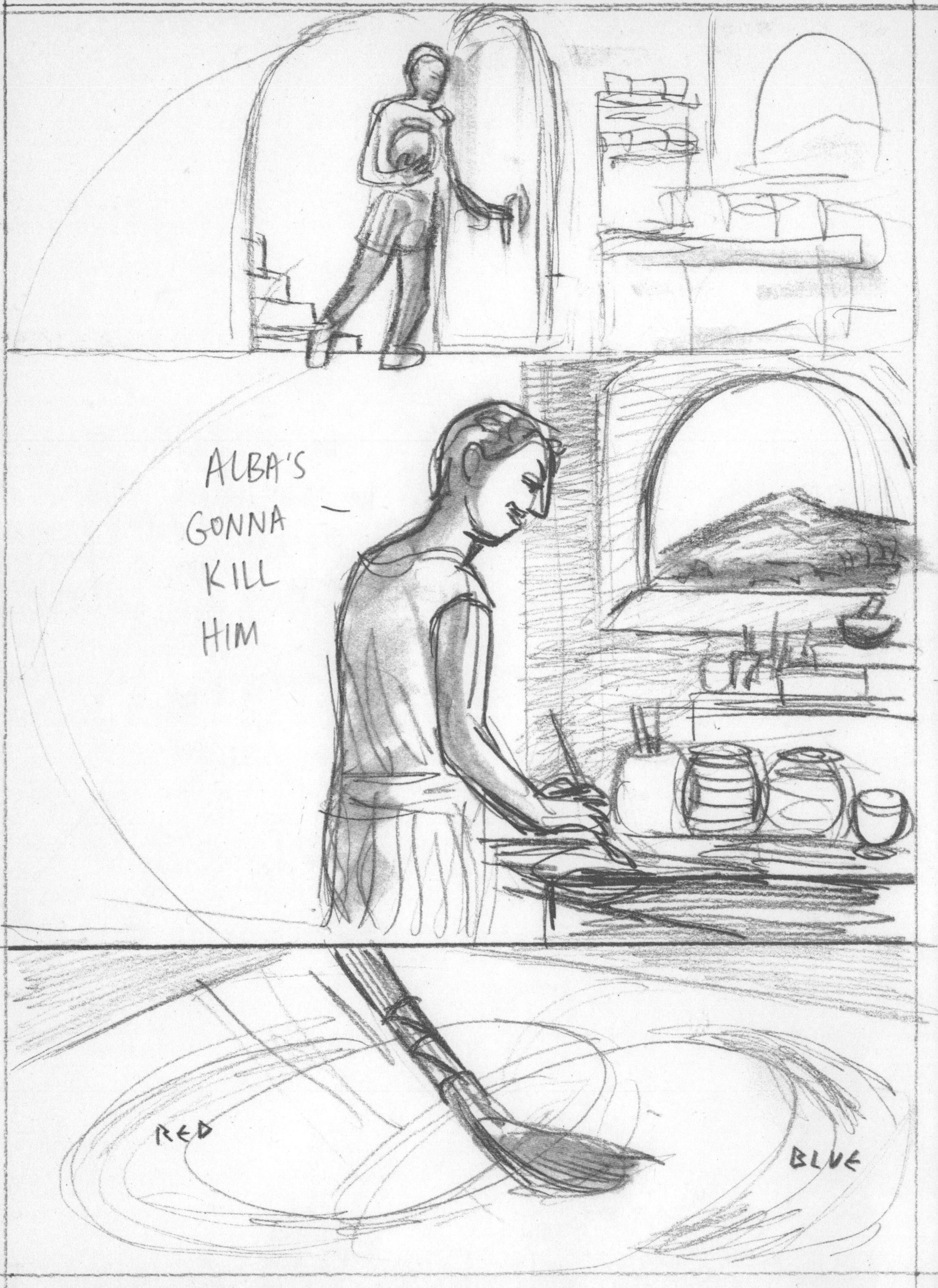
ALBA'S GONNA KILL HIM —
RED
BLUE

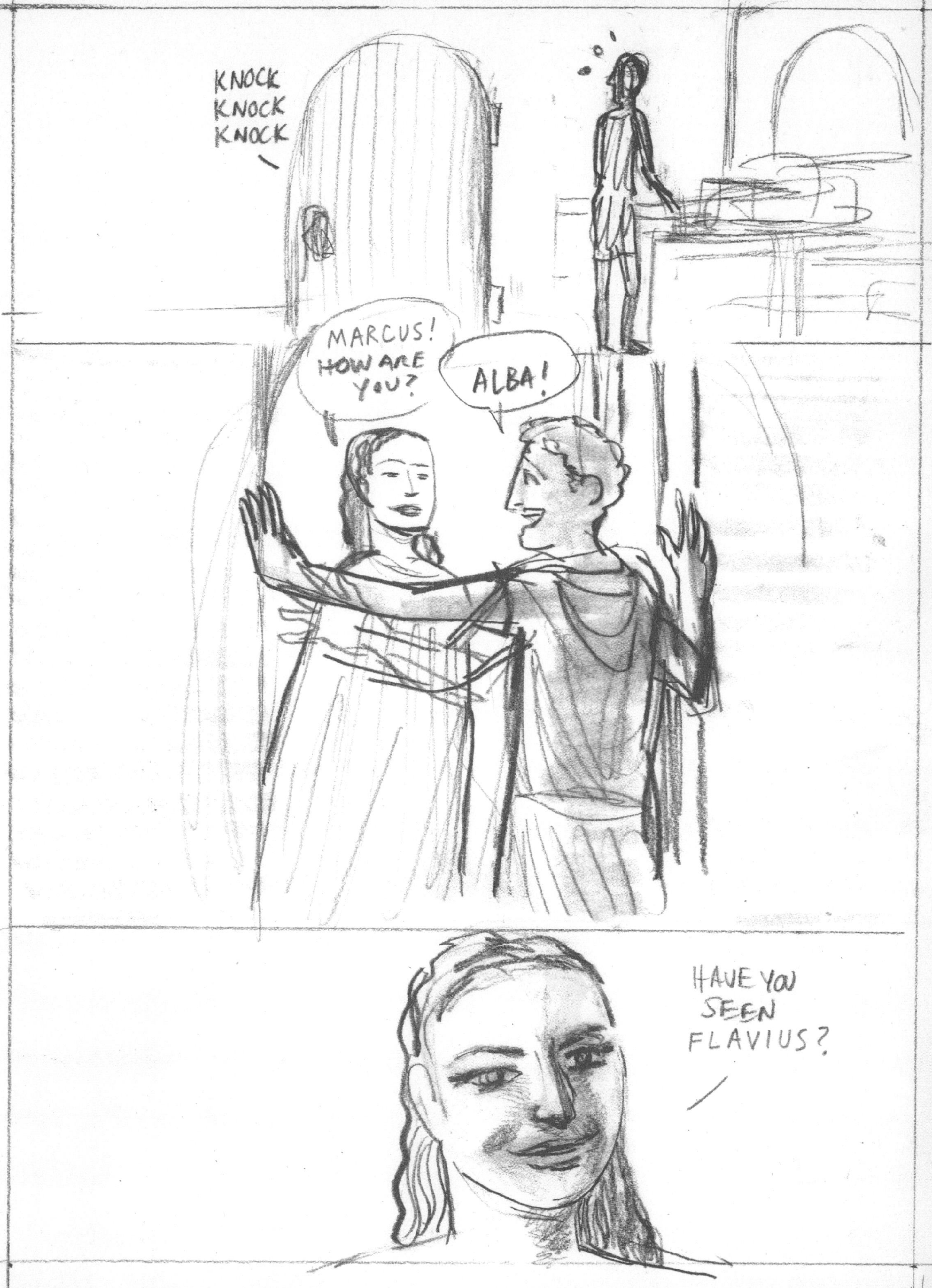
KNOCK
KNOCK
KNOCK
MARCUS! HOW ARE YOU?
ALBA!
HAVE YOU SEEN FLAVIUS?

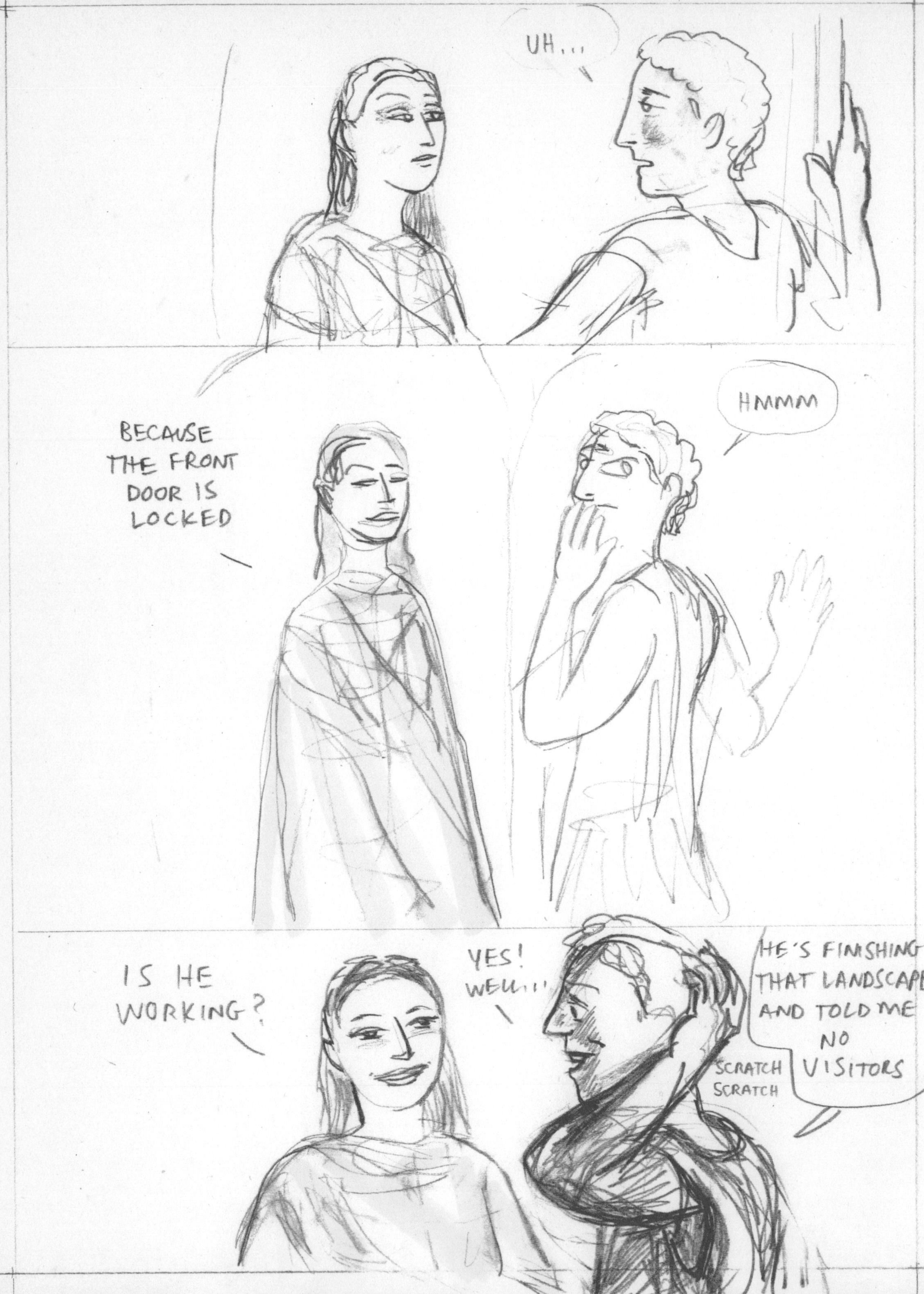
UH...
BECAUSE THE FRONT DOOR IS LOCKED
HMMM
IS HE WORKING?
YES! WELL...
HE'S FINISHING THAT LANDSCAPE AND TOLD ME NO VISITORS
SCRATCH SCRATCH

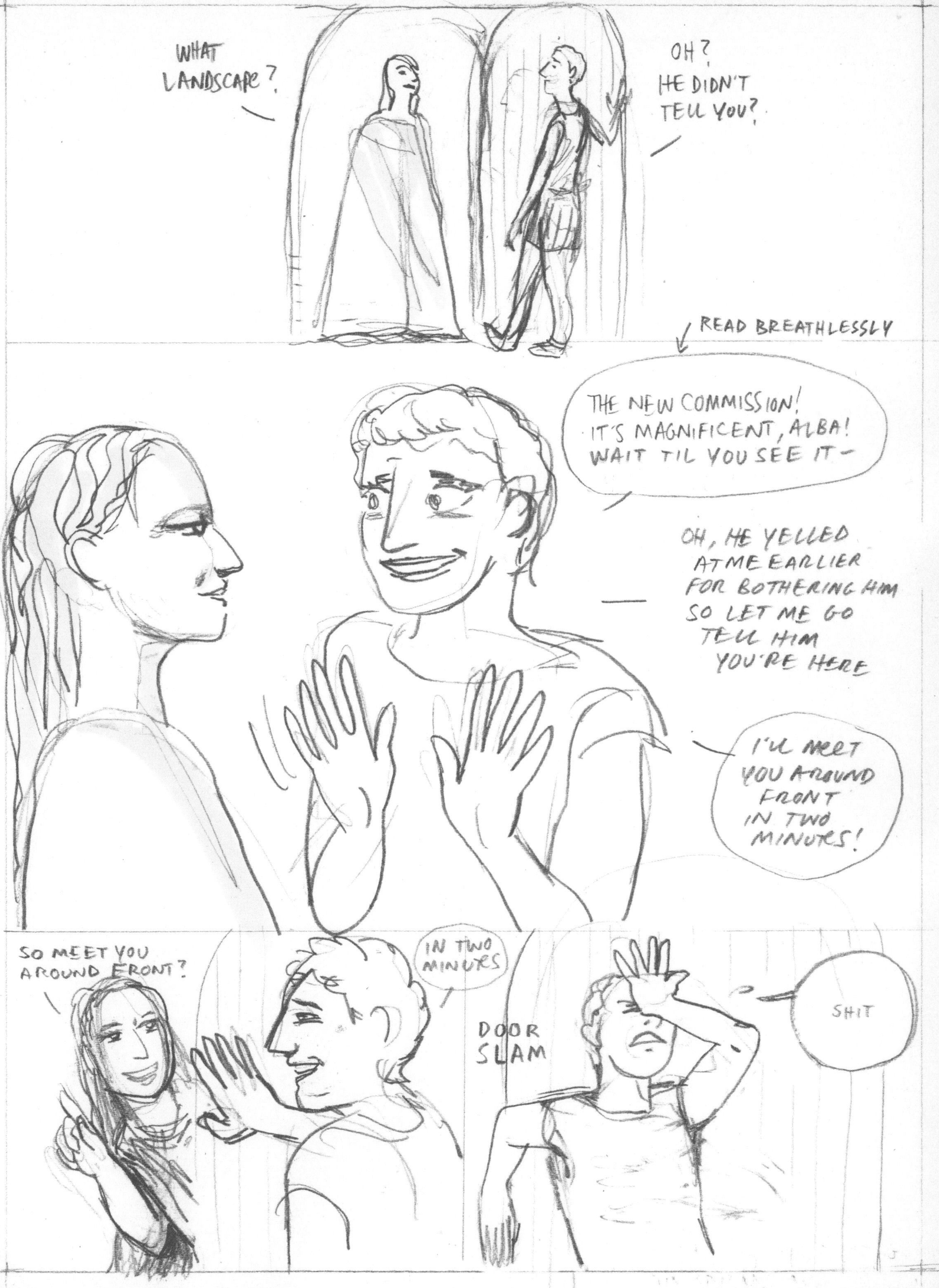
WHAT LANDSCAPE?
OH? HE DIDN'T TELL YOU?
READ BREATHLESSLY
THE NEW COMMISSION! IT'S MAGNIFICENT, ALBA! WAIT TIL YOU SEE IT-
OH, HE YELLED AT ME EARLIER FOR BOTHERING HIM SO LET ME GO TELL HIM YOU'RE HERE
I'LL MEET YOU AROUND FRONT IN TWO MINUTES!
SO MEET YOU AROUND FRONT?
IN TWO MINUTES
DOOR SLAM
SHIT

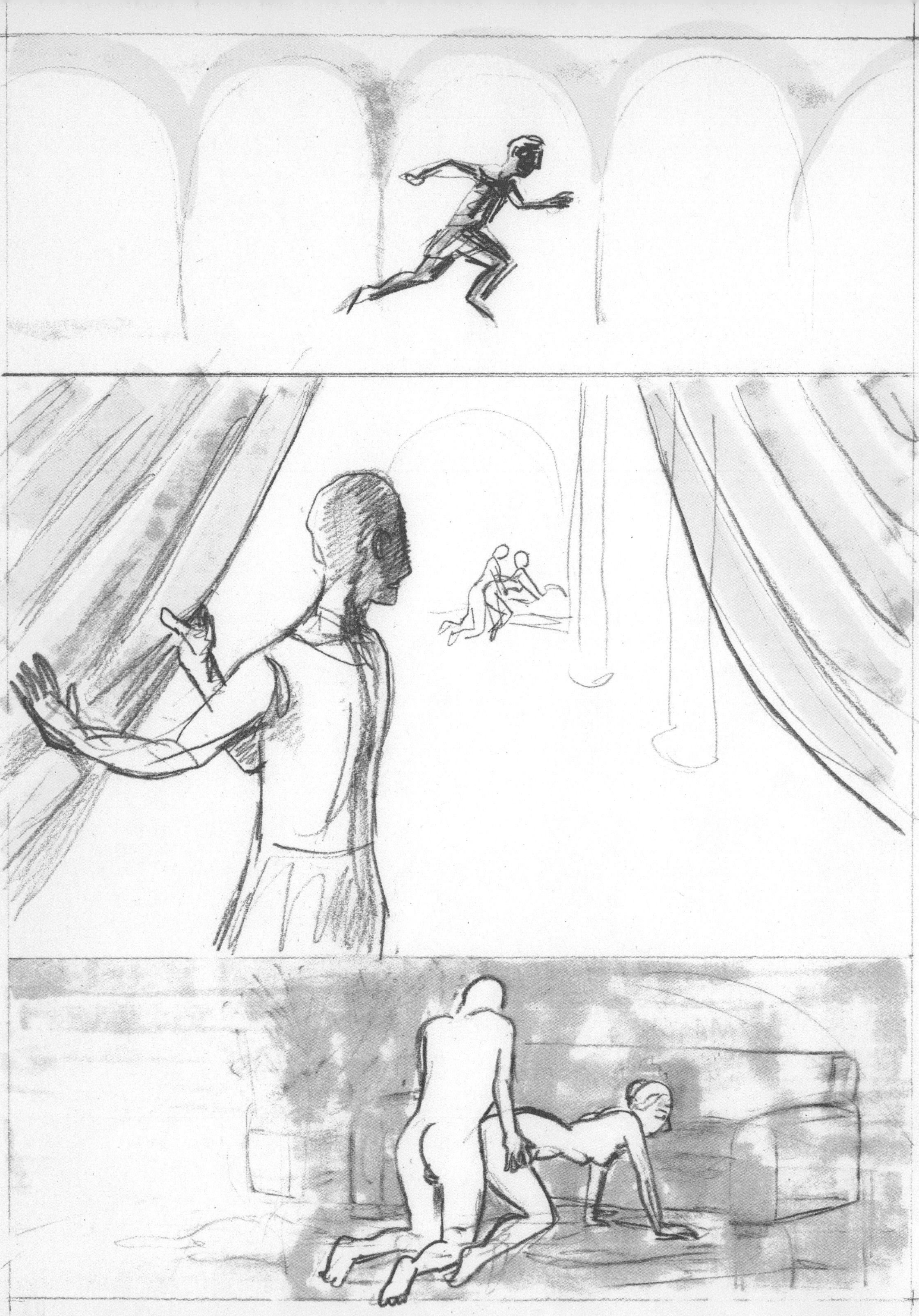

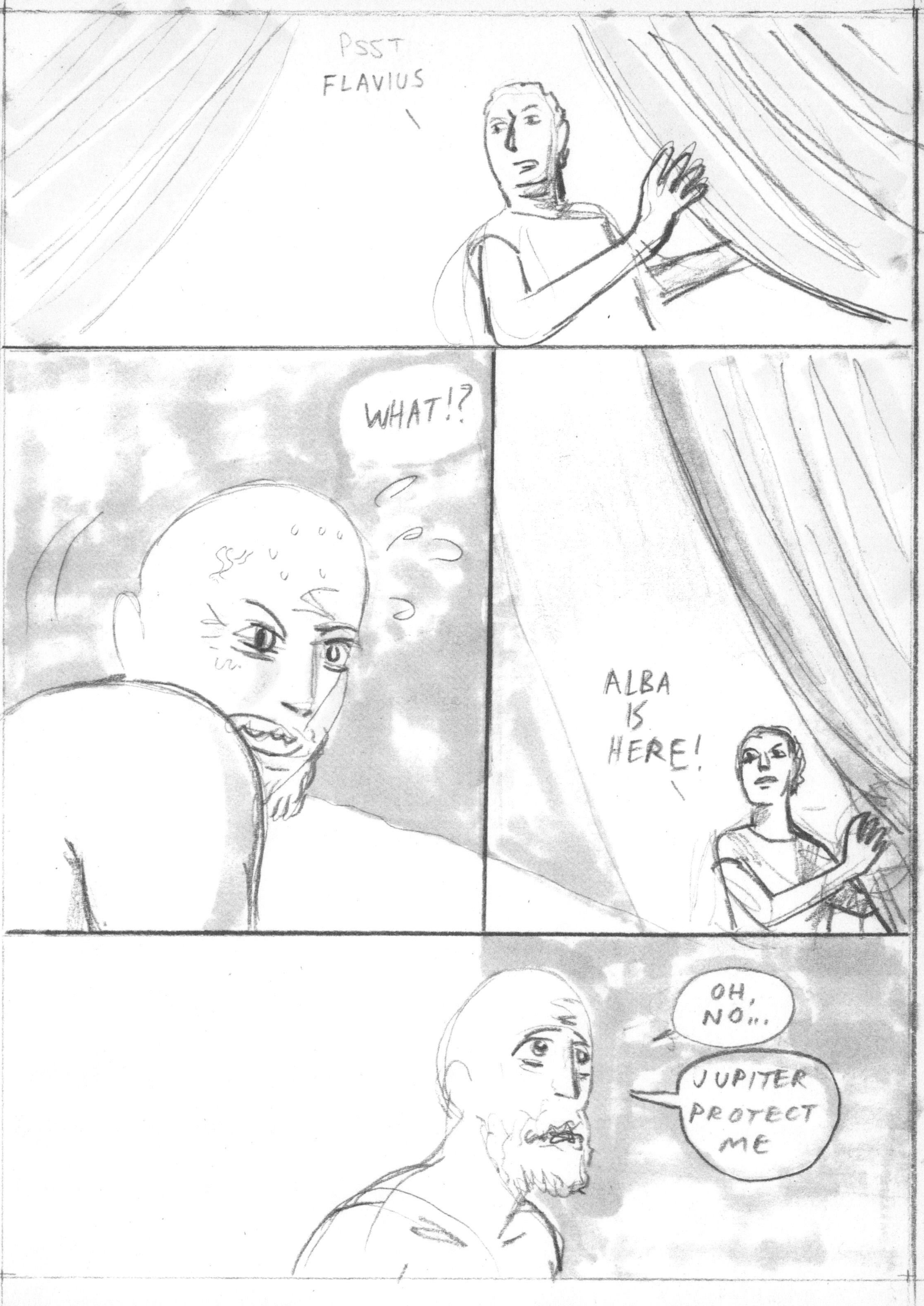
PSST
FLAVIUS
WHAT!?
ALBA IS HERE!
OH, NO...
JUPITER PROTECT ME

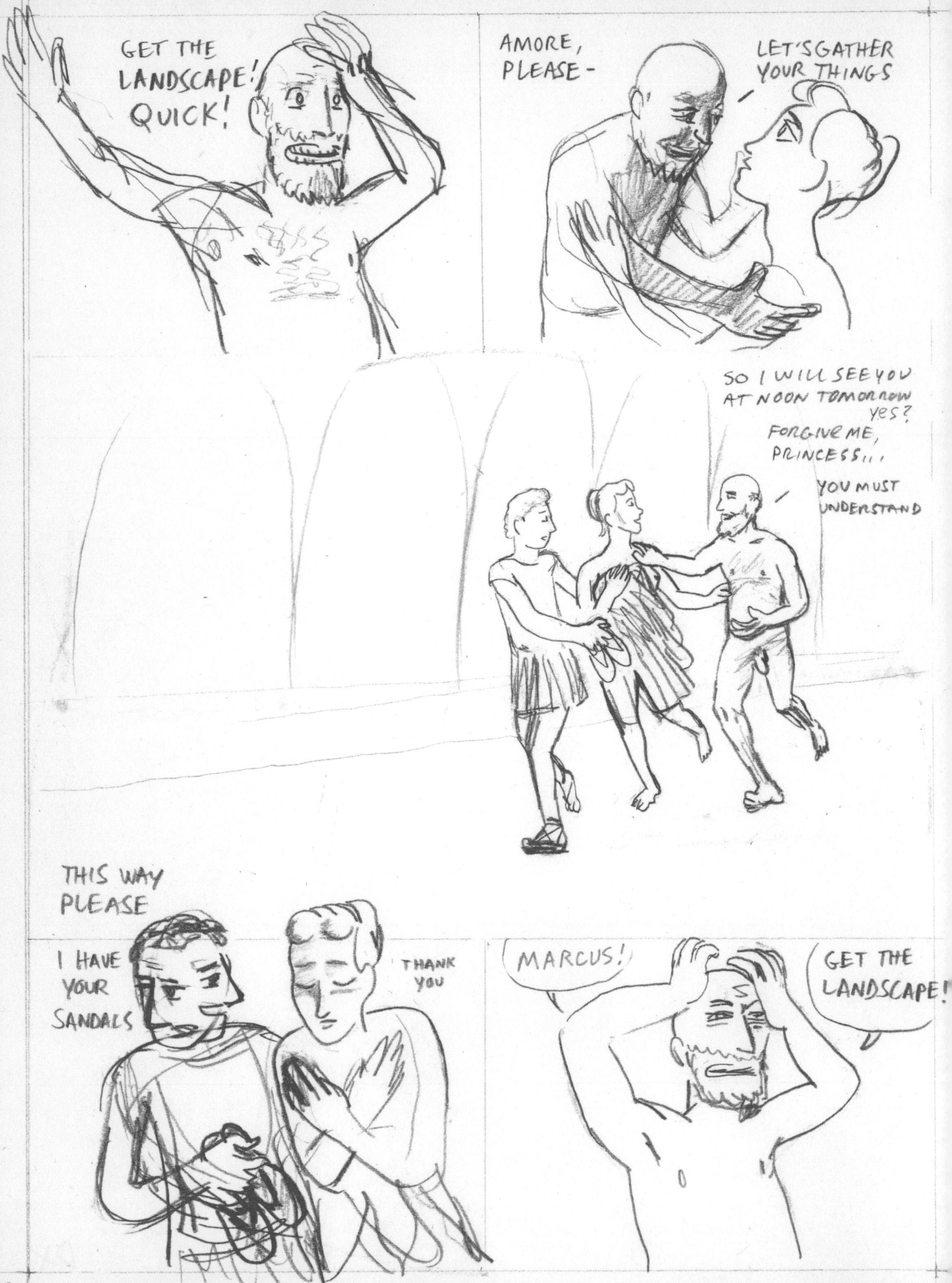

GET THE LANDSCAPE! QUICK!
AMORE, PLEASE -
LET'S GATHER YOUR THINGS
SO I WILL SEE YOU AT NOON TOMORROW YES?
FORGIVE ME, PRINCESS...
YOU MUST UNDERSTAND
THIS WAY PLEASE
I HAVE YOUR SANDALS
THANK YOU
MARCUS!
GET THE LANDSCAPE!

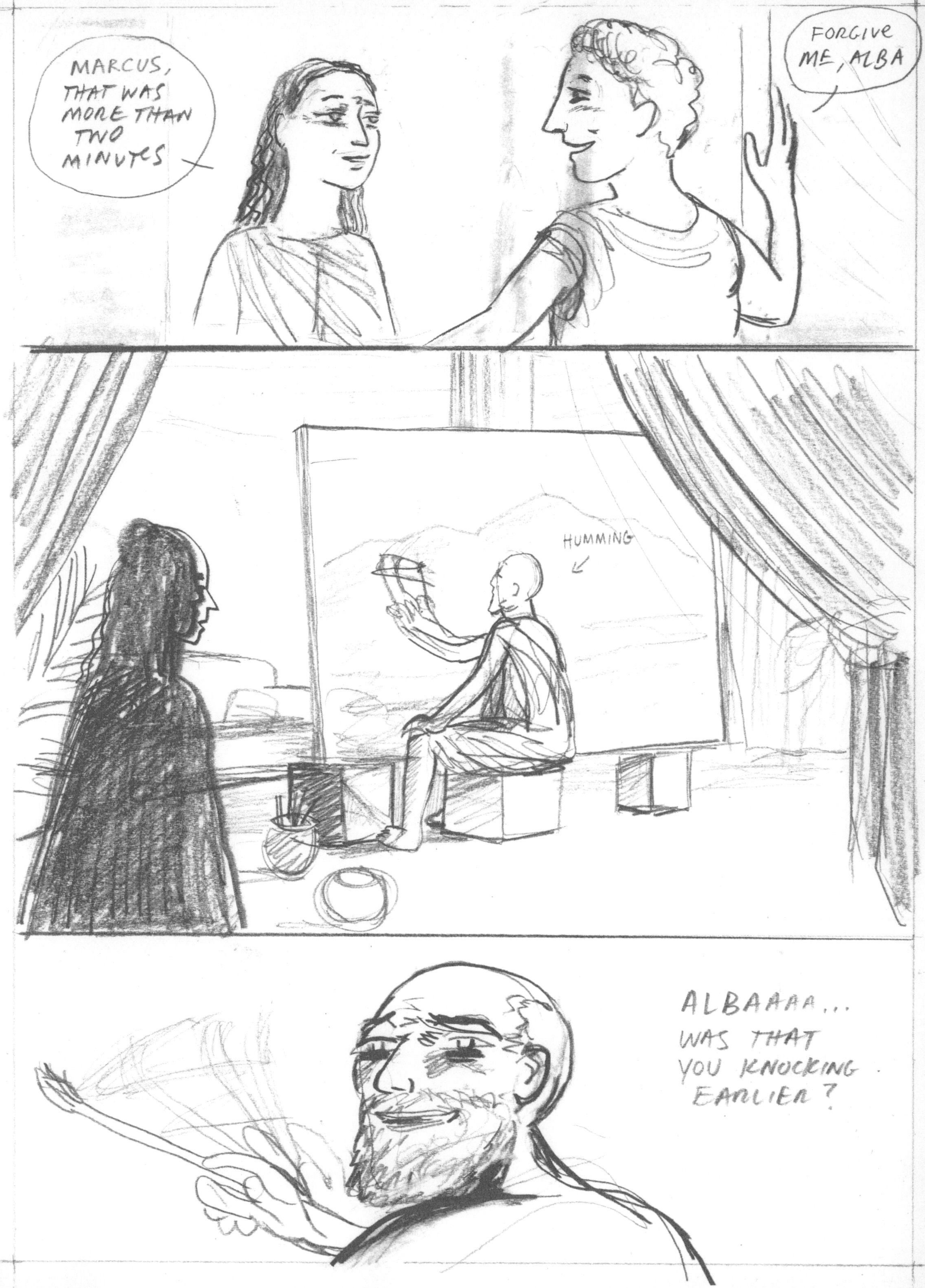
MARCUS, THAT WAS MORE THAN TWO MINUTES
FORGIVE ME, ALBA
HUMMING
ALBAAAA... WAS THAT YOU KNOCKING EARLIER?

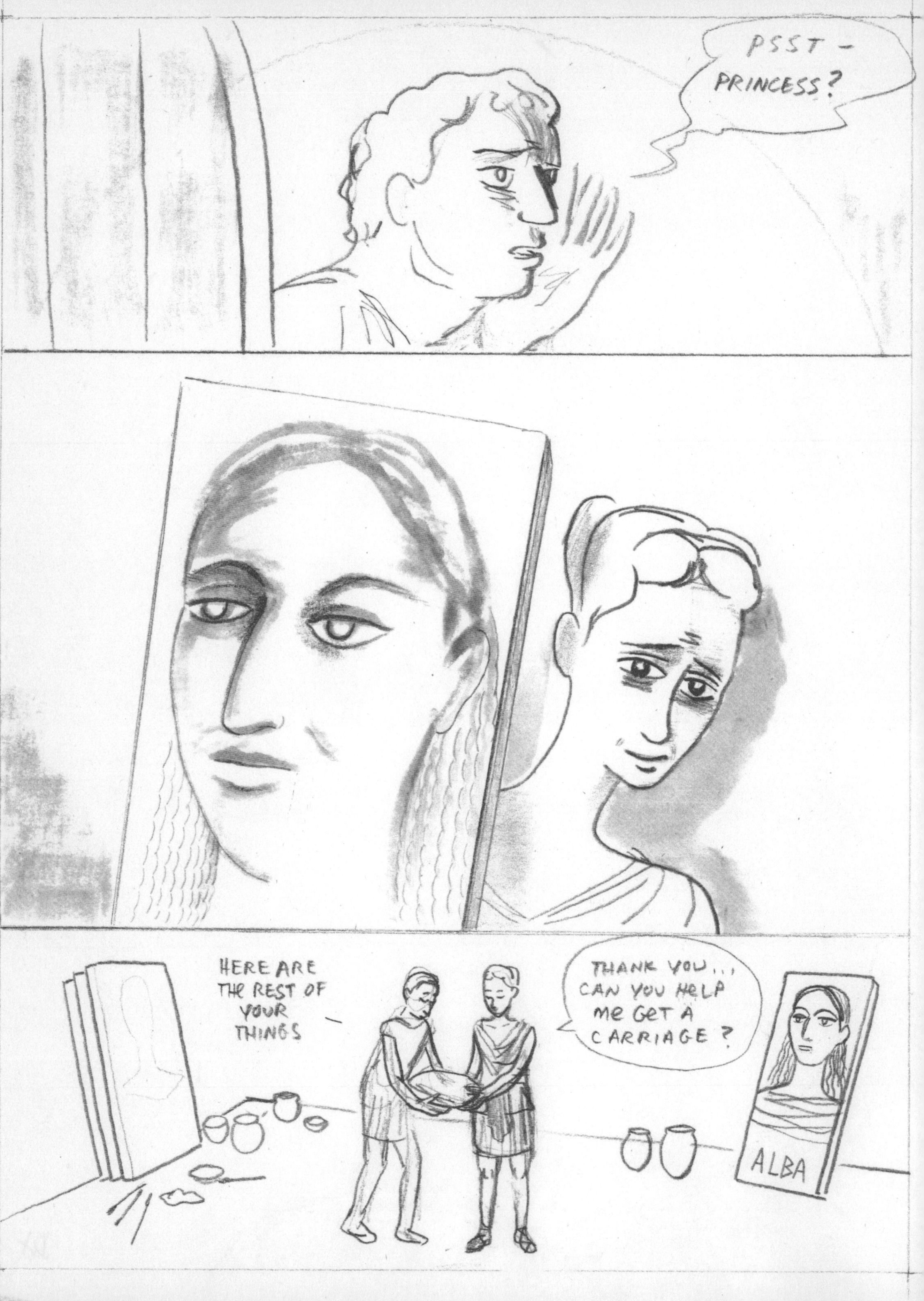
PSST - PRINCESS?
HERE ARE THE REST OF YOUR THINGS
THANK YOU... CAN YOU HELP ME GET A CARRIAGE?
ALBA

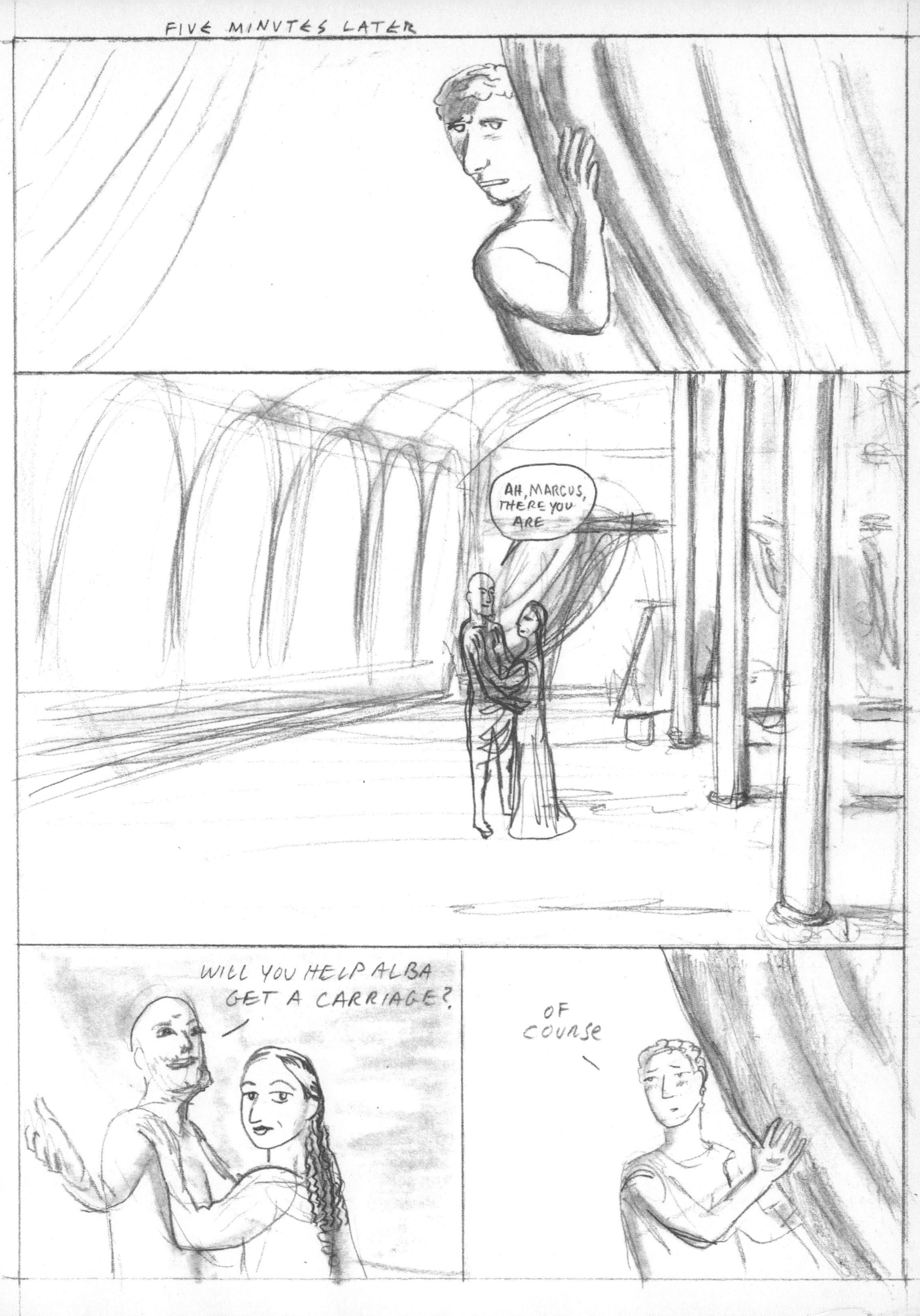
FIVE MINUTES LATER
AH, MARCUS, THERE YOU ARE
WILL YOU HELP ALBA GET A CARRIAGE?
OF COURSE

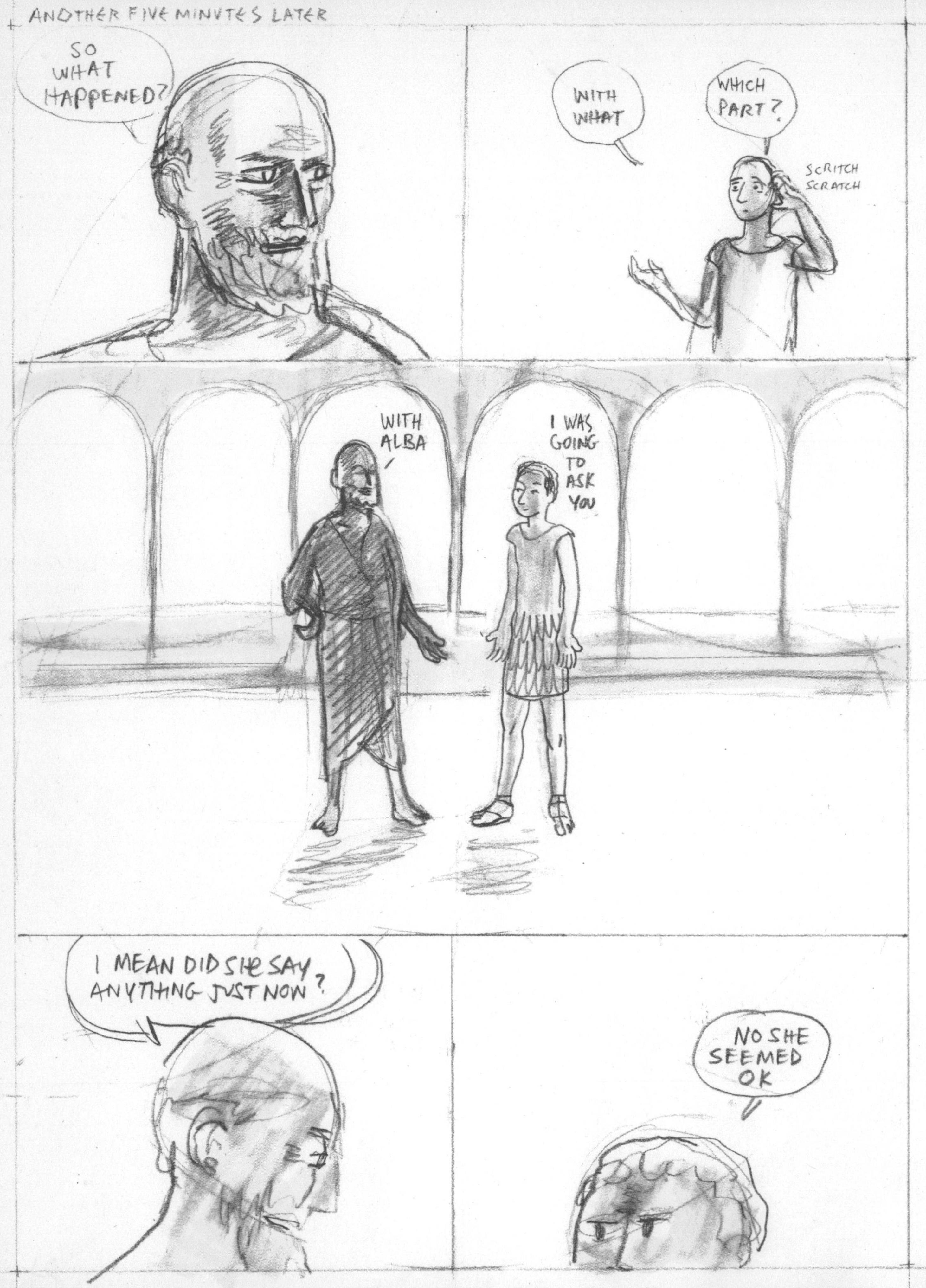
ANOTHER FIVE MINUTES LATER
SO WHAT HAPPENED?
WITH WHAT
WHICH PART?
SCRITCH SCRATCH
WITH ALBA
I WAS GOING TO ASK YOU
I MEAN DID SHE SAY ANYTHING JUST NOW?
NO SHE SEEMED OK

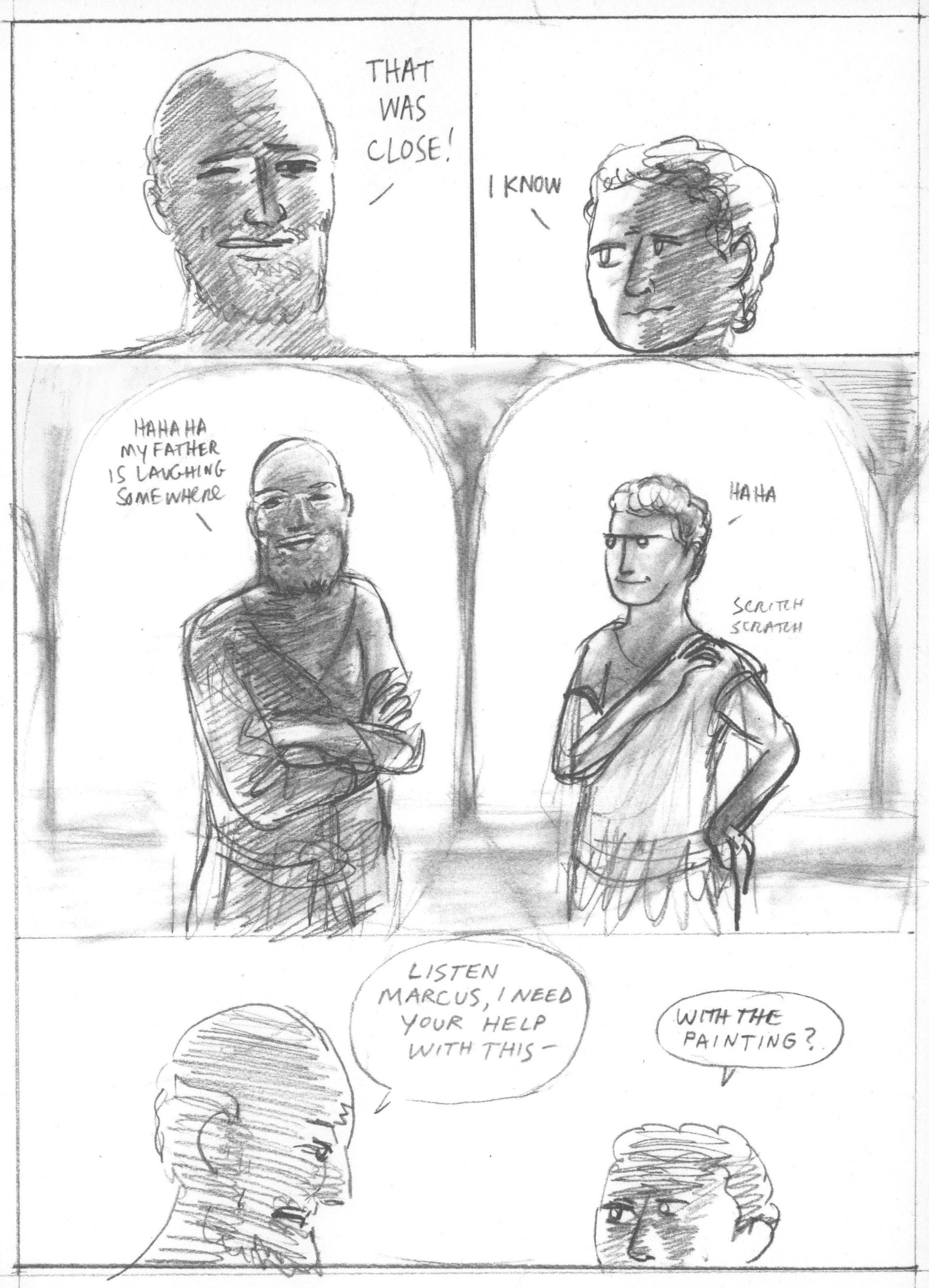
THAT WAS CLOSE!
I KNOW
HAHAHA MY FATHER IS LAUGHING SOMEWHERE
HAHA
SCRITCH SCRATCH
LISTEN MARCUS, I NEED YOUR HELP WITH THIS-
WITH THE PAINTING?

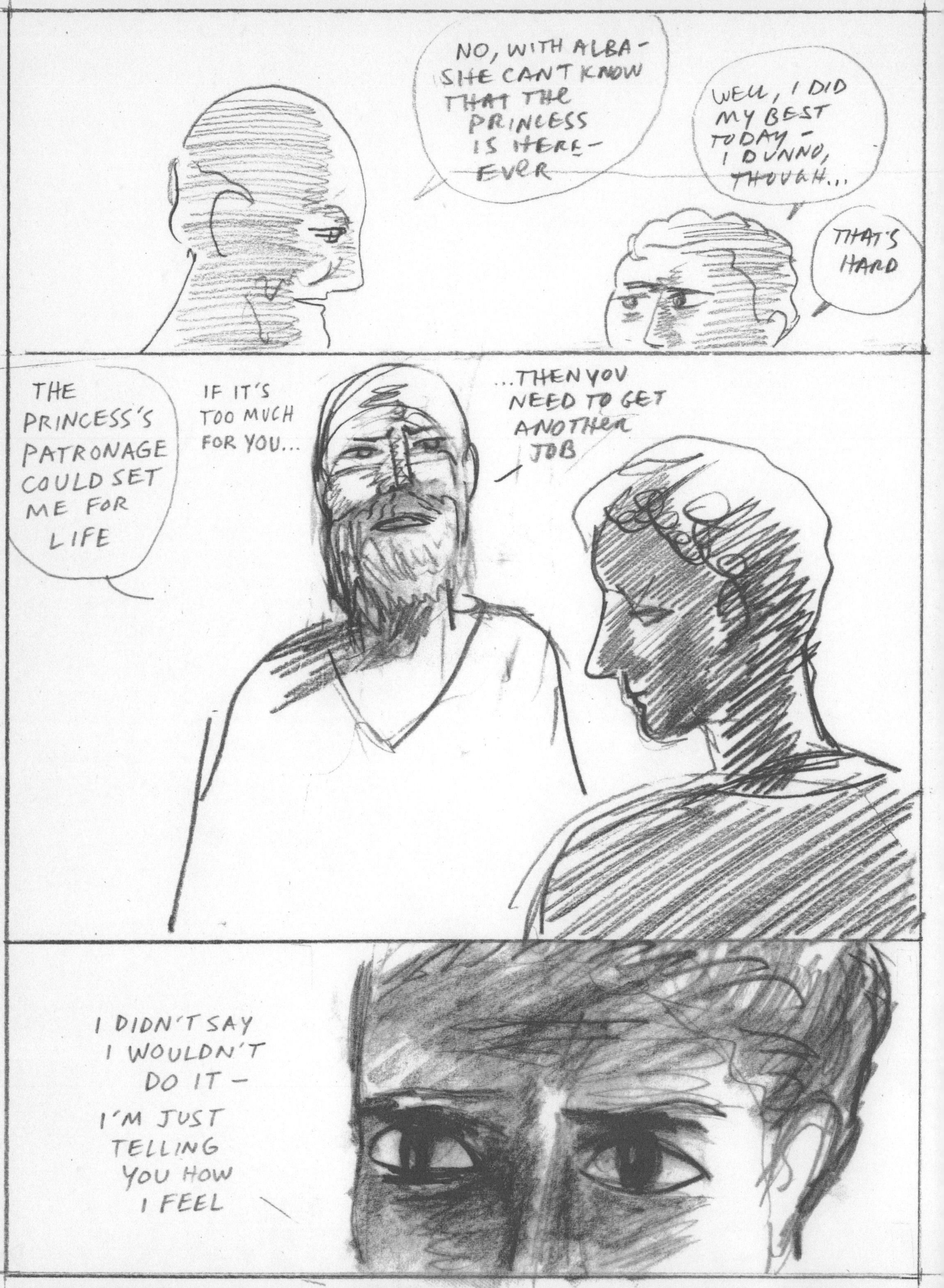
NO, WITH ALBA-SHE CAN'T KNOW THAT THE PRINCESS IS HERE-EVER
WELL, I DID MY BEST TODAY-I DUNNO, THOUGH...
THAT'S HARD
THE PRINCESS'S PATRONAGE COULD SET ME FOR LIFE
IF IT'S TOO MUCH FOR YOU...
...THEN YOU NEED TO GET ANOTHER JOB
I DIDN'T SAY I WOULDN'T DO IT -
I'M JUST TELLING YOU HOW I FEEL

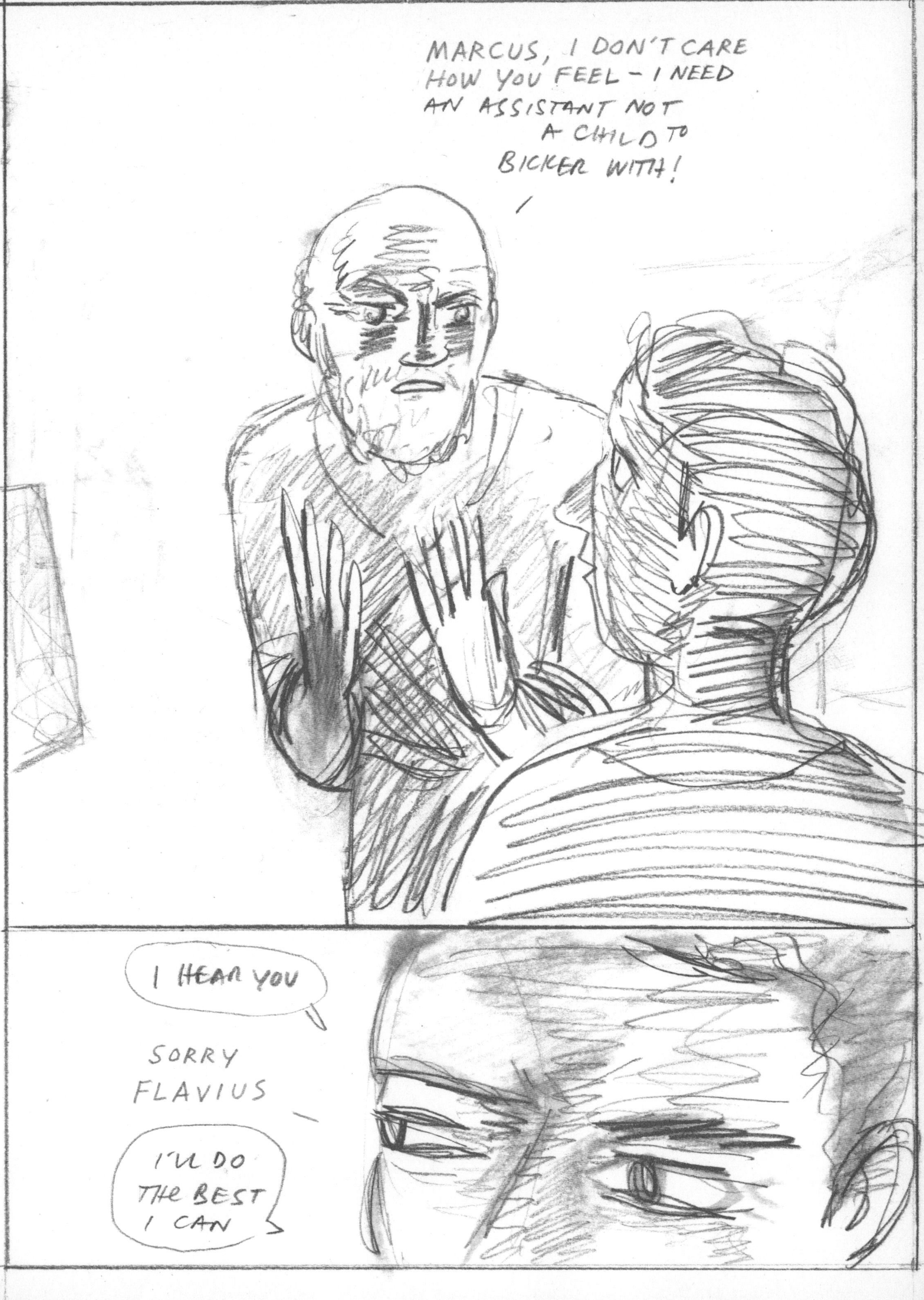
MARCUS, I DON'T CARE HOW YOU FEEL - I NEED AN ASSISTANT NOT A CHILD TO BICKER WITH!
I HEAR YOU
SORRY FLAVIUS
I'LL DO THE BEST I CAN

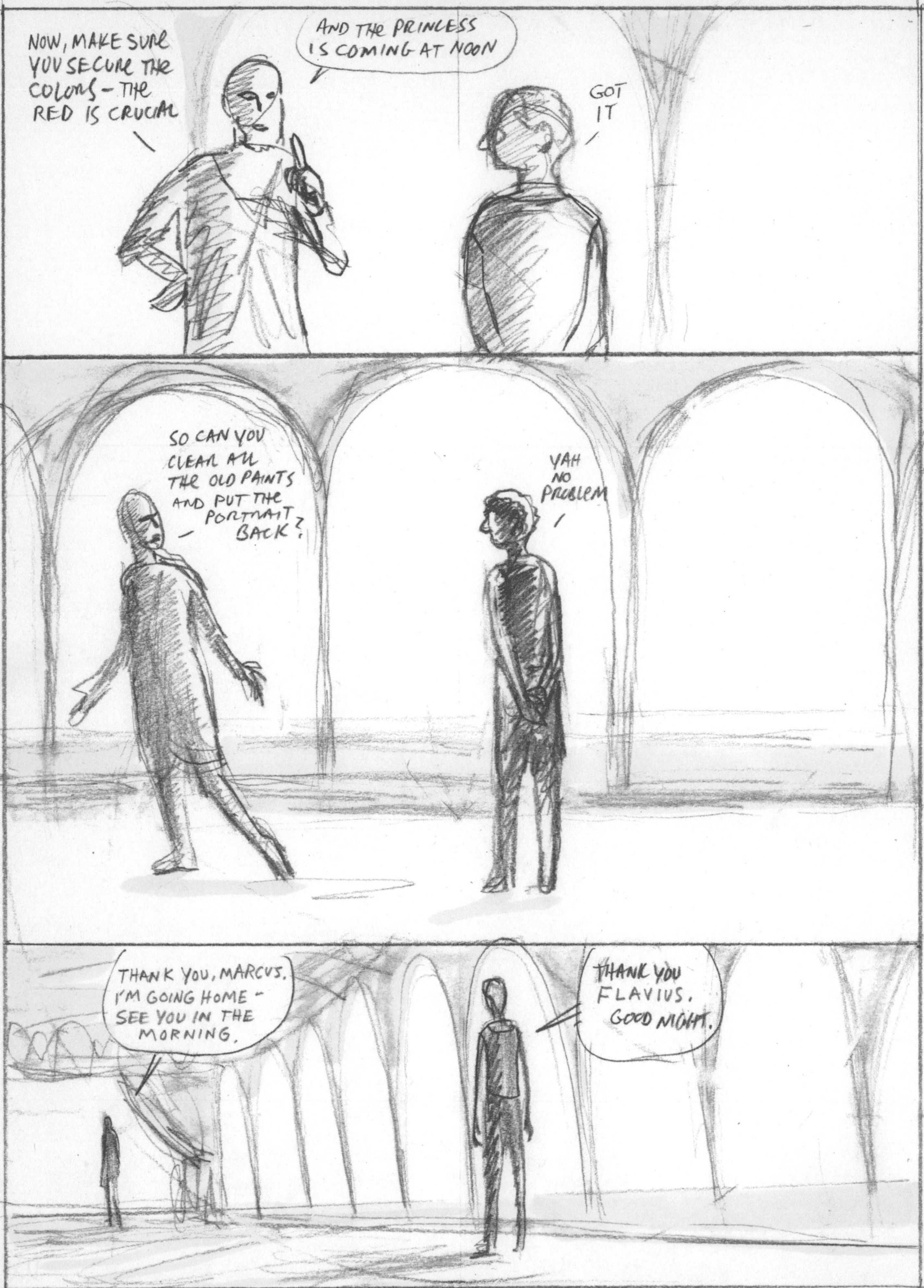
NOW, MAKE SURE YOU SECURE THE COLORS – THE RED IS CRUCIAL
AND THE PRINCESS IS COMING AT NOON
GOT IT
SO CAN YOU CLEAR ALL THE OLD PAINTS AND PUT THE PORTRAIT BACK?
YAH NO PROBLEM
THANK YOU, MARCUS. I'M GOING HOME – SEE YOU IN THE MORNING.
THANK YOU FLAVIUS. GOOD NIGHT.

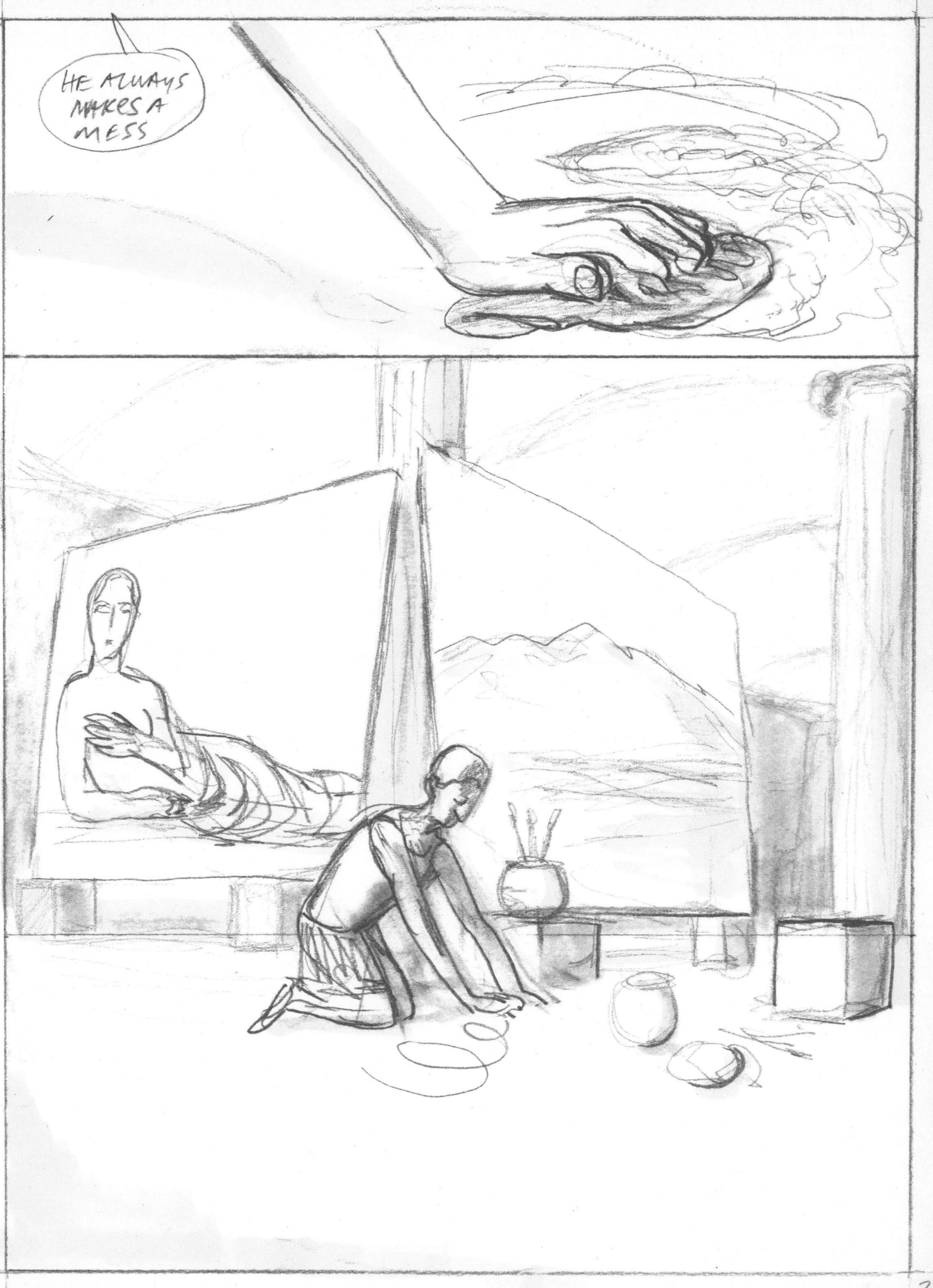
HE ALWAYS MAKES A MESS

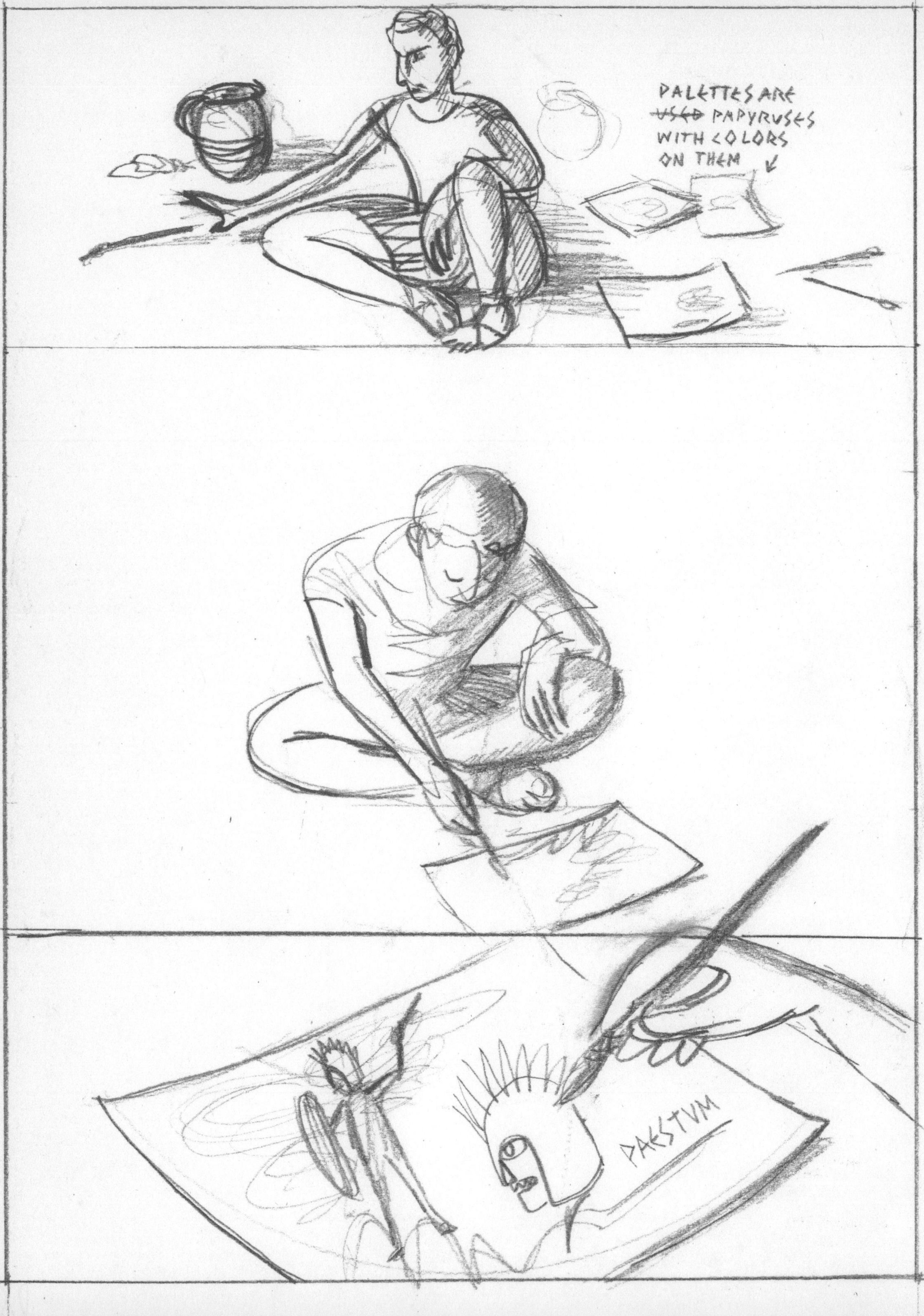
PALETTES ARE ~~USED~~ PAPYRUSES WITH COLORS ON THEM ↓
PAESTUM

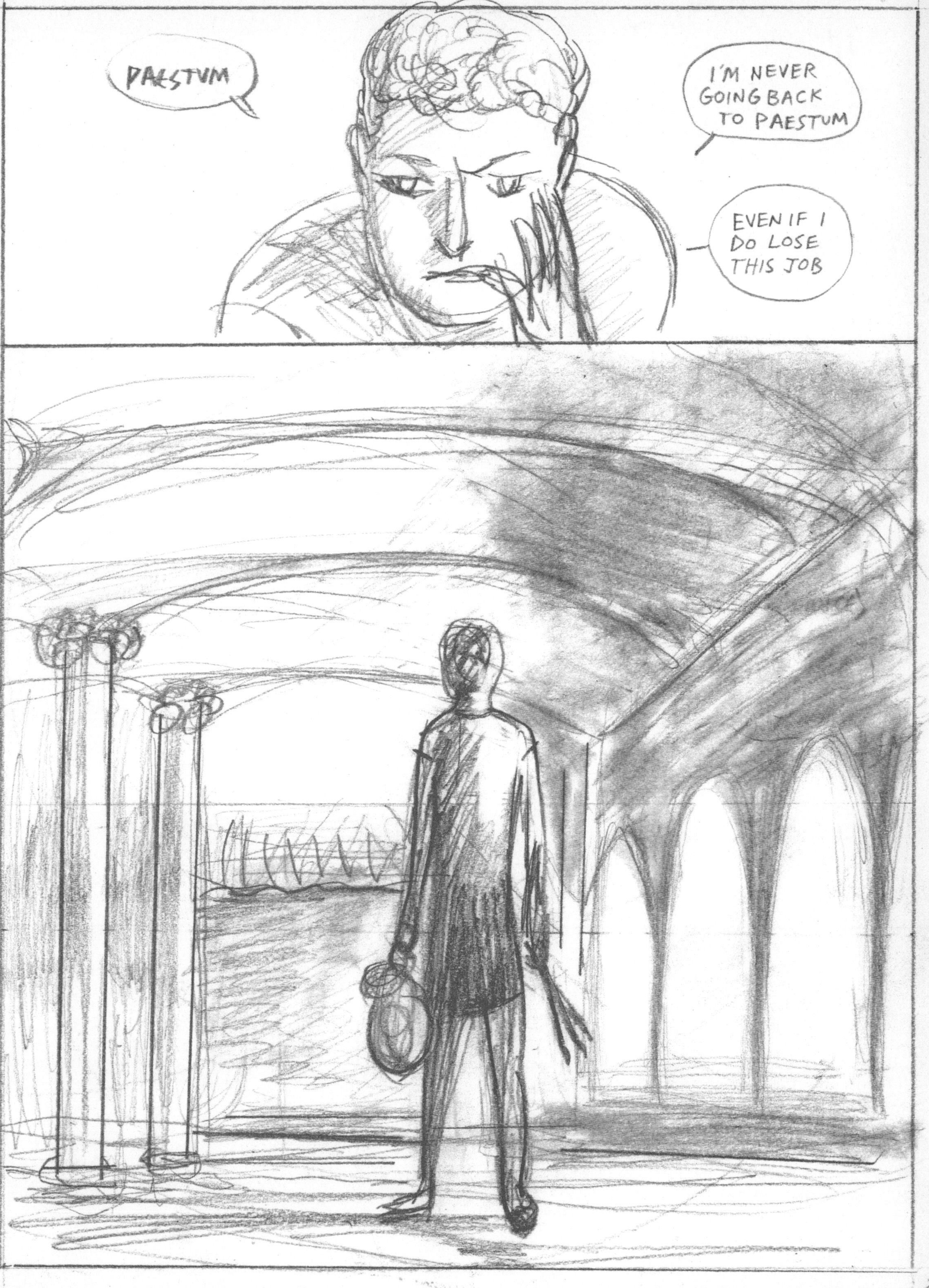
PAESTUM
I'M NEVER GOING BACK TO PAESTUM
EVEN IF I DO LOSE THIS JOB

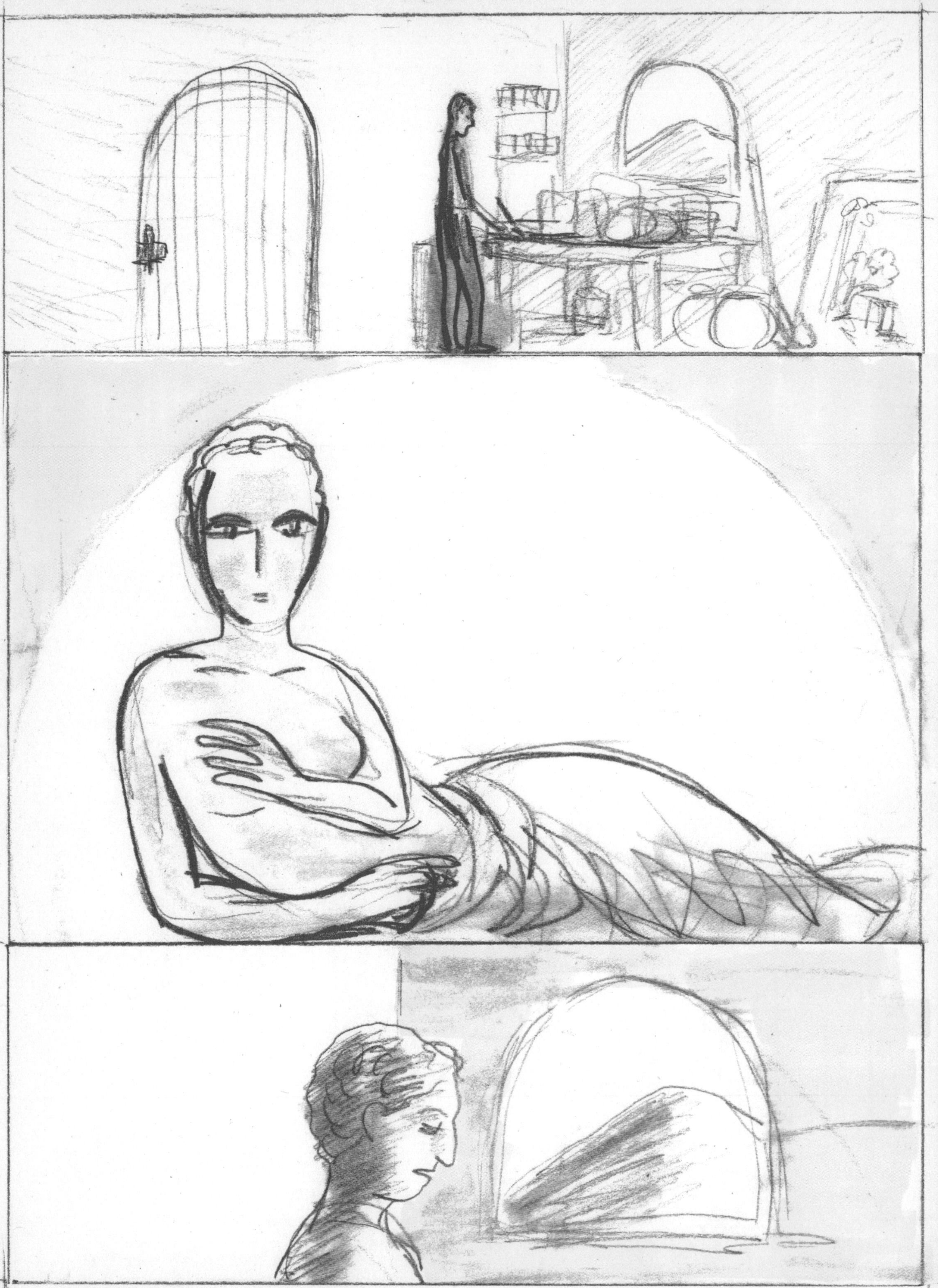

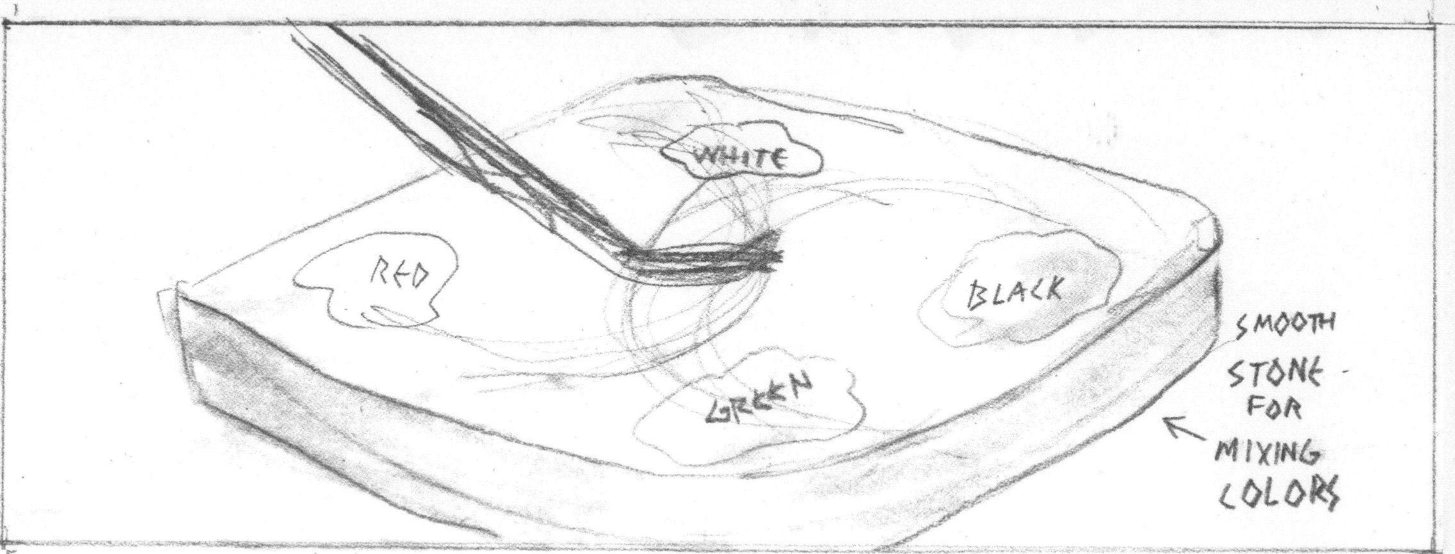
WHITE
RED
BLACK
GREEN
SMOOTH STONE FOR MIXING COLORS

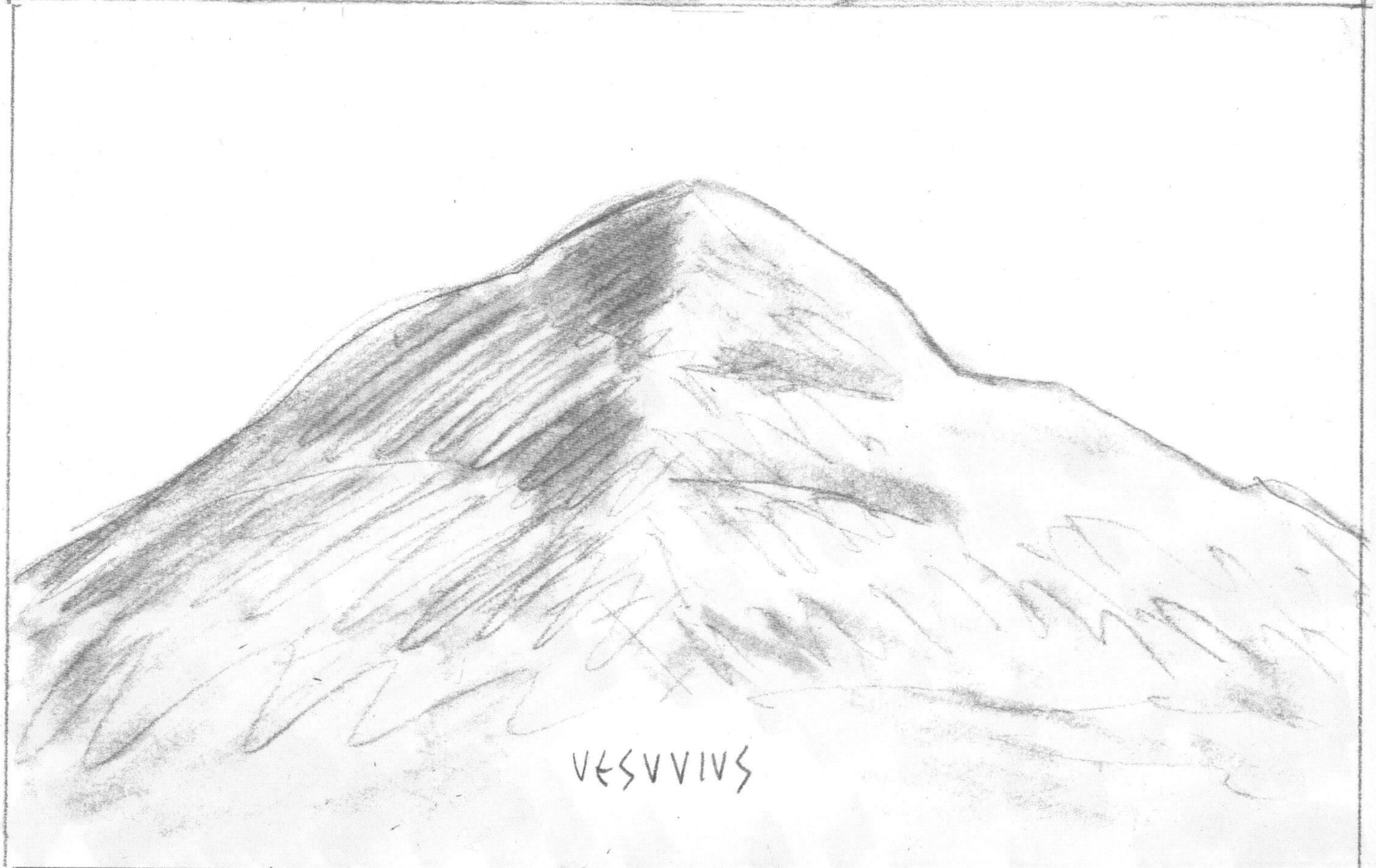
VESVVIVS

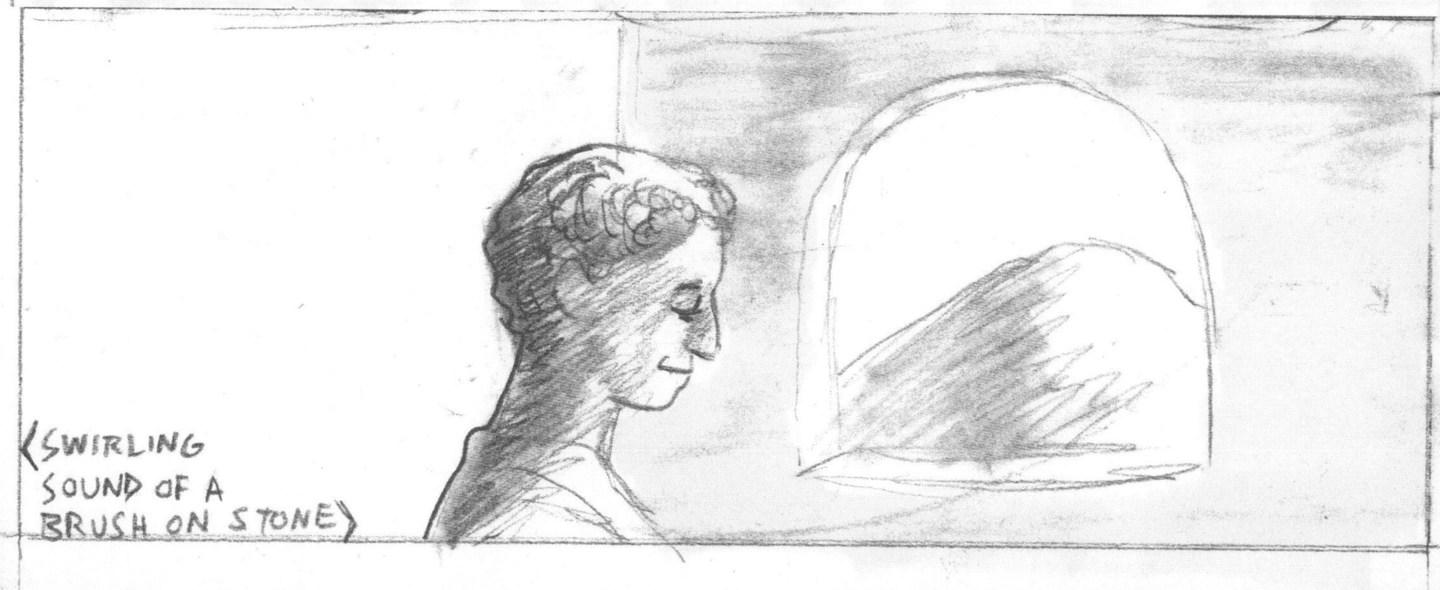
<SWIRLING SOUND OF A BRUSH ON STONE>

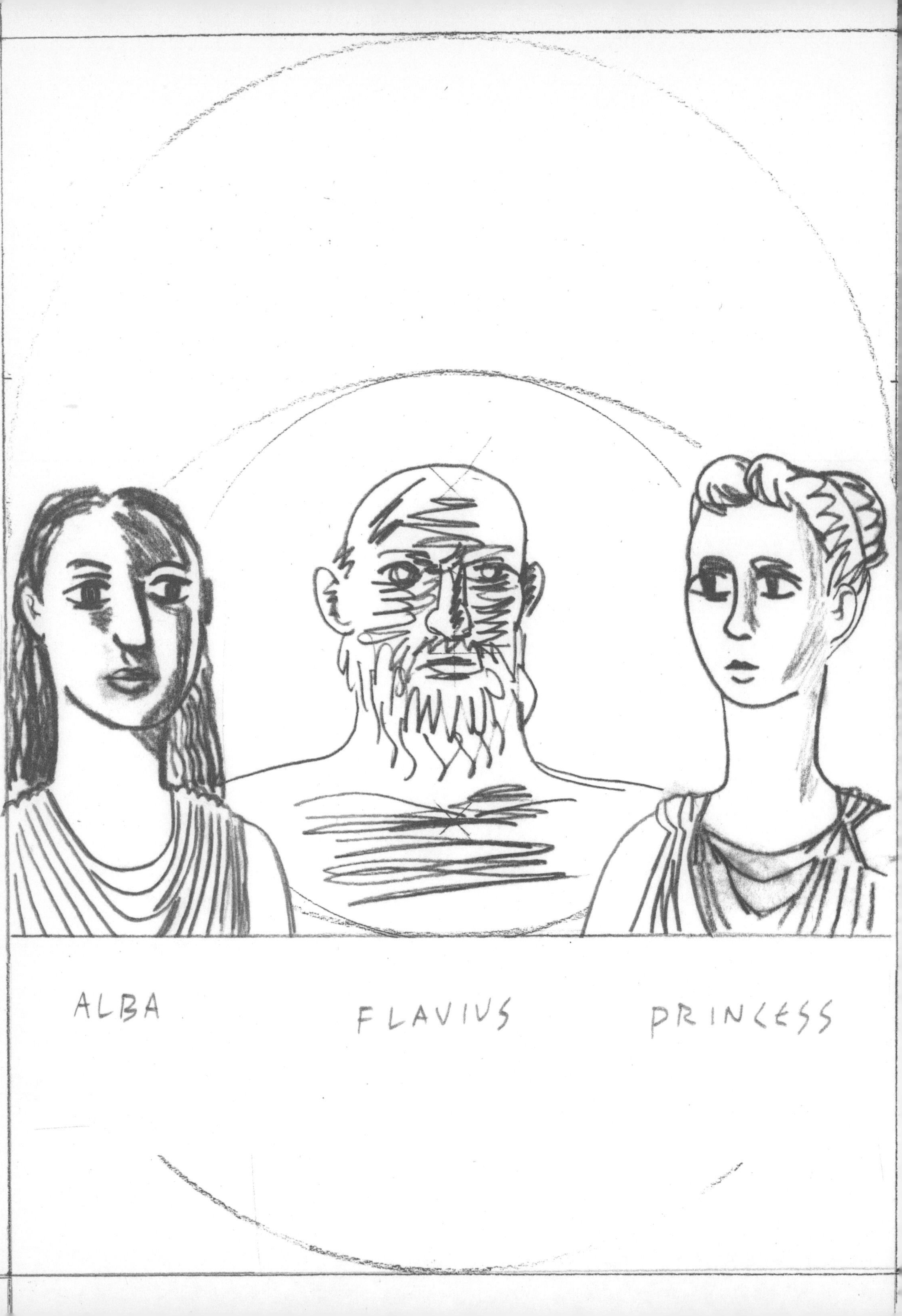
ALBA
FLAVIUS
PRINCESS

LUCIA

33

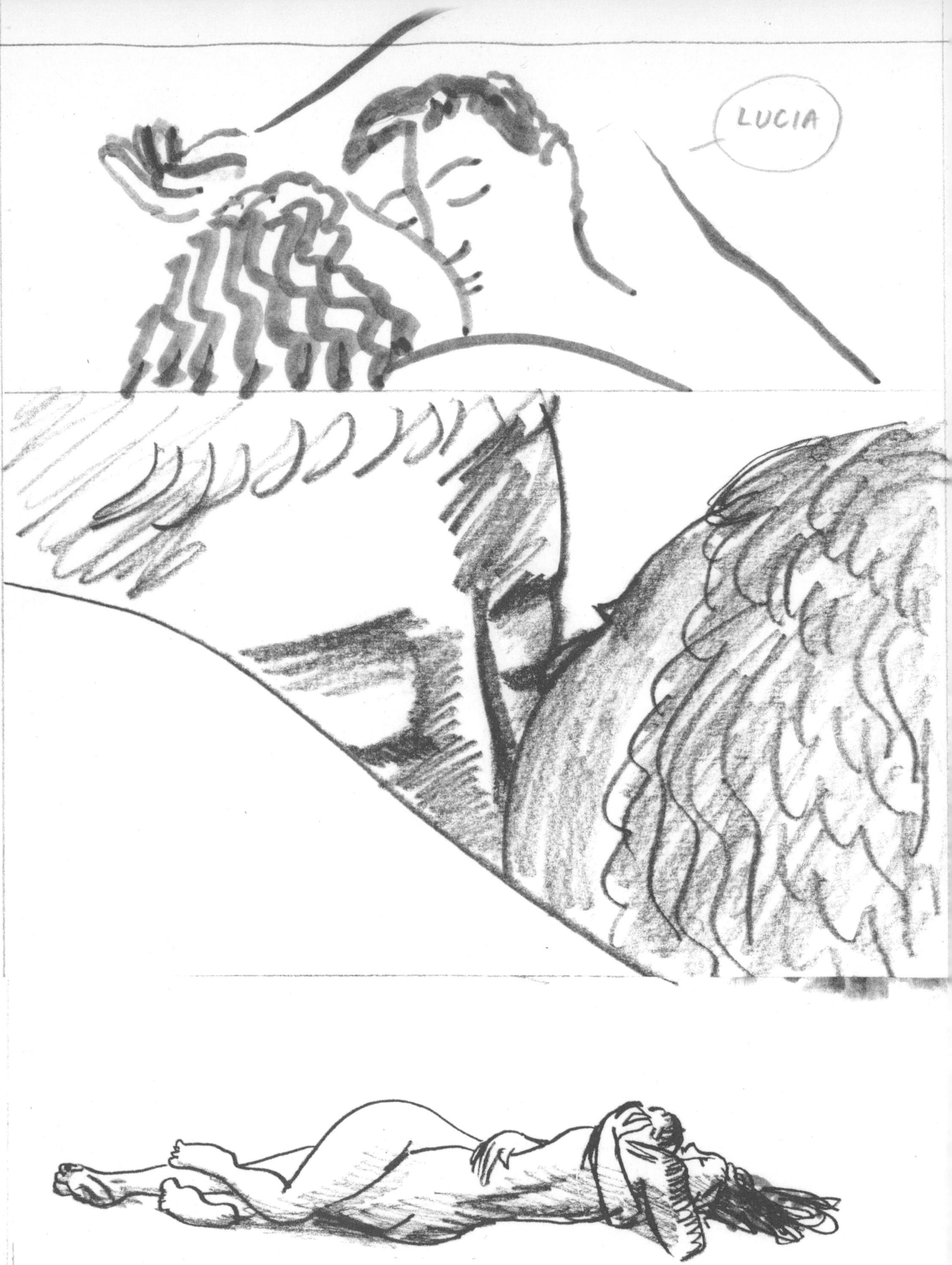
LUCIA

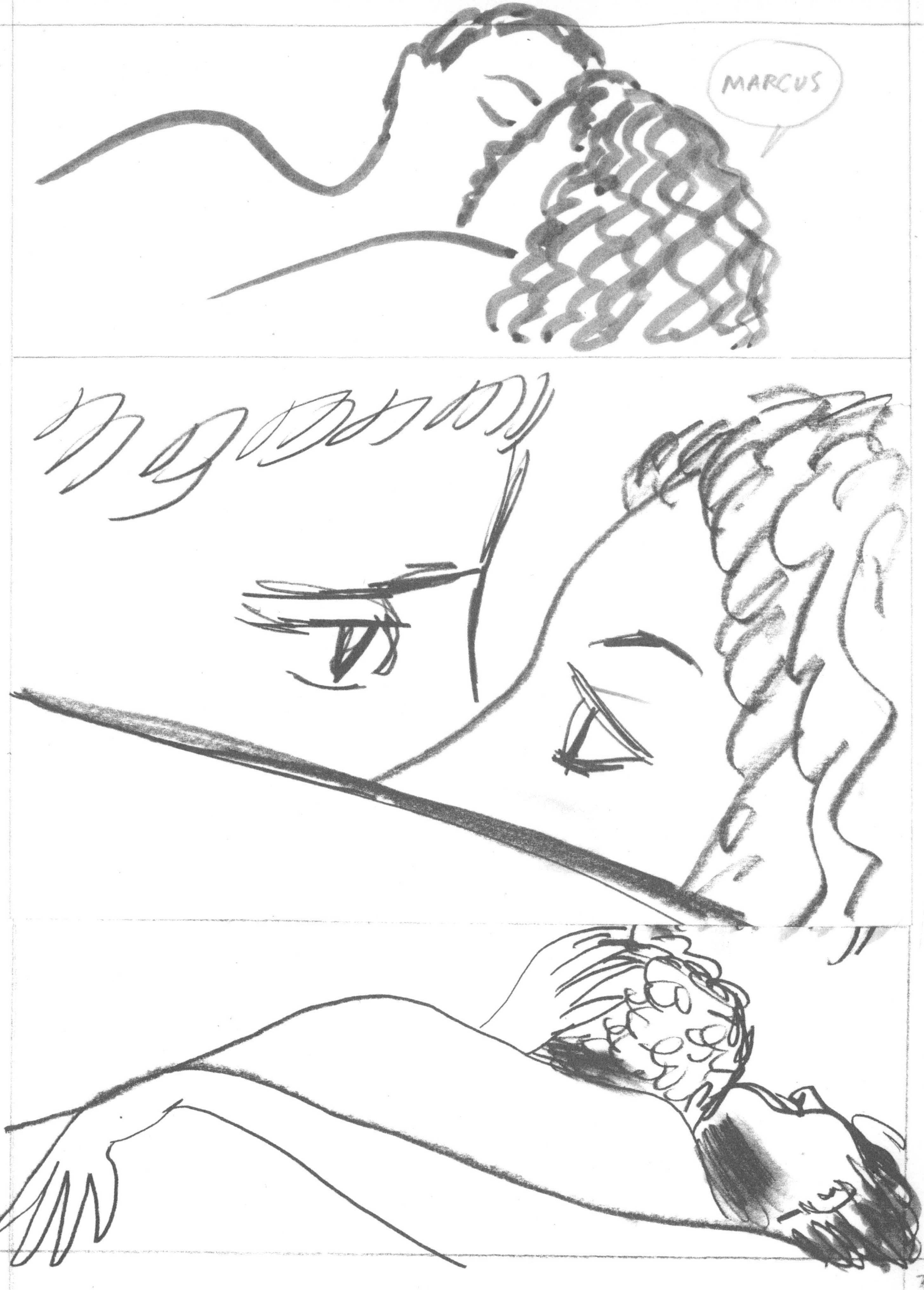
MARCUS

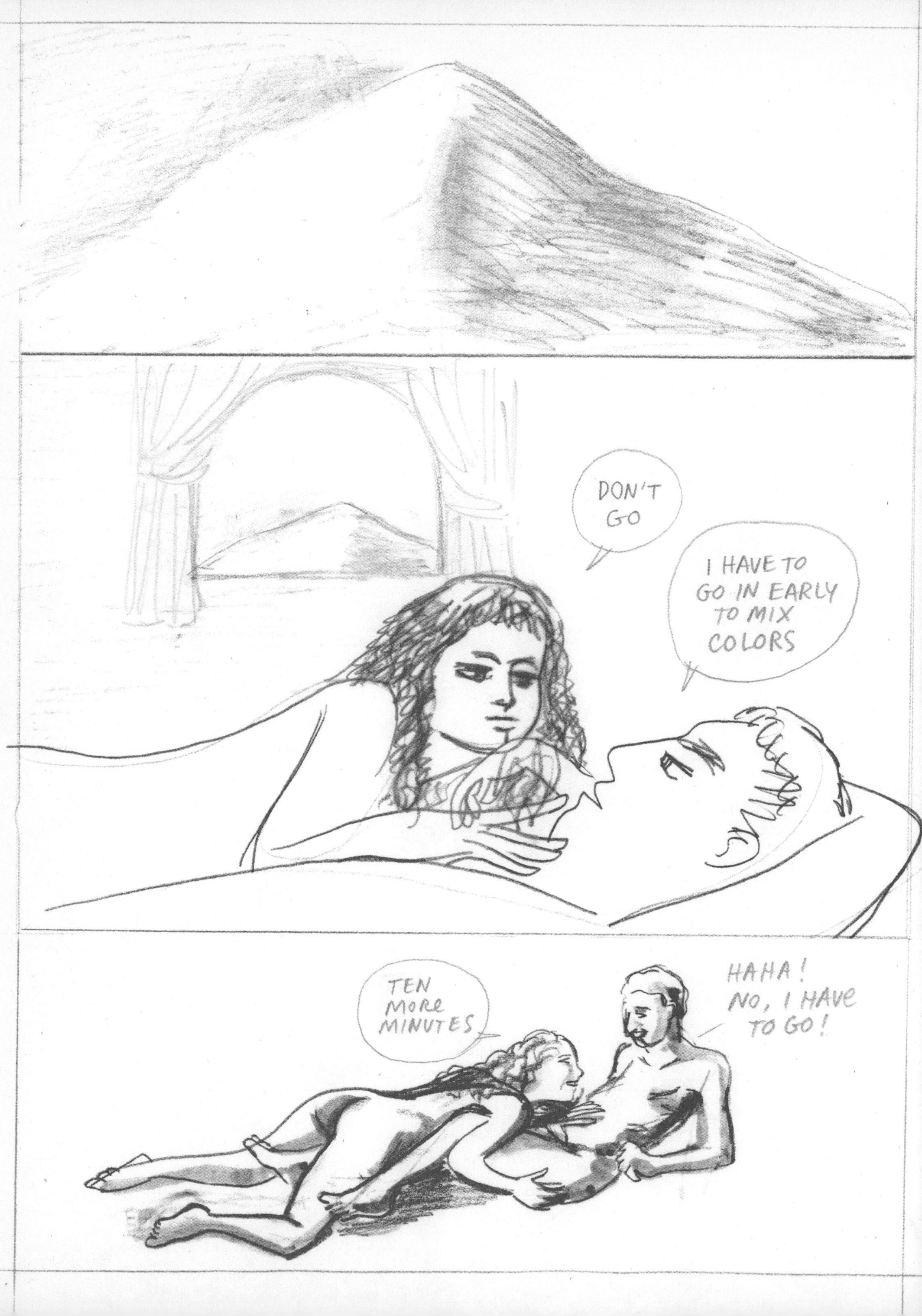
DON'T GO
I HAVE TO GO IN EARLY TO MIX COLORS
TEN MORE MINUTES
HAHA! NO, I HAVE TO GO!

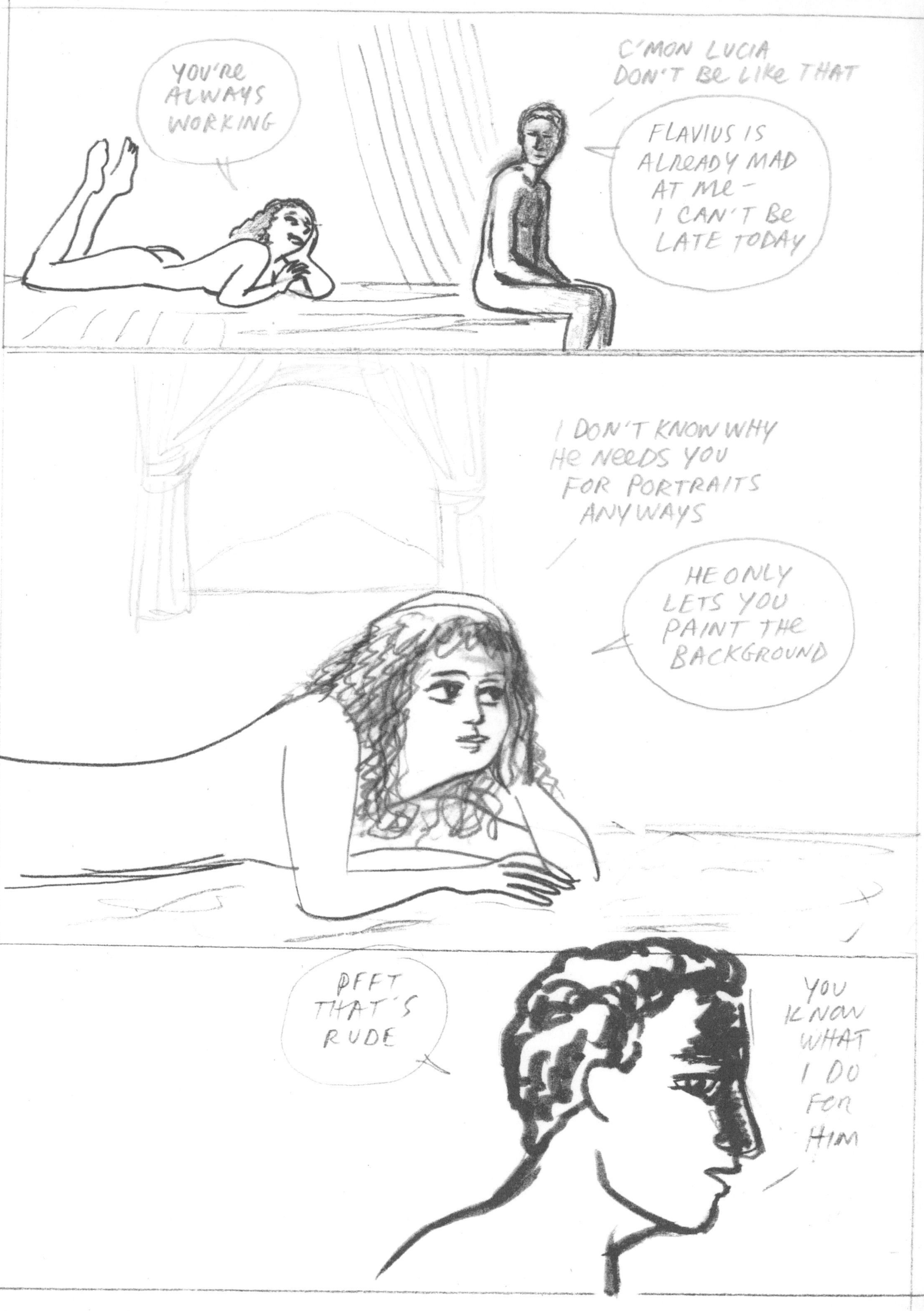
YOU'RE ALWAYS WORKING
C'MON LUCIA DON'T BE LIKE THAT
FLAVIUS IS ALREADY MAD AT ME- I CAN'T BE LATE TODAY
I DON'T KNOW WHY HE NEEDS YOU FOR PORTRAITS ANYWAYS
HE ONLY LETS YOU PAINT THE BACKGROUND
PFFT THAT'S RUDE
YOU KNOW WHAT I DO FOR HIM

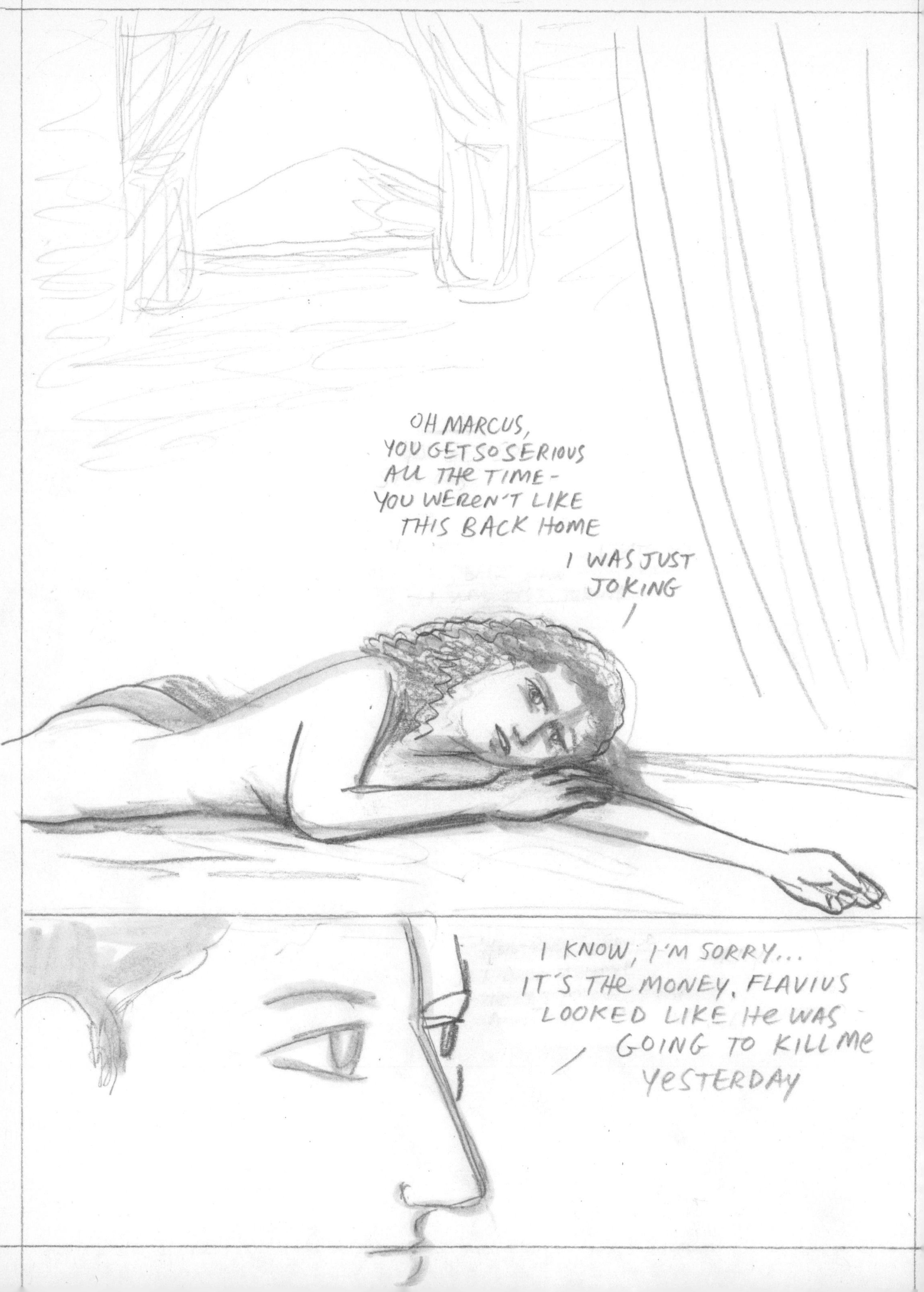
OH MARCUS, YOU GET SO SERIOUS ALL THE TIME- YOU WEREN'T LIKE THIS BACK HOME
I WAS JUST JOKING
I KNOW, I'M SORRY... IT'S THE MONEY. FLAVIUS LOOKED LIKE HE WAS GOING TO KILL ME YESTERDAY

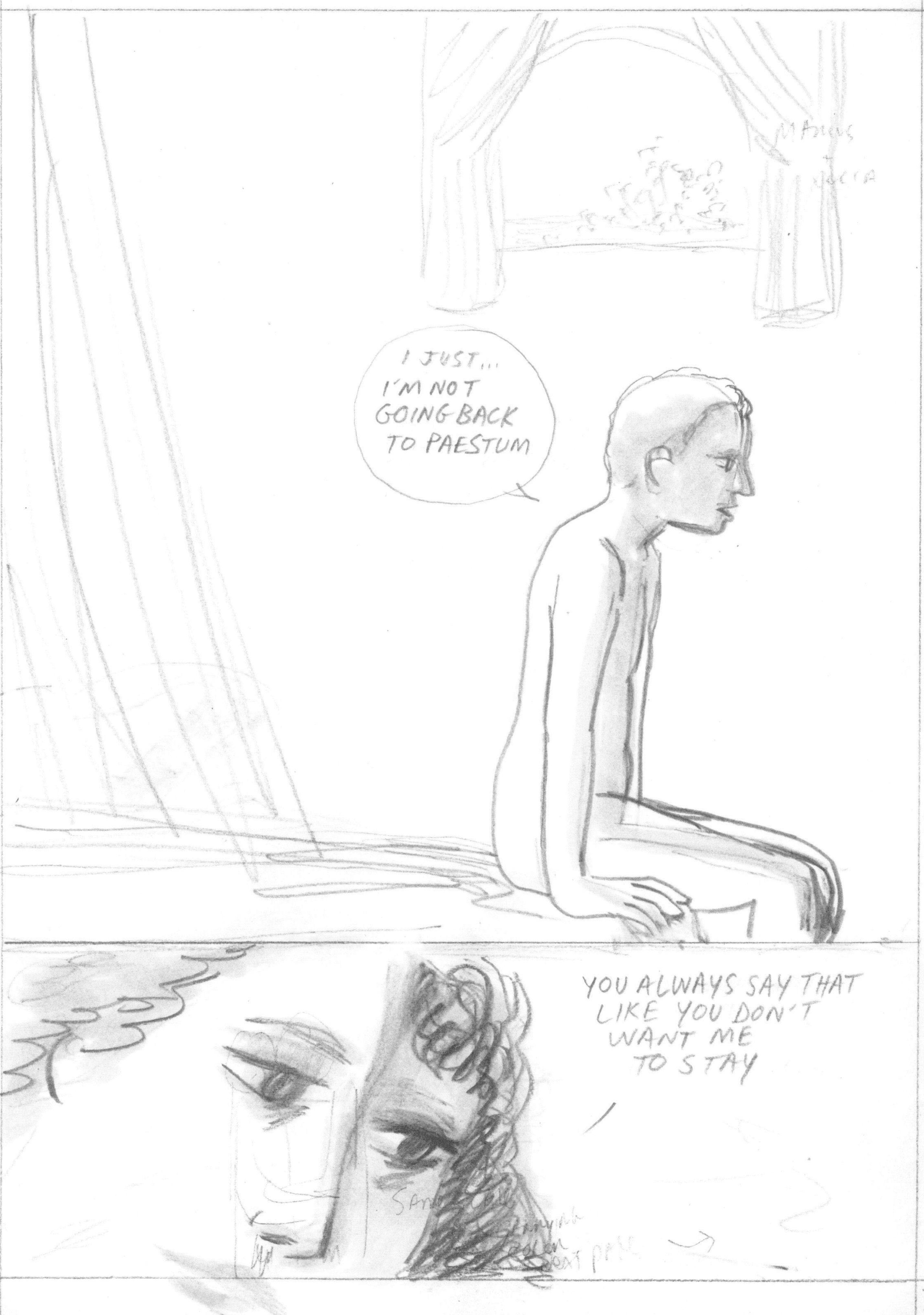
I JUST... I'M NOT GOING BACK TO PAESTUM
YOU ALWAYS SAY THAT LIKE YOU DON'T WANT ME TO STAY

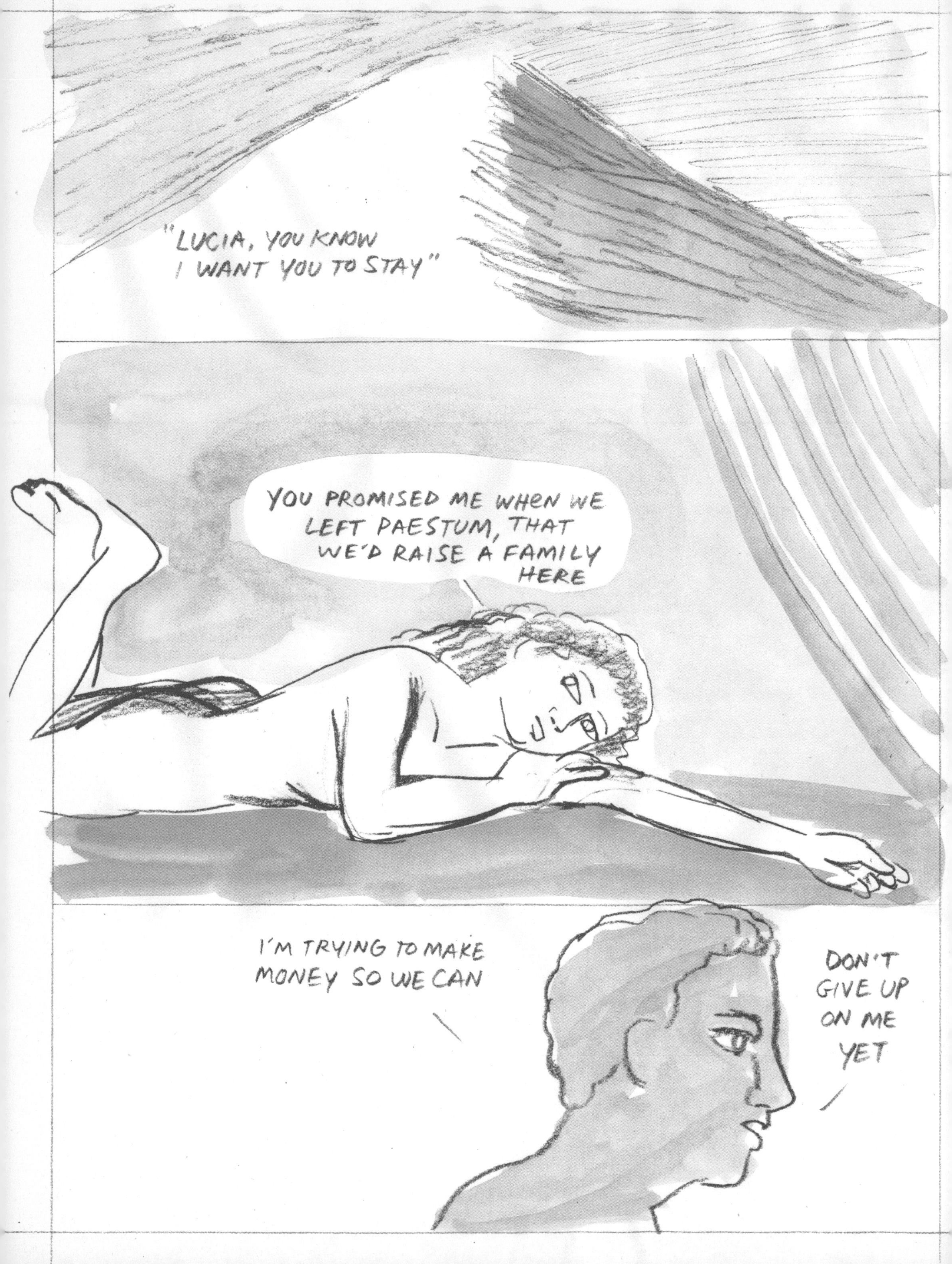
"LUCIA, YOU KNOW
I WANT YOU TO STAY"
YOU PROMISED ME WHEN WE LEFT PAESTUM, THAT WE'D RAISE A FAMILY HERE
I'M TRYING TO MAKE MONEY SO WE CAN
DON'T GIVE UP ON ME YET

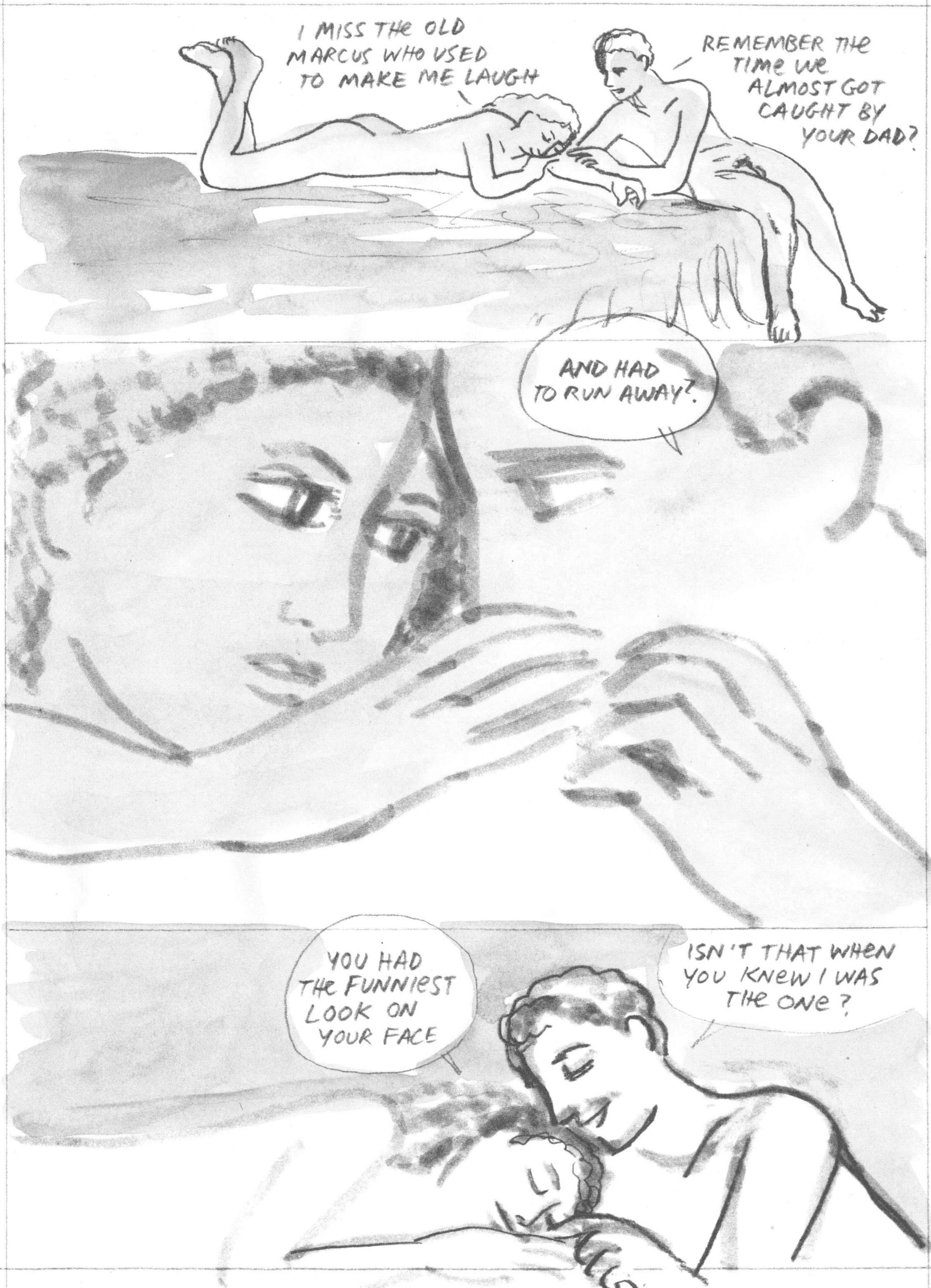
I MISS THE OLD MARCUS WHO USED TO MAKE ME LAUGH
REMEMBER THE TIME WE ALMOST GOT CAUGHT BY YOUR DAD?
AND HAD TO RUN AWAY?
YOU HAD THE FUNNIEST LOOK ON YOUR FACE
ISN'T THAT WHEN YOU KNEW I WAS THE ONE?

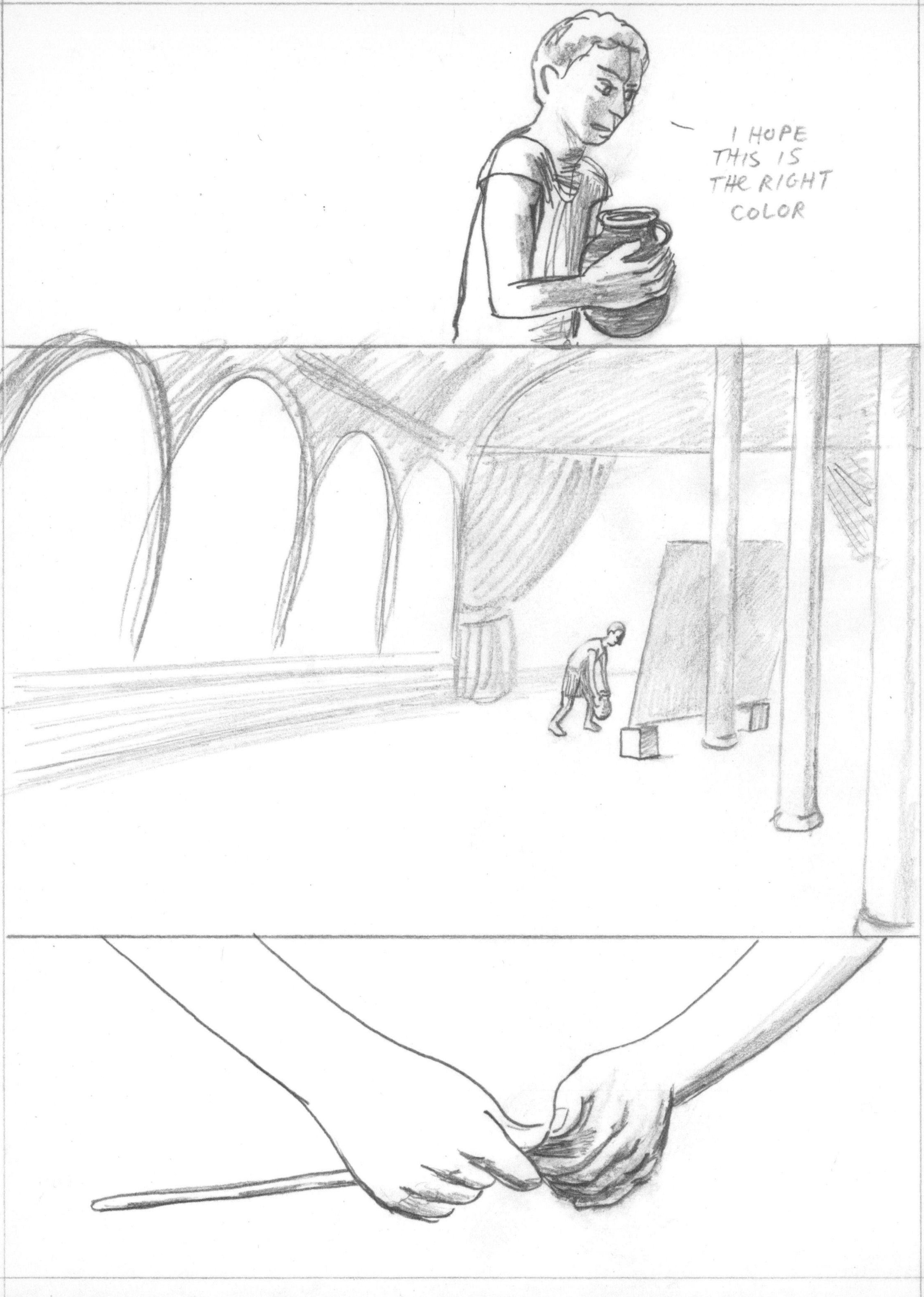
I HOPE THIS IS THE RIGHT COLOR

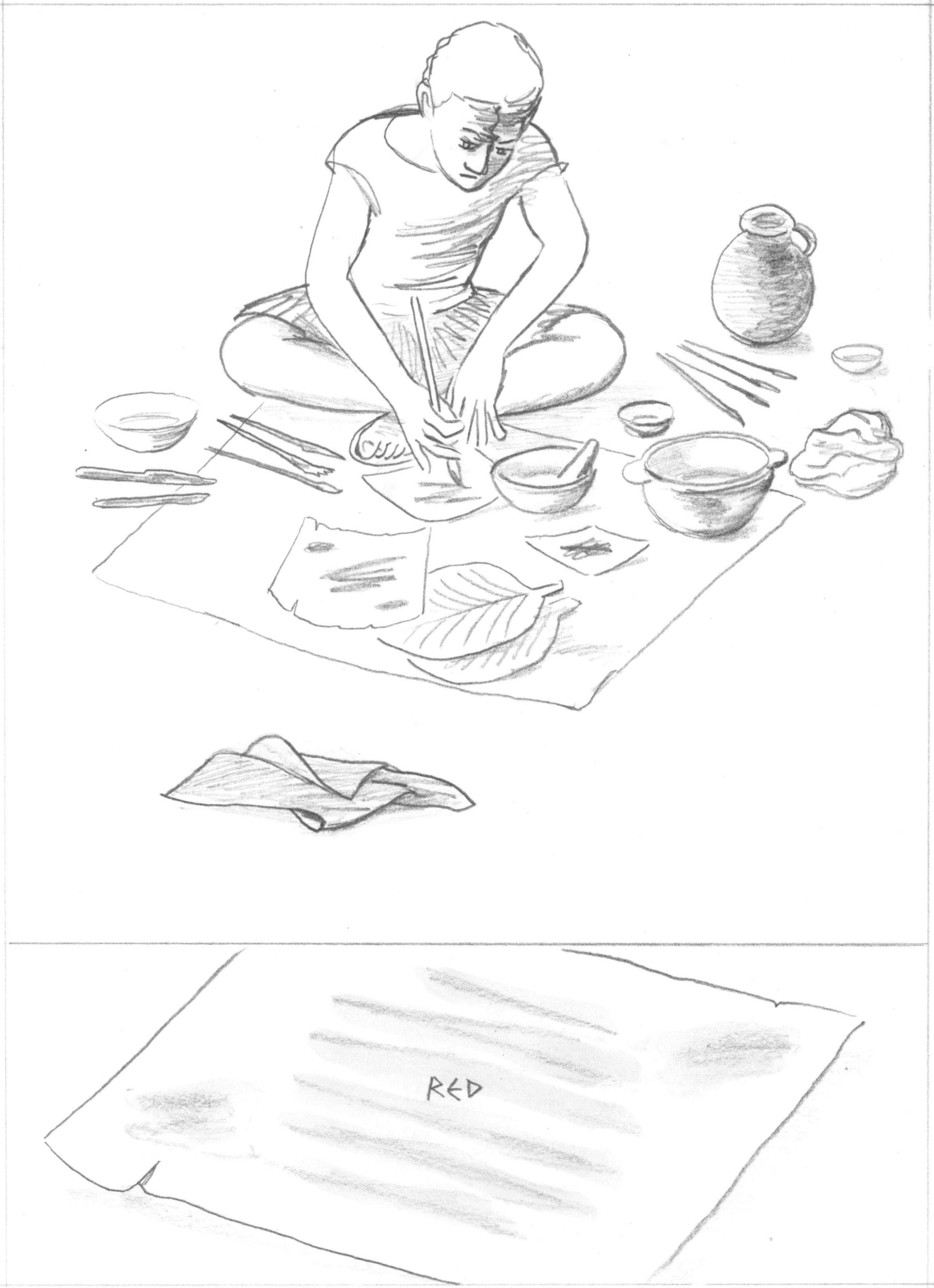
RED

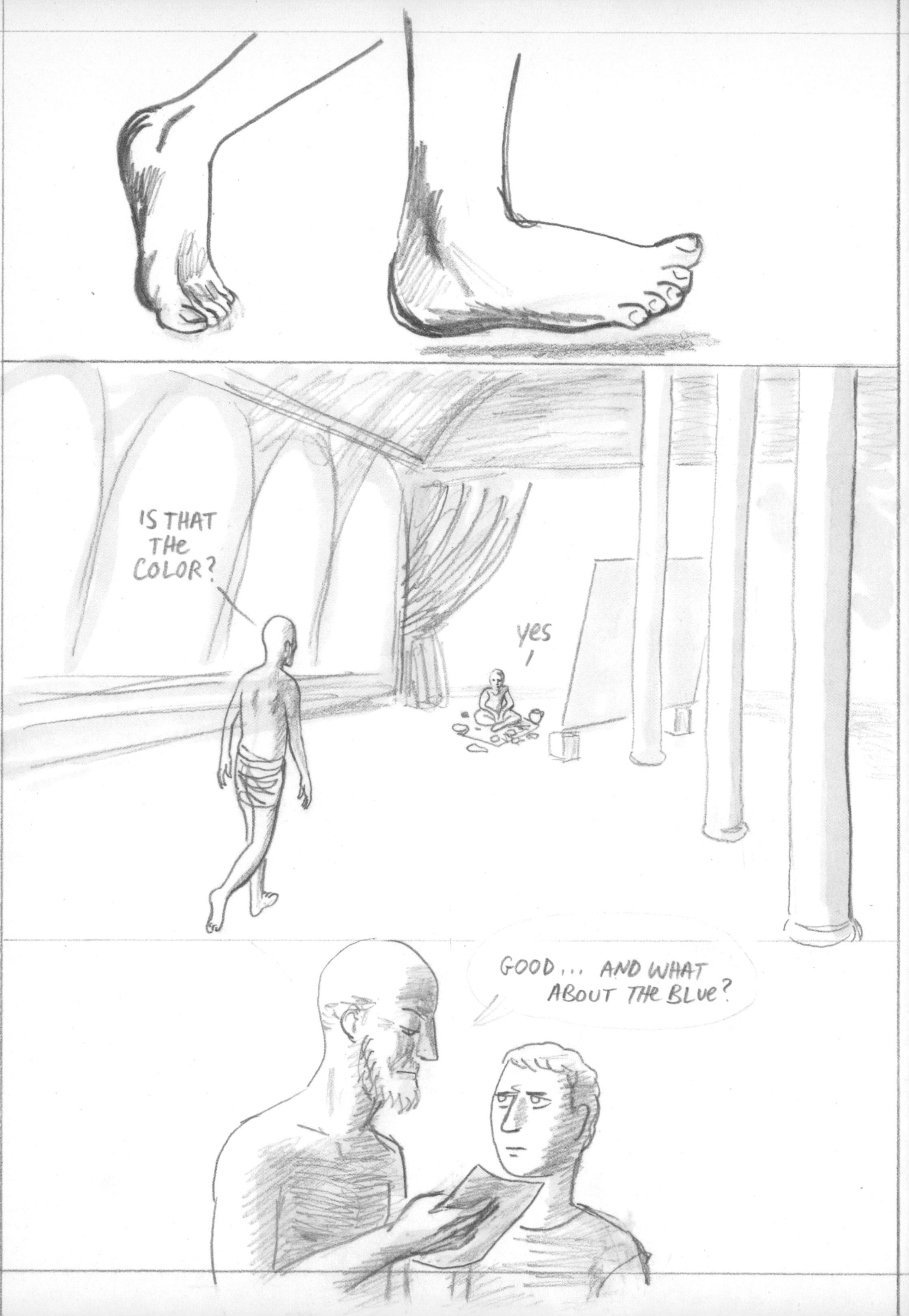
IS THAT THE COLOR?
yes
GOOD... AND WHAT ABOUT THE BLUE?

IS THIS
THE NEW
ONE?

YAH, THE
SAME AS
BEFORE

GOOD

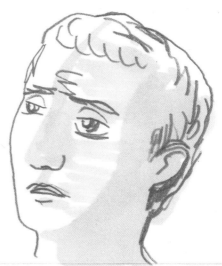

DID YOU SEE
THE CEREMONY
TODAY?

NO, I WAS
MIXING COLORS

I HEARD THAT
THE WATERS
OF THE TEMPLE
HAVE STOPPED

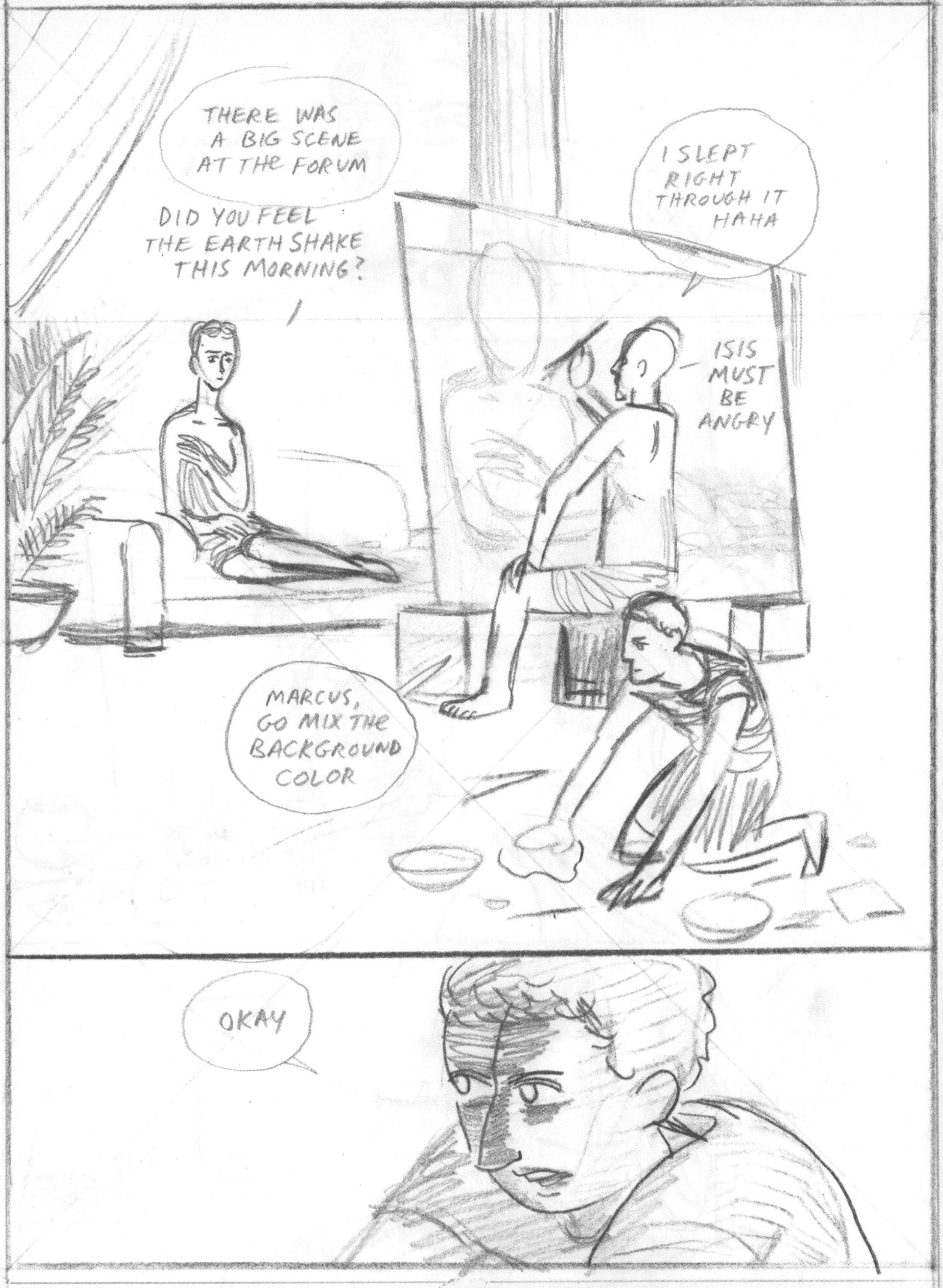
THERE WAS A BIG SCENE AT THE FORUM
DID YOU FEEL THE EARTH SHAKE THIS MORNING?
I SLEPT RIGHT THROUGH IT HAHA
ISIS MUST BE ANGRY
MARCUS, GO MIX THE BACKGROUND COLOR
OKAY

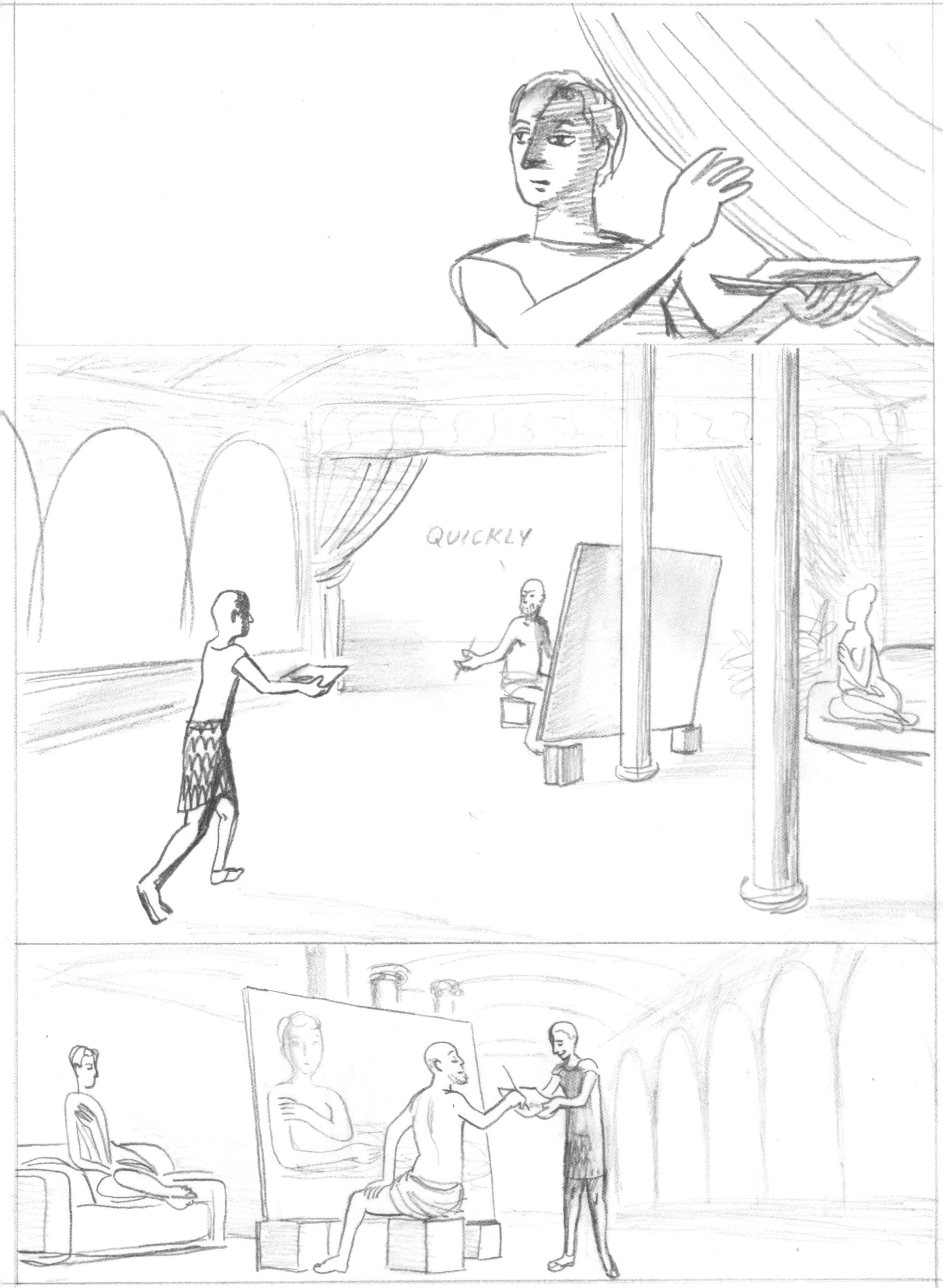
QUICKLY

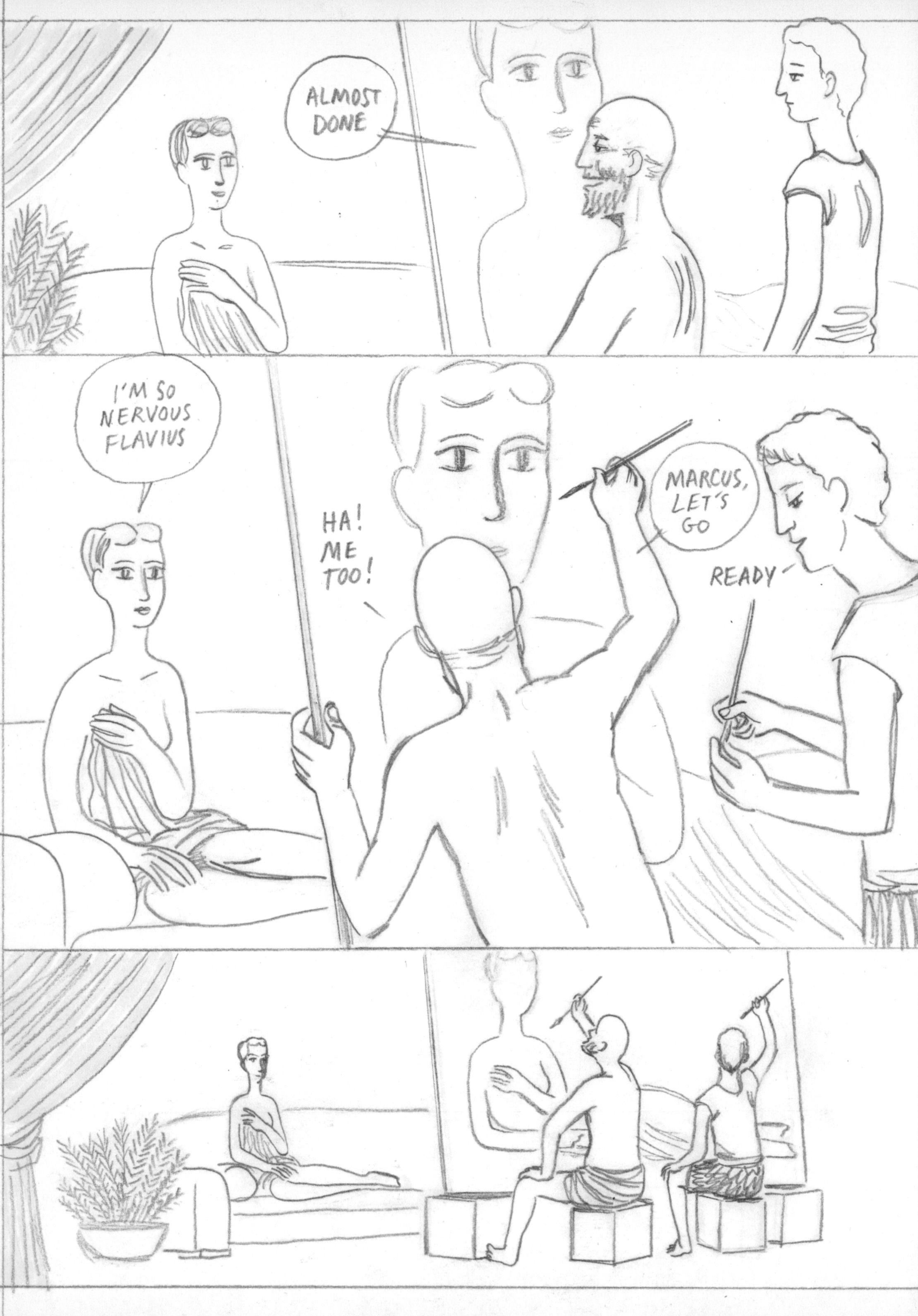
ALMOST DONE
I'M SO NERVOUS FLAVIUS
HA! ME TOO!
MARCUS, LET'S GO
READY

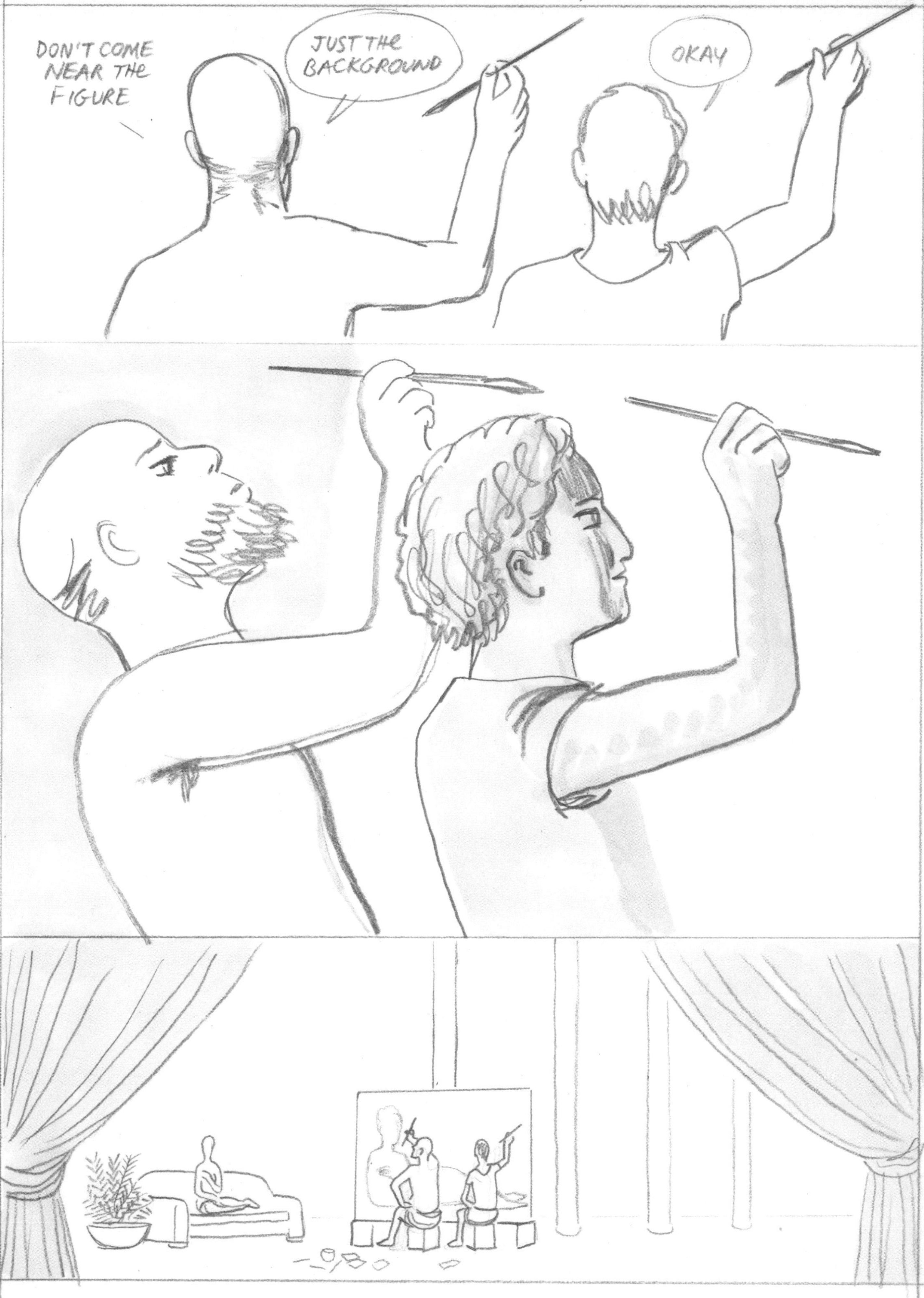
DON'T COME NEAR THE FIGURE
JUST THE BACKGROUND
OKAY

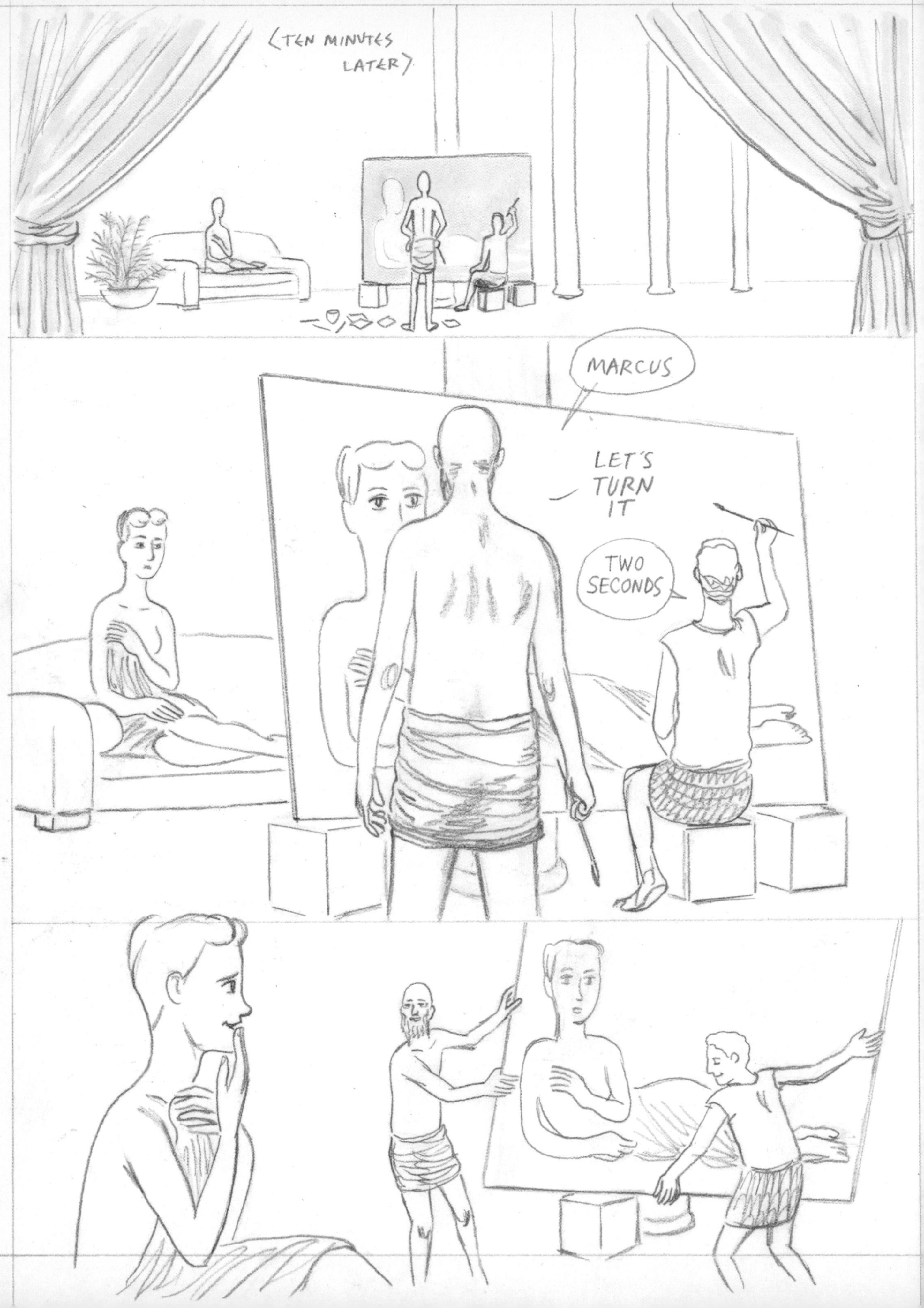

<TEN MINUTES LATER>
MARCUS
LET'S TURN IT
TWO SECONDS

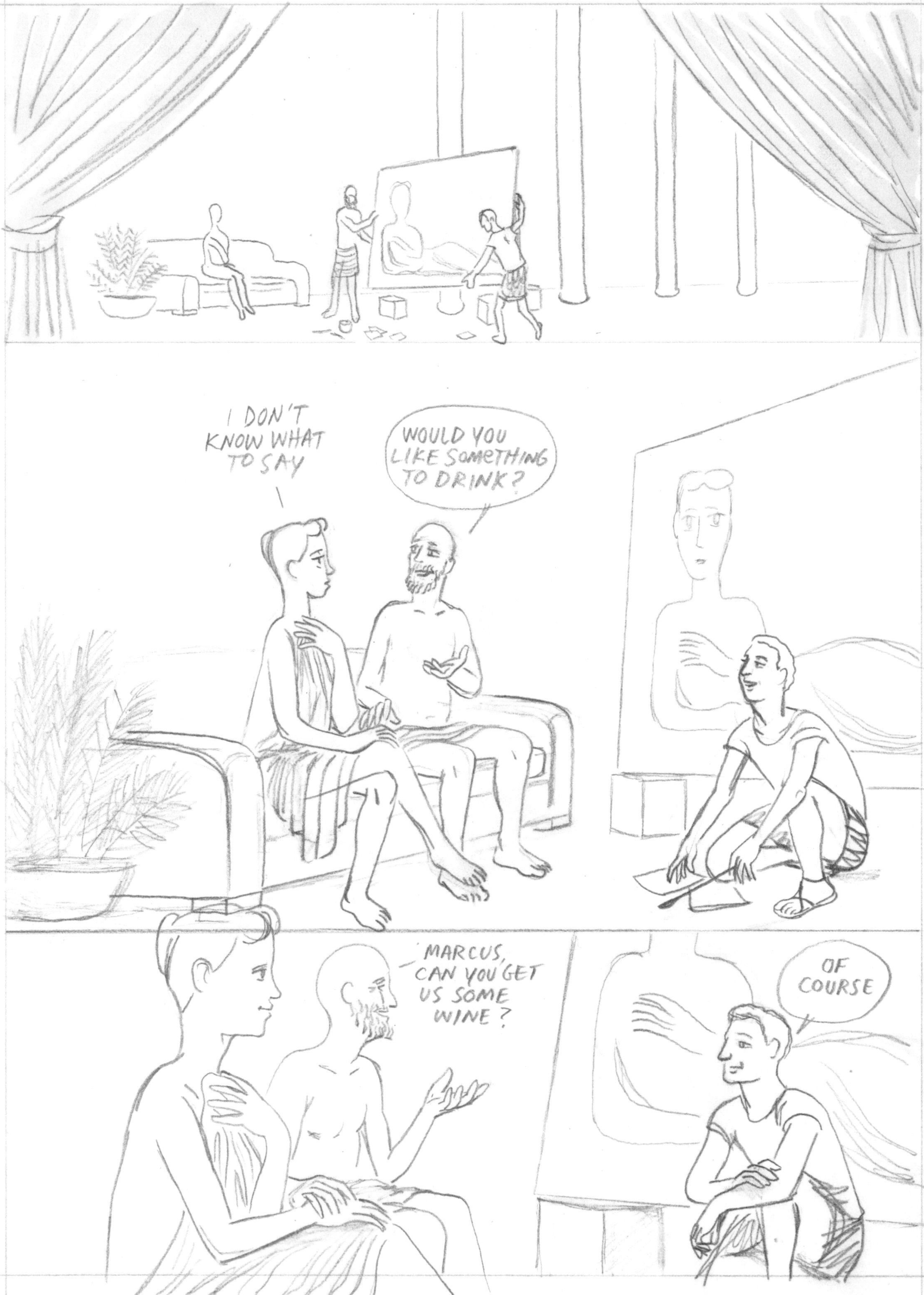
I DON'T KNOW WHAT TO SAY
WOULD YOU LIKE SOMETHING TO DRINK?
MARCUS, CAN YOU GET US SOME WINE?
OF COURSE

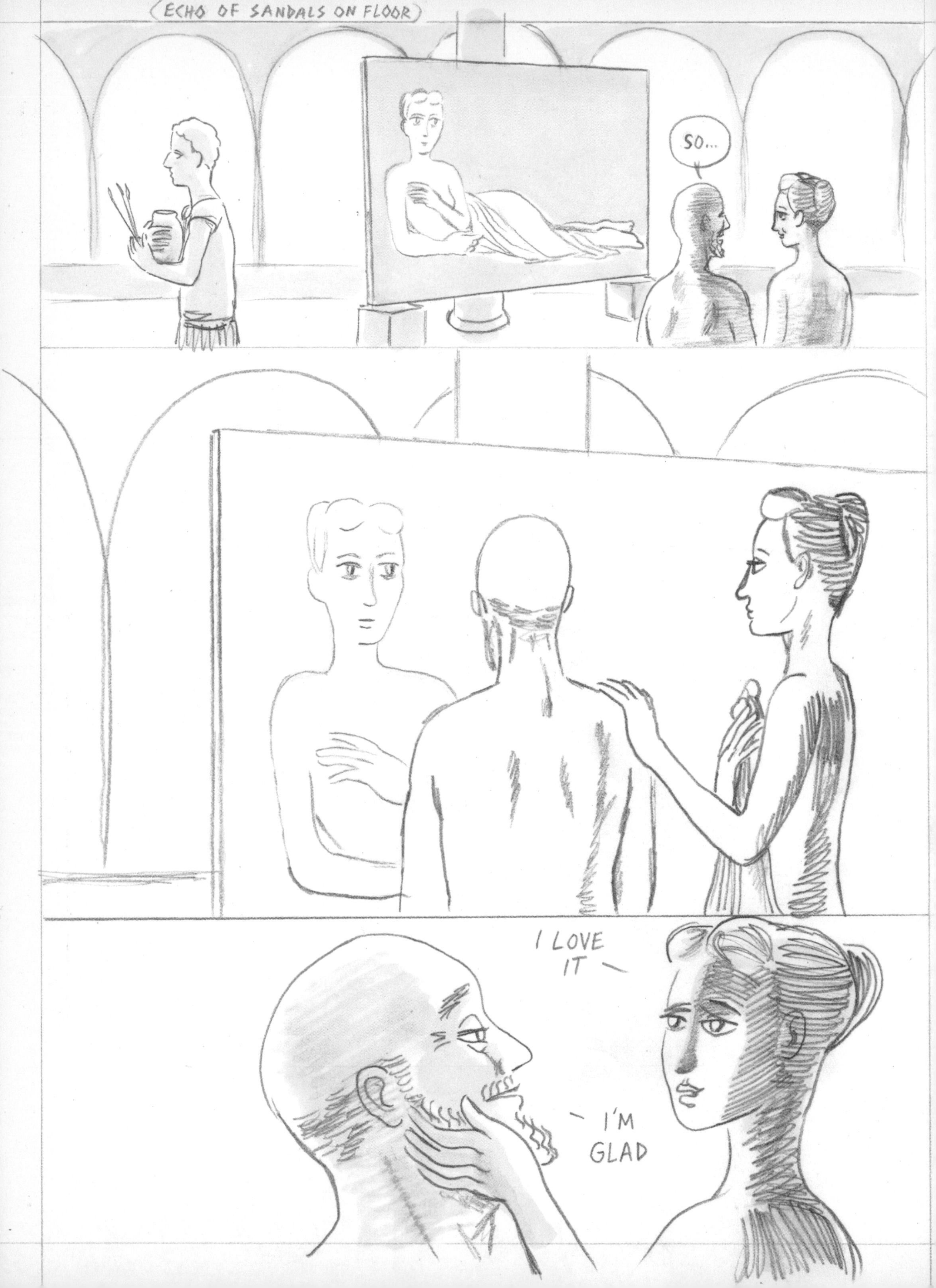
(ECHO OF SANDALS ON FLOOR)
SO...
I LOVE IT –
– I'M GLAD

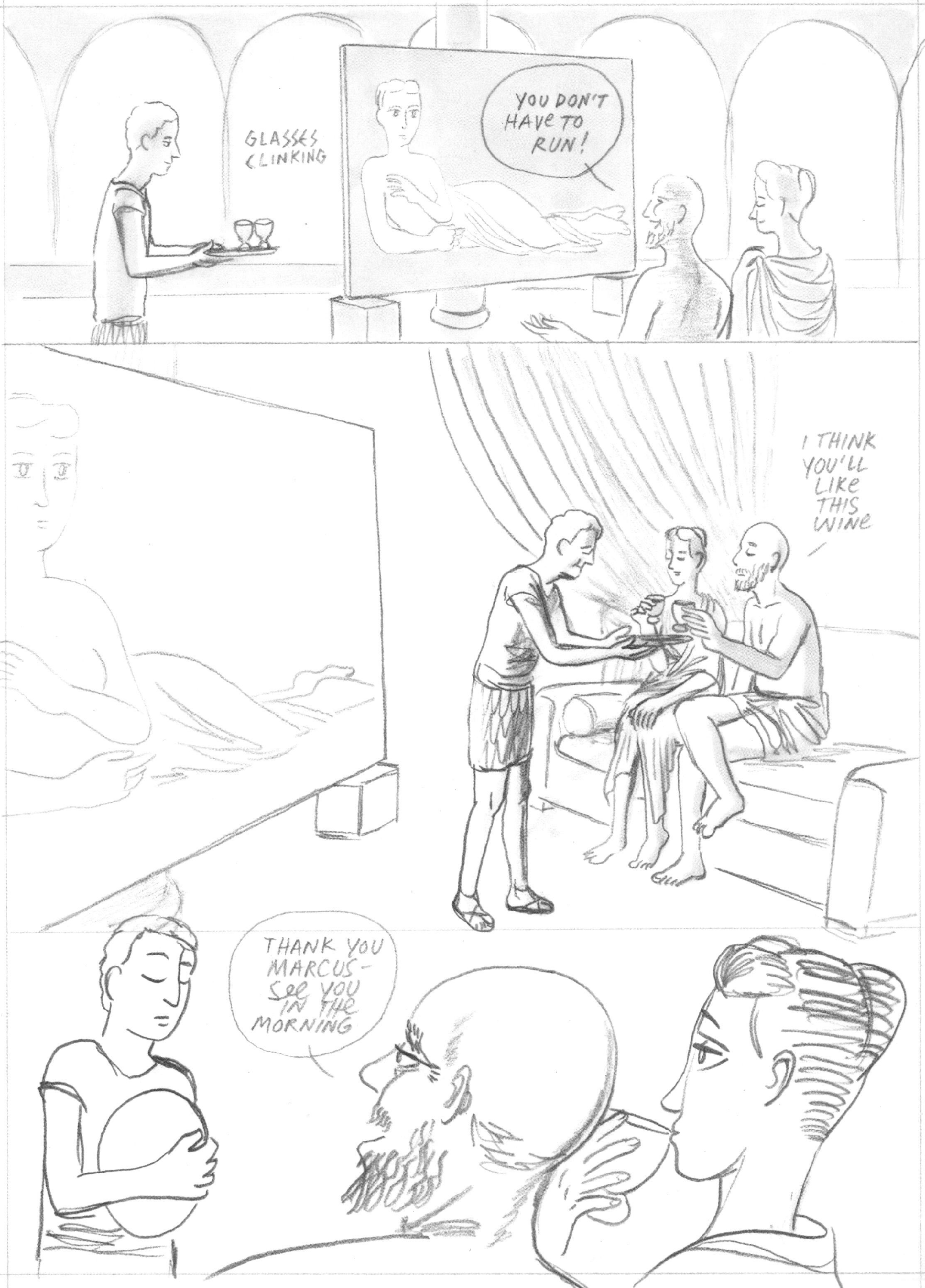
GLASSES CLINKING
YOU DON'T HAVE TO RUN!
I THINK YOU'LL LIKE THIS WINE
THANK YOU MARCUS- SEE YOU IN THE MORNING

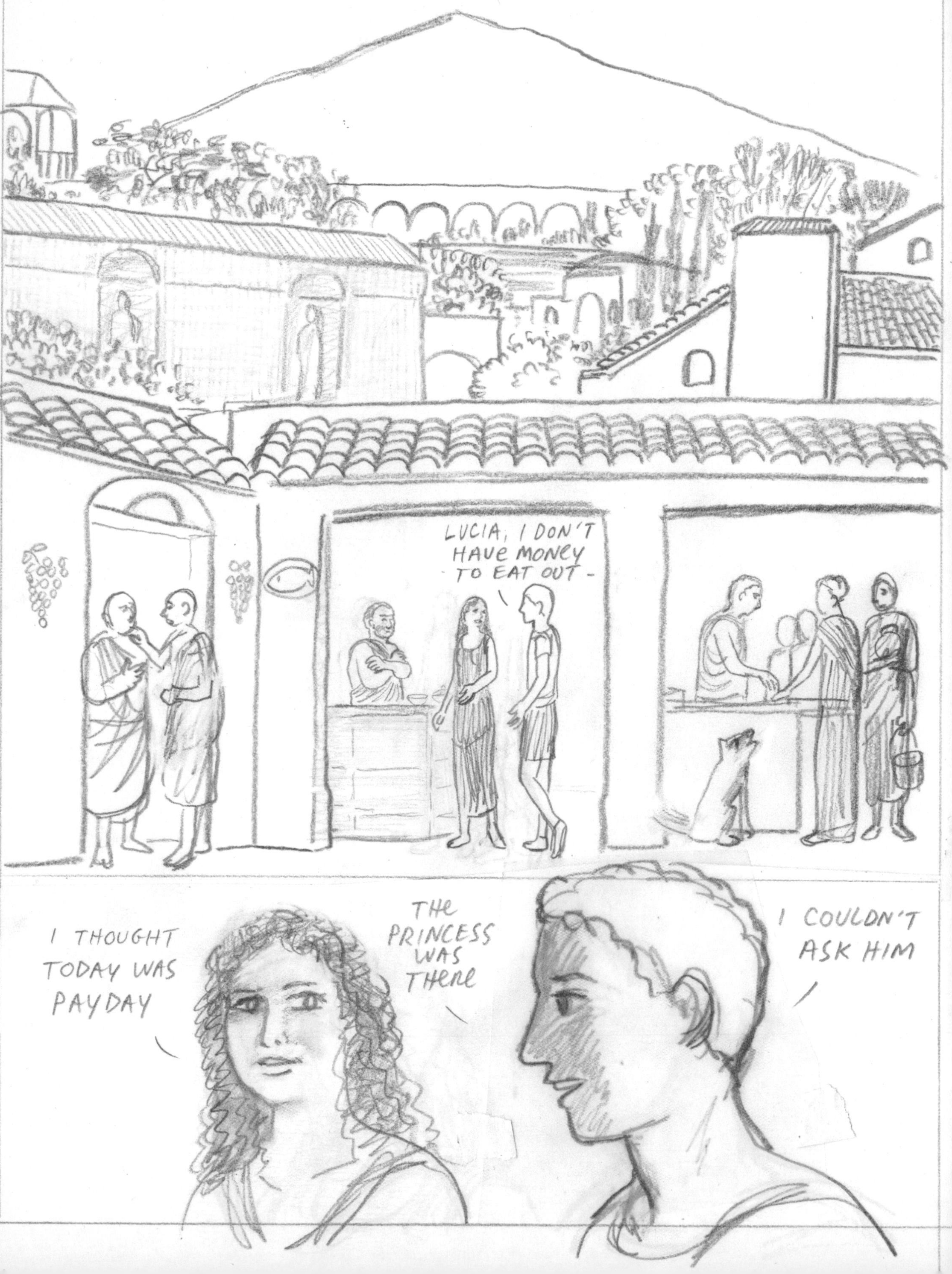
LUCIA, I DON'T HAVE MONEY TO EAT OUT -
I THOUGHT TODAY WAS PAYDAY
THE PRINCESS WAS THERE
I COULDN'T ASK HIM

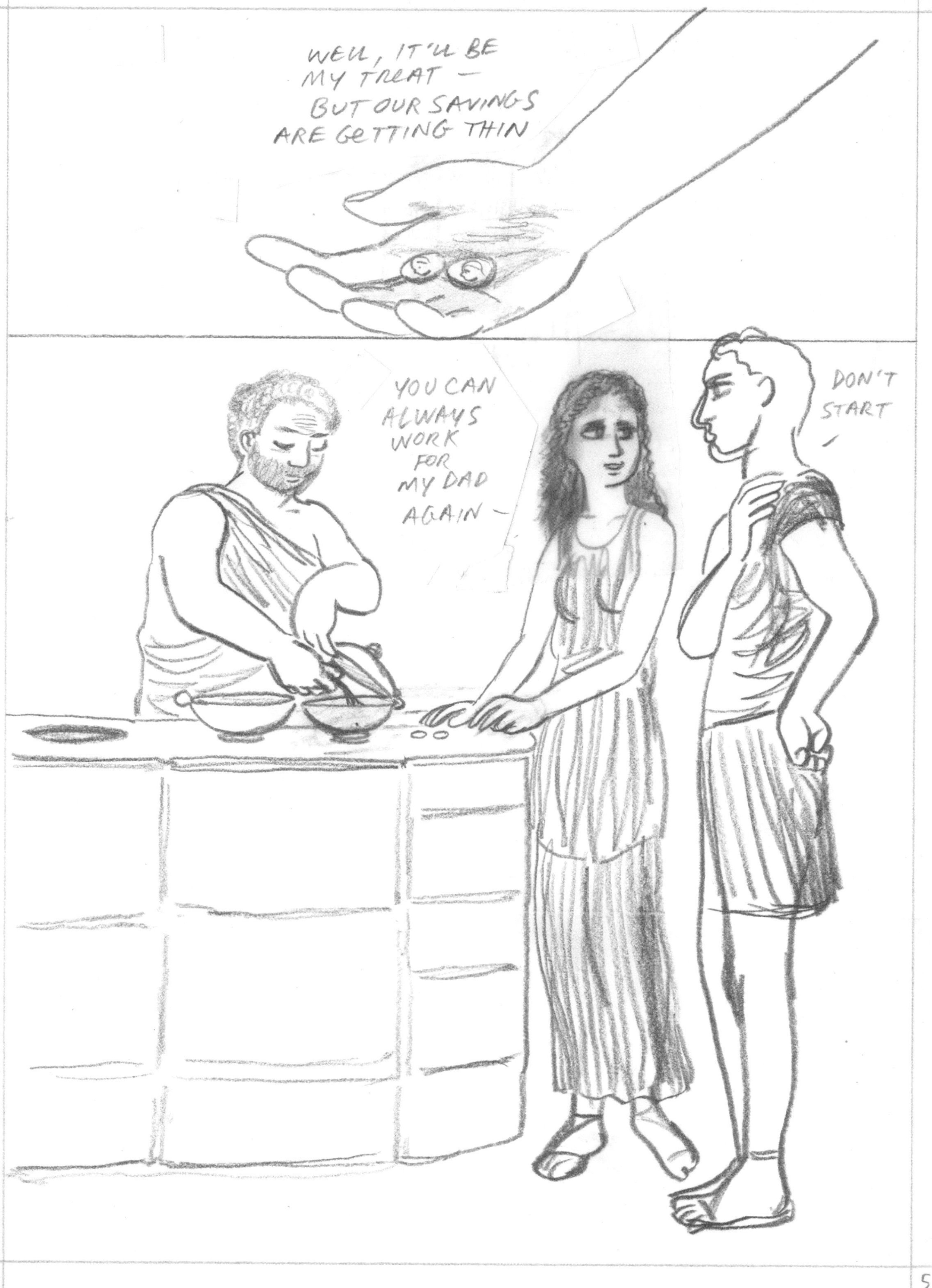
WELL, IT'LL BE MY TREAT — BUT OUR SAVINGS ARE GETTING THIN
YOU CAN ALWAYS WORK FOR MY DAD AGAIN —
DON'T START

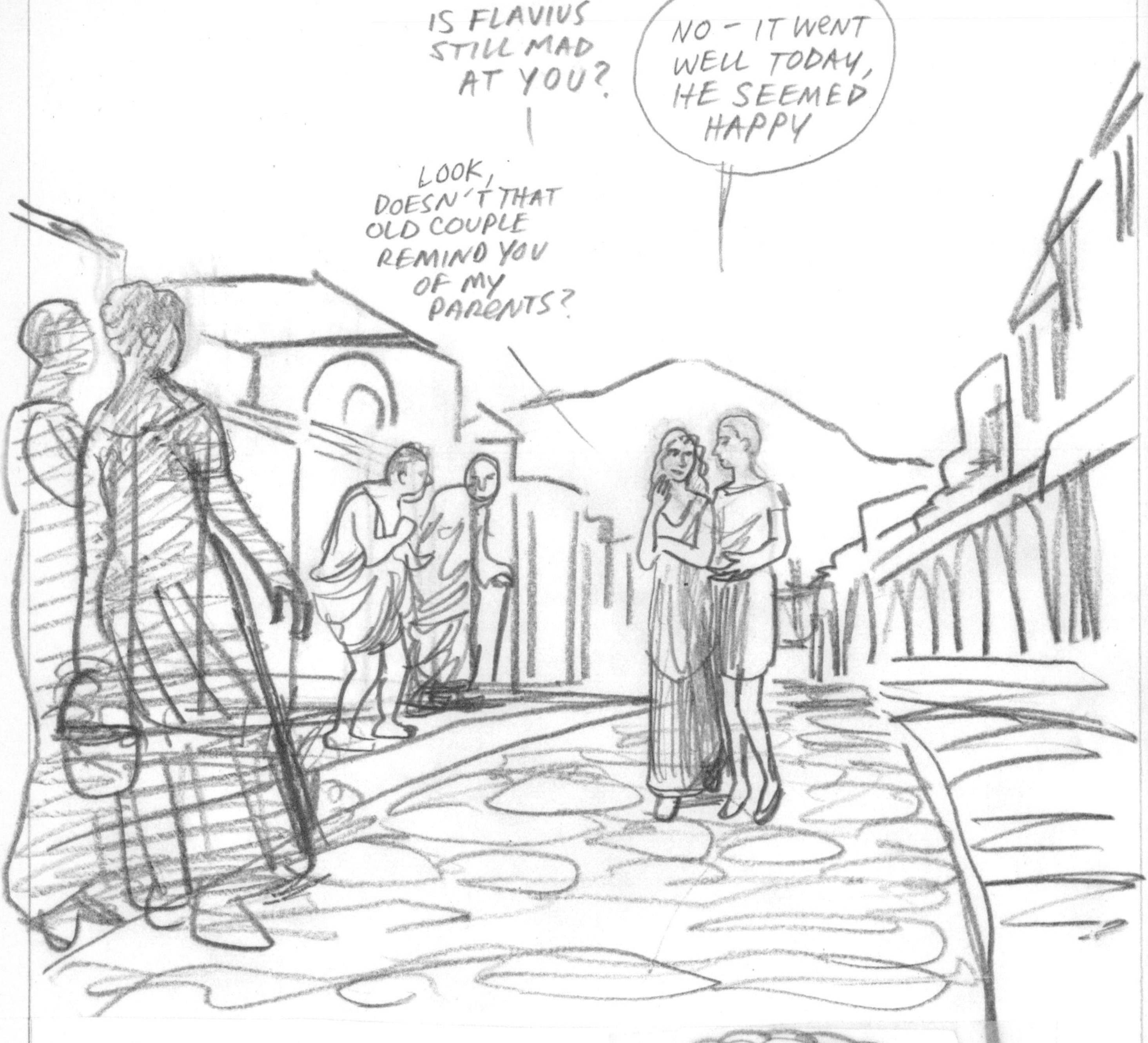
IS FLAVIUS STILL MAD AT YOU?
LOOK, DOESN'T THAT OLD COUPLE REMIND YOU OF MY PARENTS?
NO - IT WENT WELL TODAY, HE SEEMED HAPPY

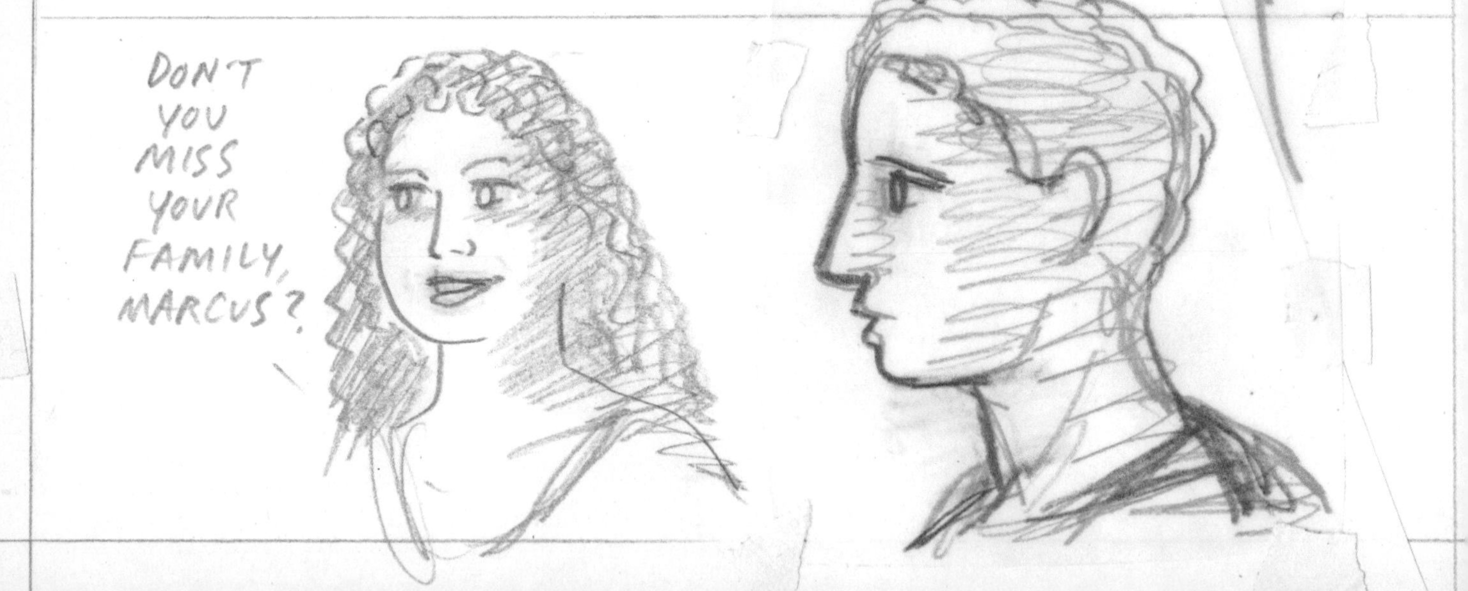
DON'T YOU MISS YOUR FAMILY, MARCUS?

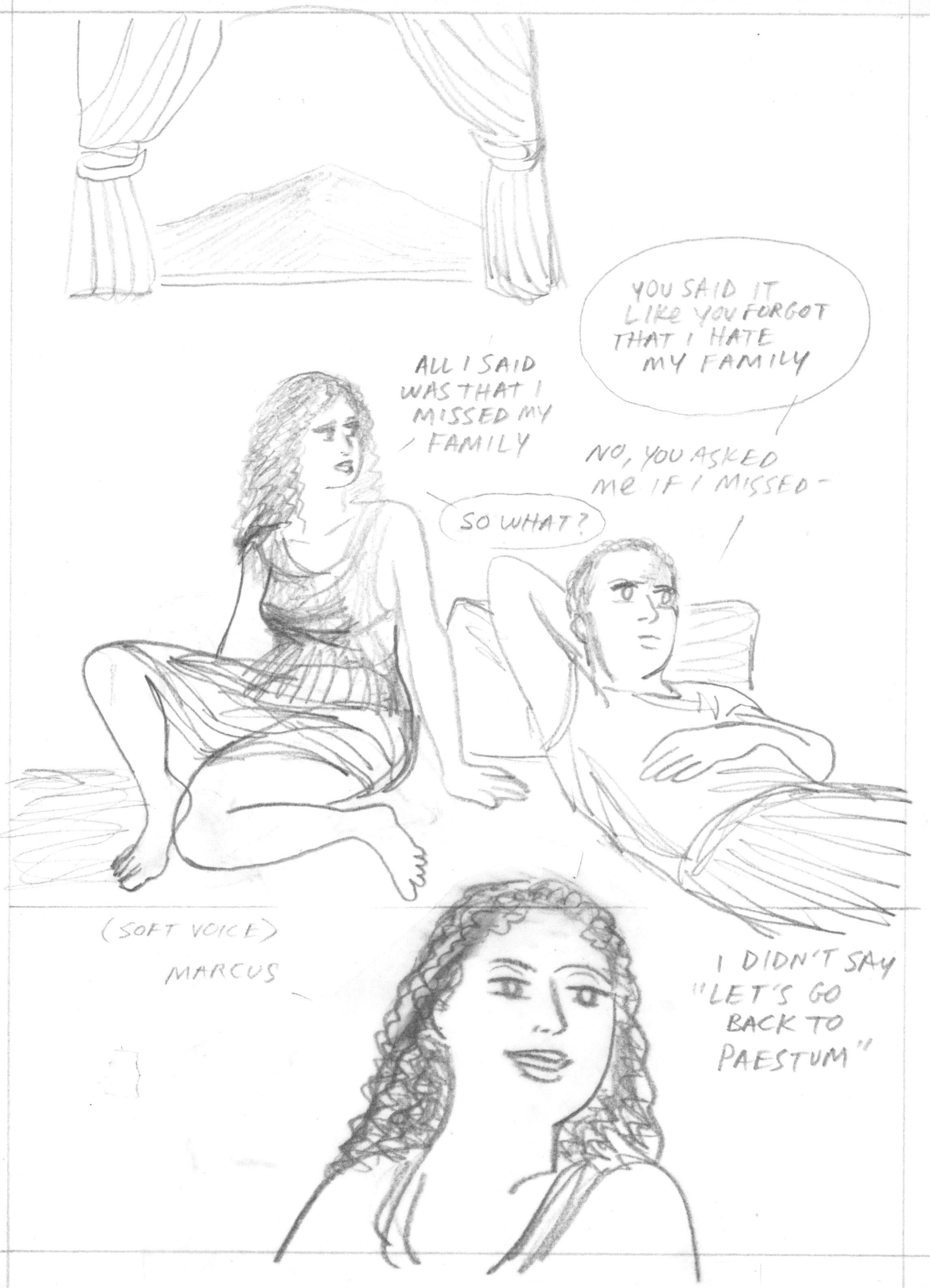
ALL I SAID WAS THAT I MISSED MY FAMILY
NO, YOU ASKED ME IF I MISSED-
SO WHAT?
YOU SAID IT LIKE YOU FORGOT THAT I HATE MY FAMILY
(SOFT VOICE) MARCUS
I DIDN'T SAY "LET'S GO BACK TO PAESTUM"

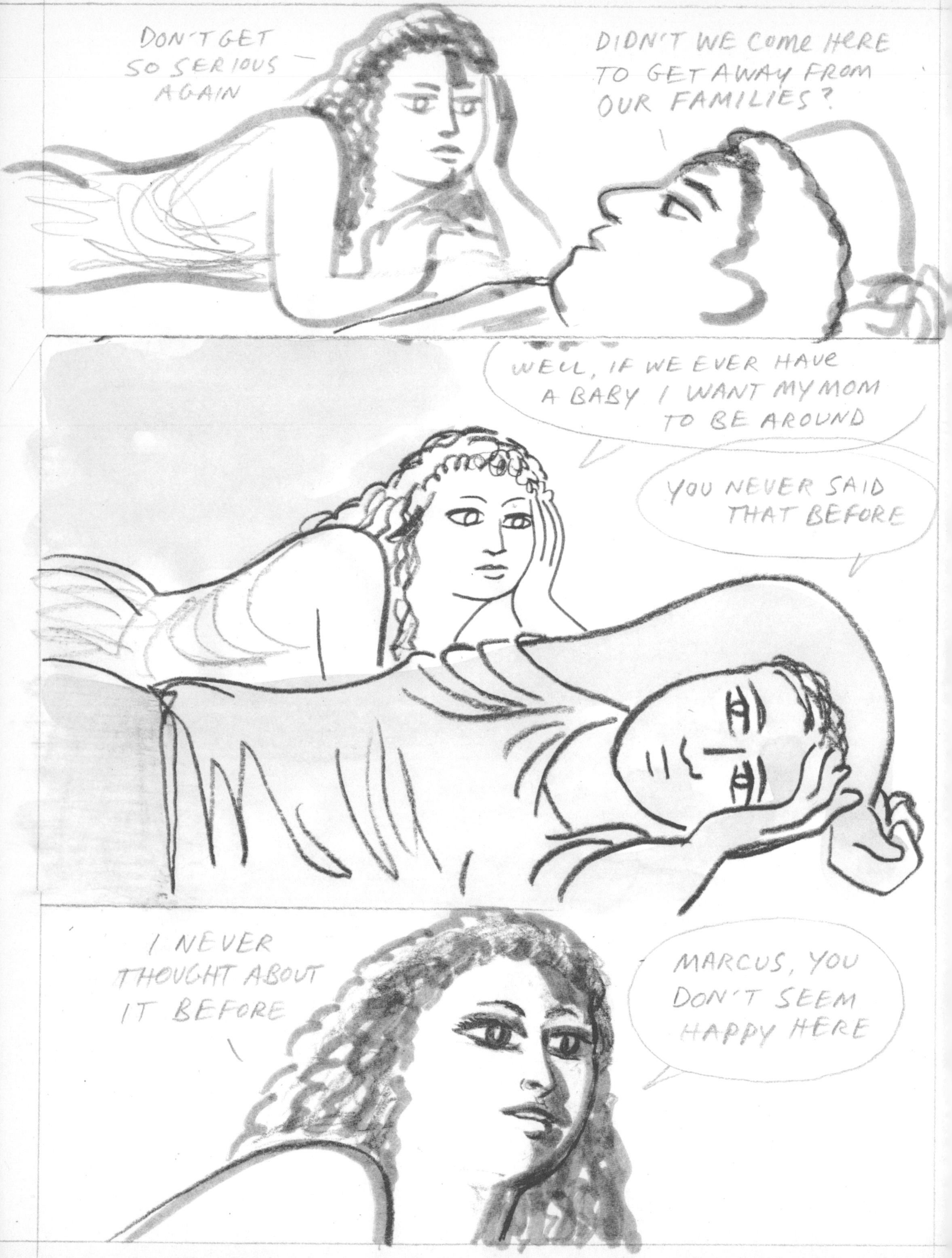

DON'T GET SO SERIOUS AGAIN
DIDN'T WE COME HERE TO GET AWAY FROM OUR FAMILIES?
WELL, IF WE EVER HAVE A BABY I WANT MY MOM TO BE AROUND
YOU NEVER SAID THAT BEFORE
I NEVER THOUGHT ABOUT IT BEFORE
MARCUS, YOU DON'T SEEM HAPPY HERE

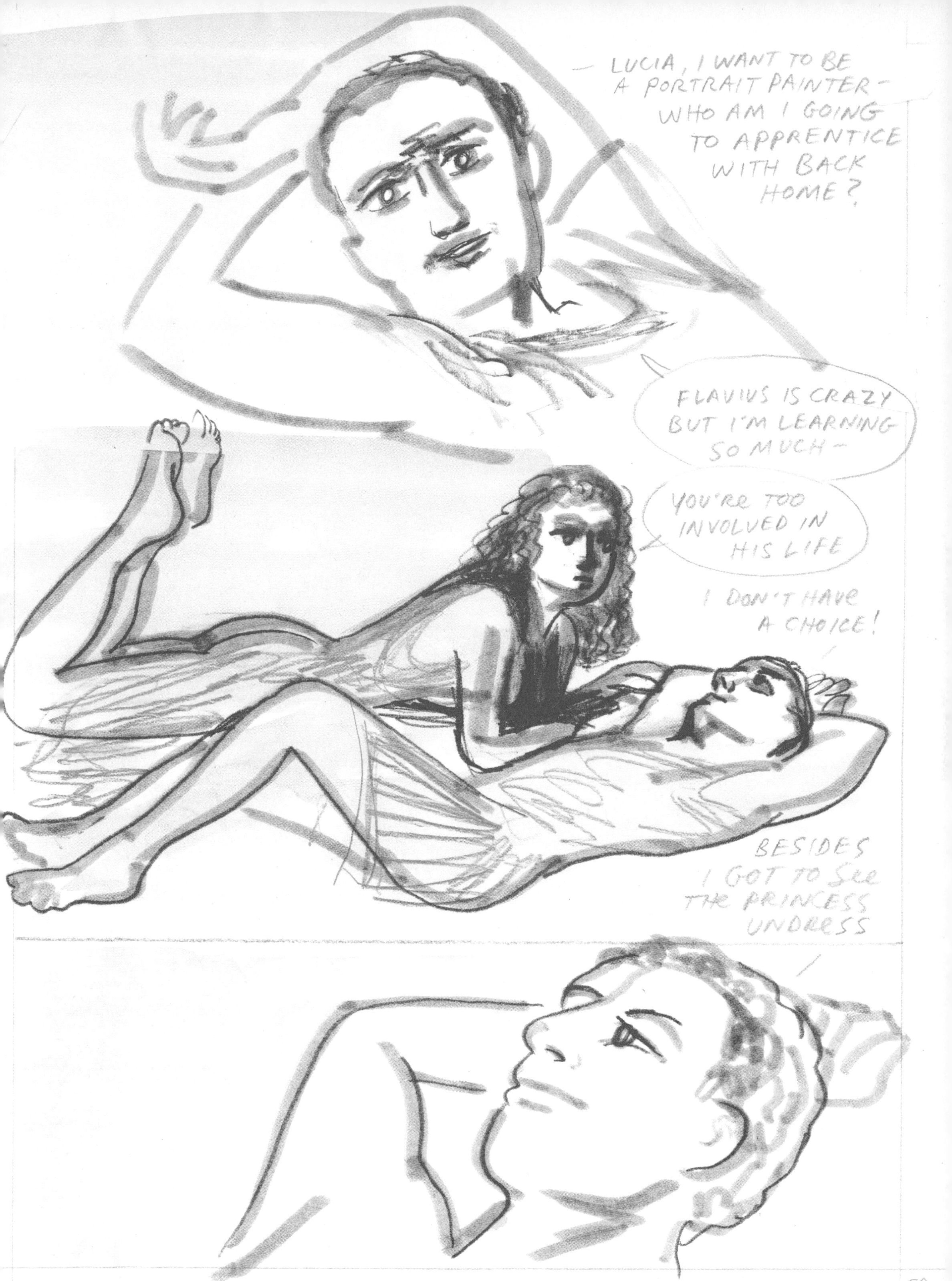

LUCIA, I WANT TO BE A PORTRAIT PAINTER - WHO AM I GOING TO APPRENTICE WITH BACK HOME?
FLAVIUS IS CRAZY BUT I'M LEARNING SO MUCH -
YOU'RE TOO INVOLVED IN HIS LIFE
I DON'T HAVE A CHOICE!
BESIDES I GOT TO SEE THE PRINCESS UNDRESS

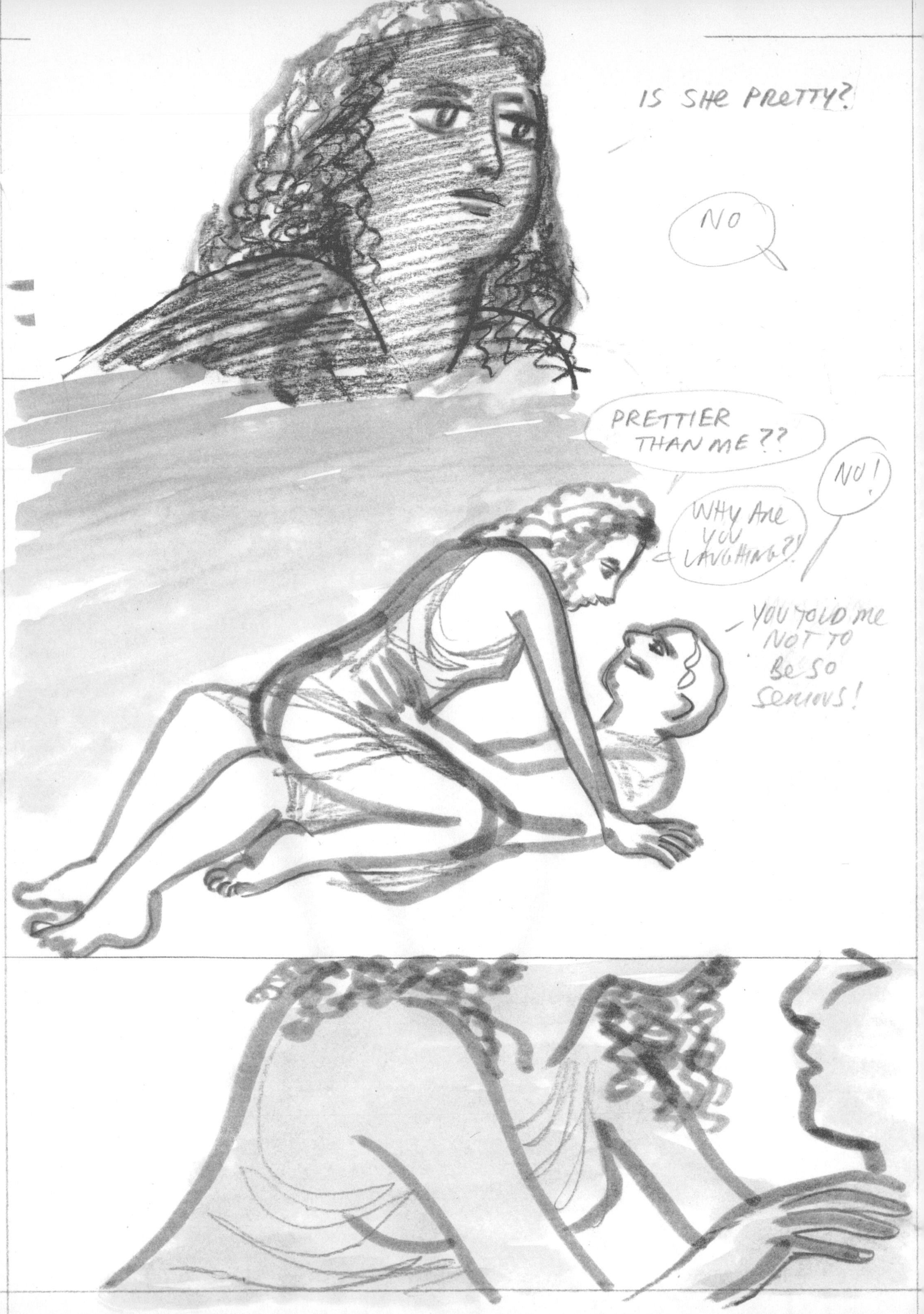
IS SHE PRETTY?
NO
PRETTIER THAN ME??
NO!
WHY ARE YOU LAUGHING?!
YOU TOLD ME NOT TO BE SO SERIOUS!

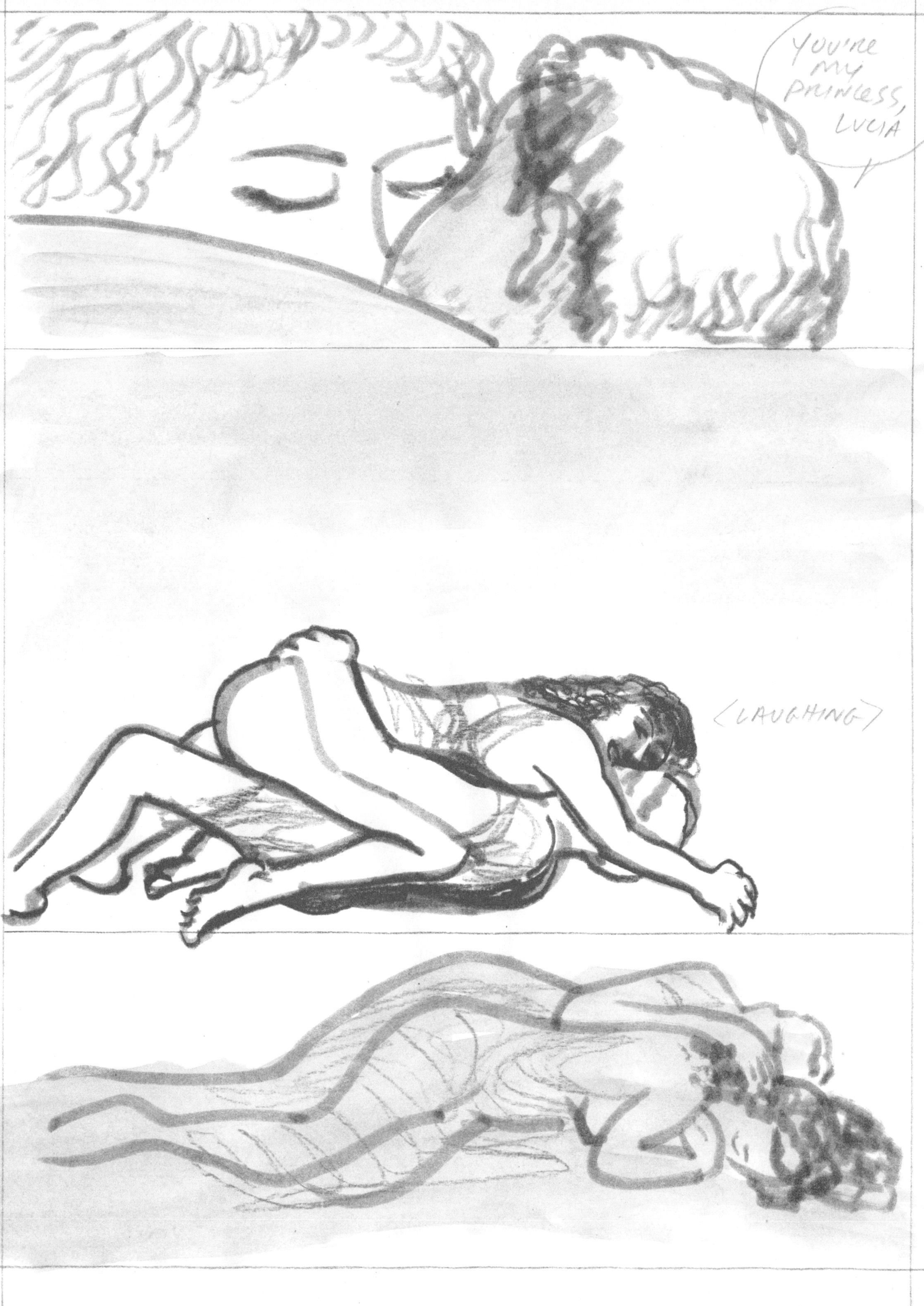
YOU'RE MY PRINCESS, LUCIA
<LAUGHING>

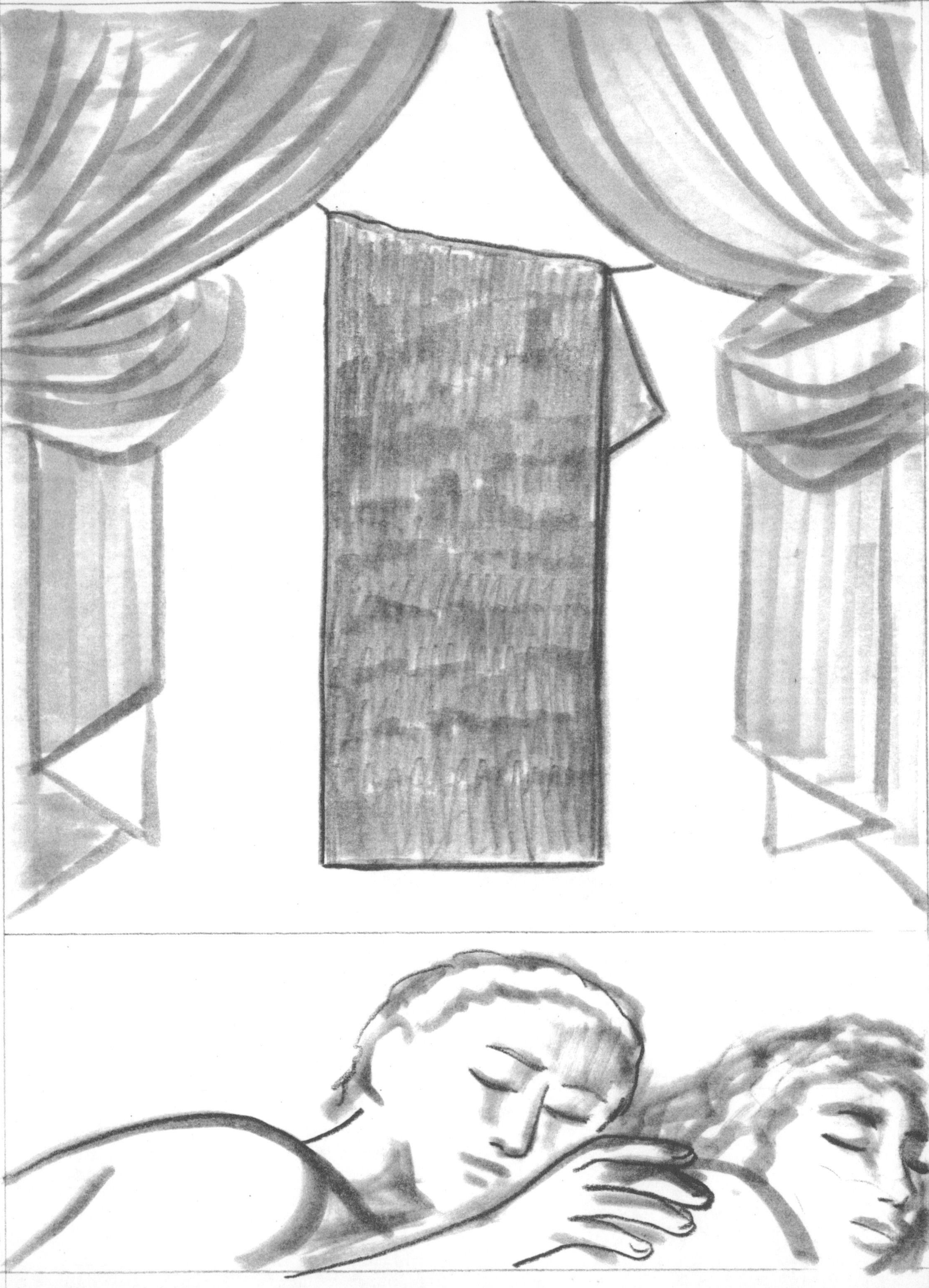

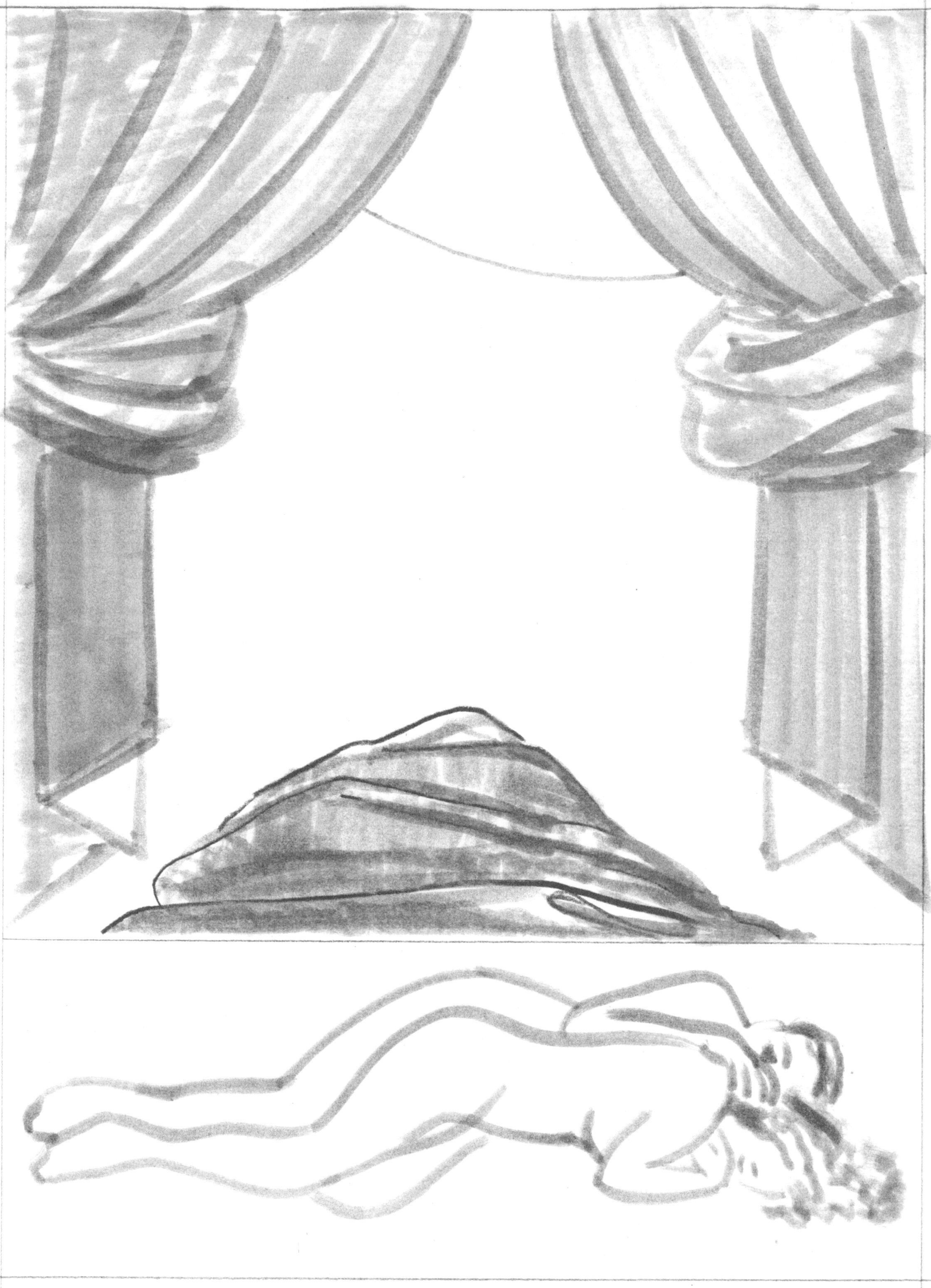

<AFTER ARGUING IN THE MIDDLE OF THE NIGHT FOR AN HOUR>

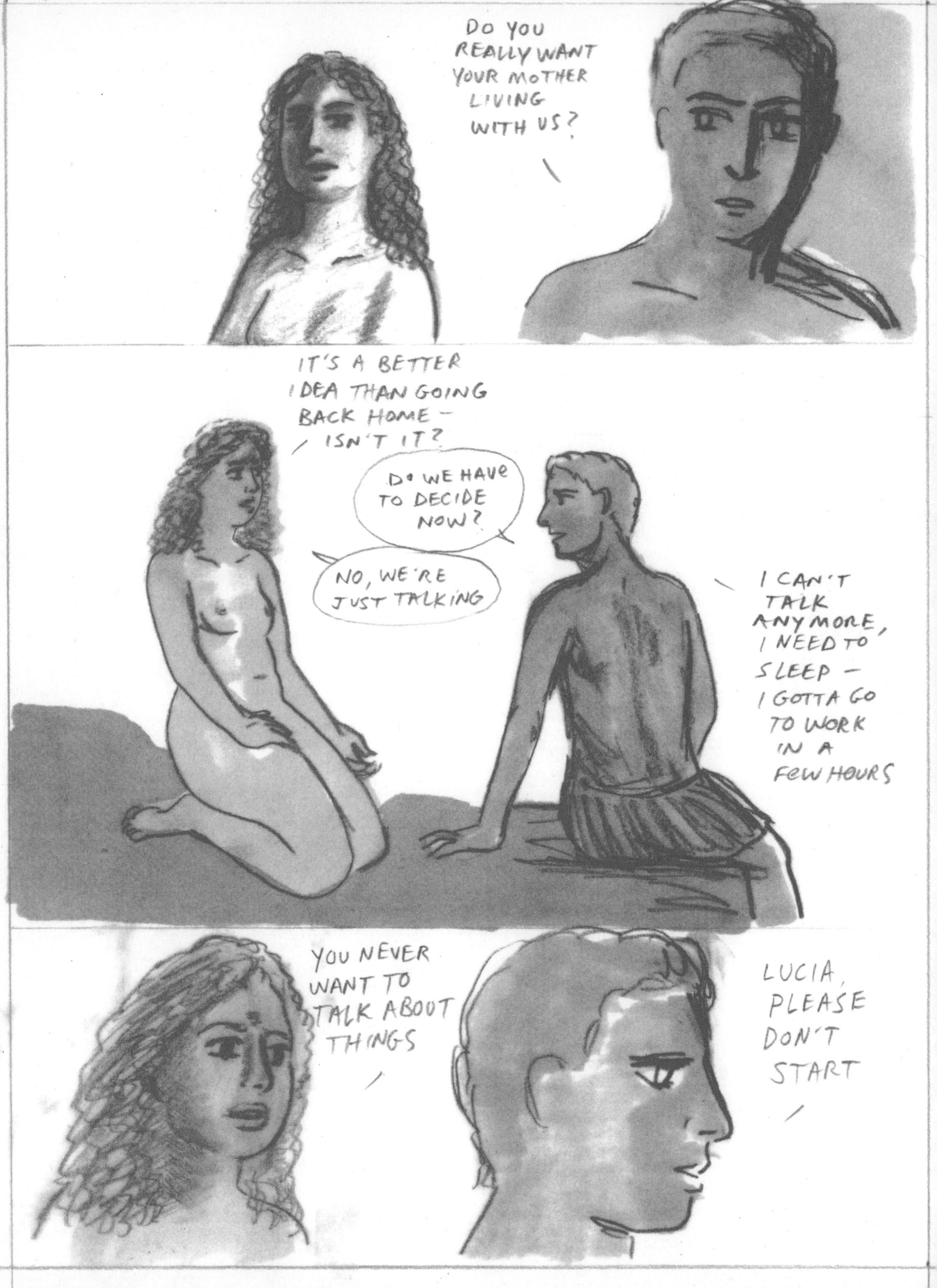
DO YOU REALLY WANT YOUR MOTHER LIVING WITH US?
IT'S A BETTER IDEA THAN GOING BACK HOME - ISN'T IT?
DO WE HAVE TO DECIDE NOW?
NO, WE'RE JUST TALKING
I CAN'T TALK ANYMORE, I NEED TO SLEEP - I GOTTA GO TO WORK IN A FEW HOURS
YOU NEVER WANT TO TALK ABOUT THINGS
LUCIA, PLEASE DON'T START

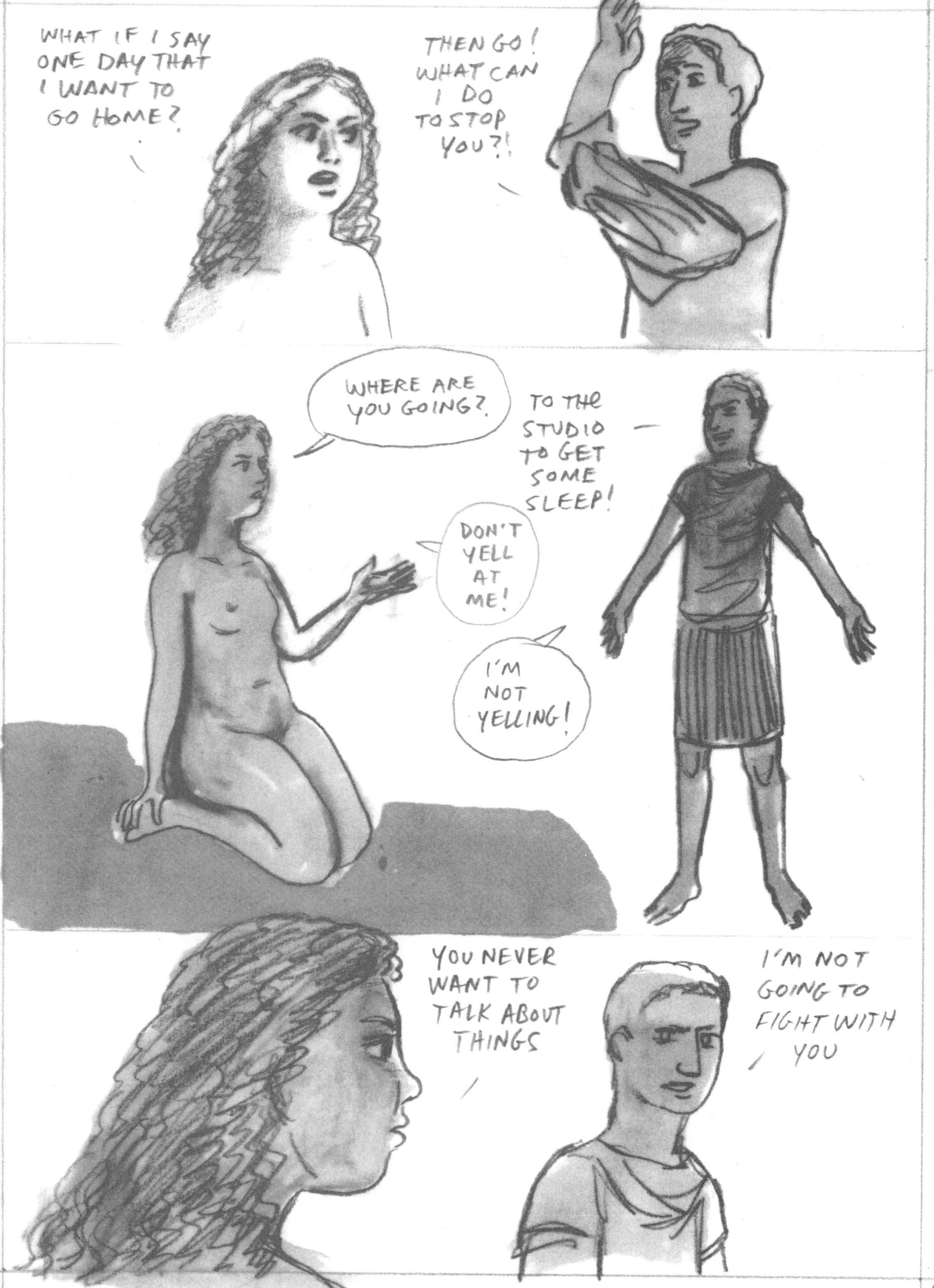
WHAT IF I SAY ONE DAY THAT I WANT TO GO HOME?
THEN GO! WHAT CAN I DO TO STOP YOU?!
WHERE ARE YOU GOING?
TO THE STUDIO TO GET SOME SLEEP!
DON'T YELL AT ME!
I'M NOT YELLING!
YOU NEVER WANT TO TALK ABOUT THINGS
I'M NOT GOING TO FIGHT WITH YOU

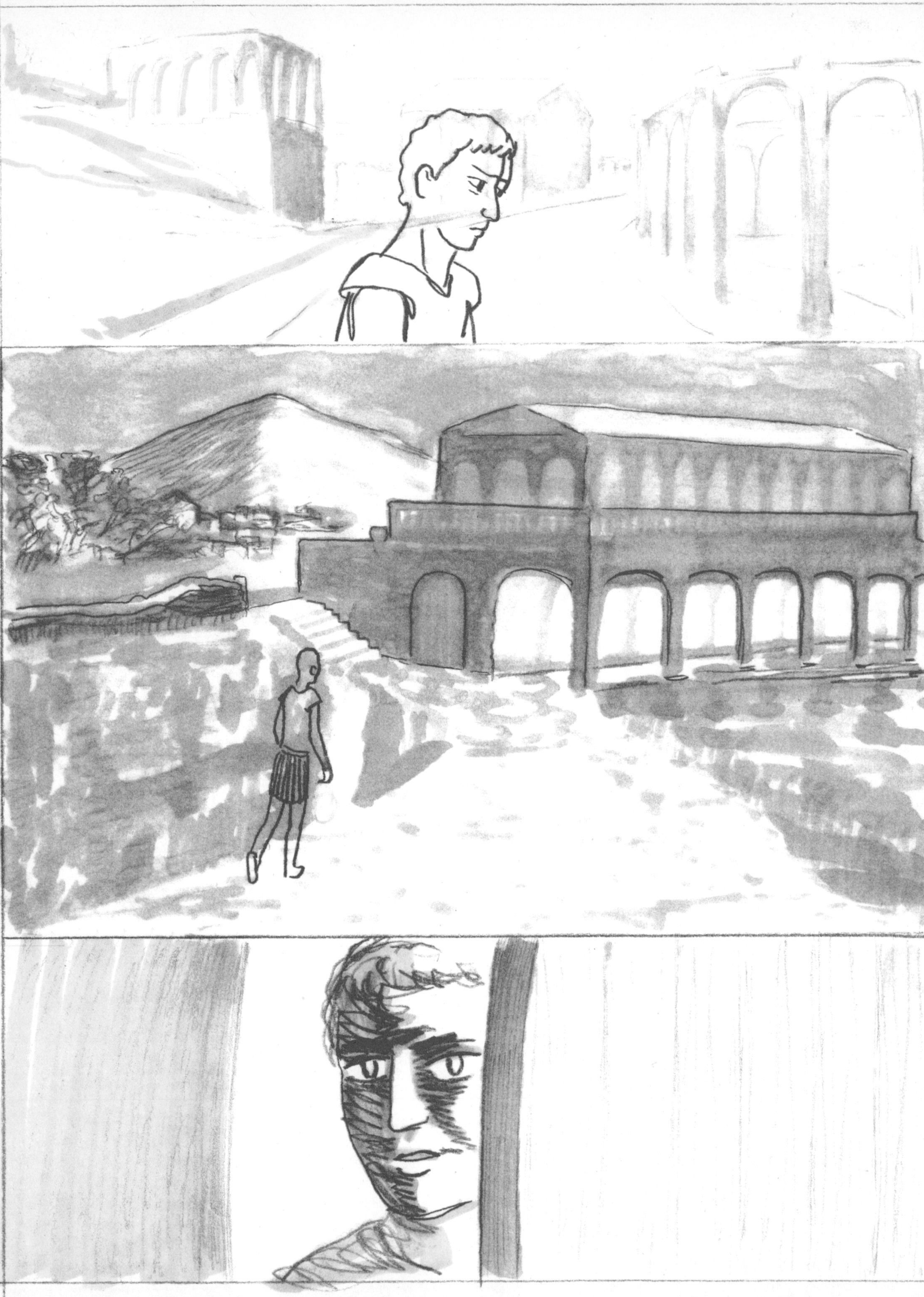

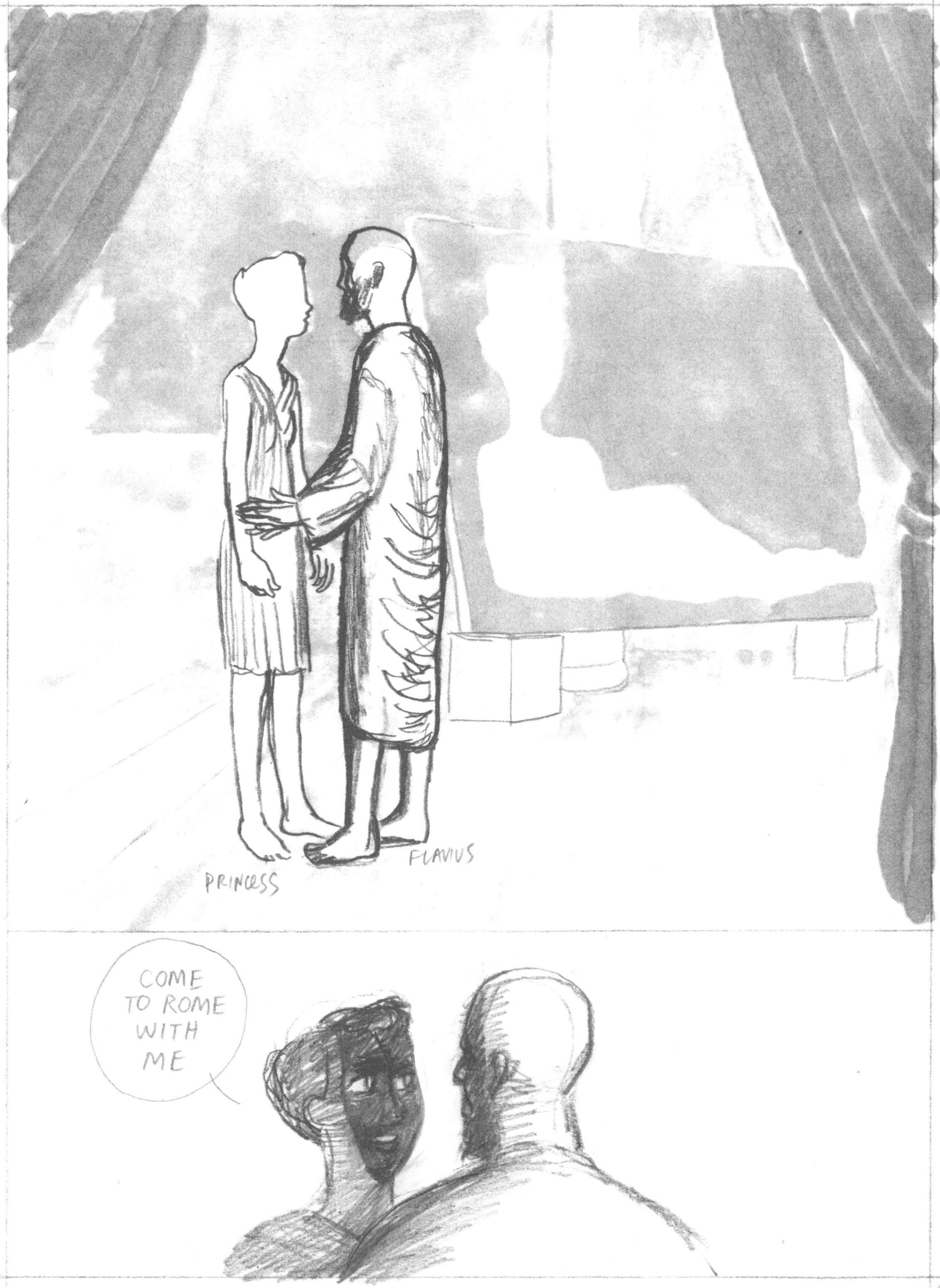
PRINCESS
FLAVIUS
COME TO ROME WITH ME

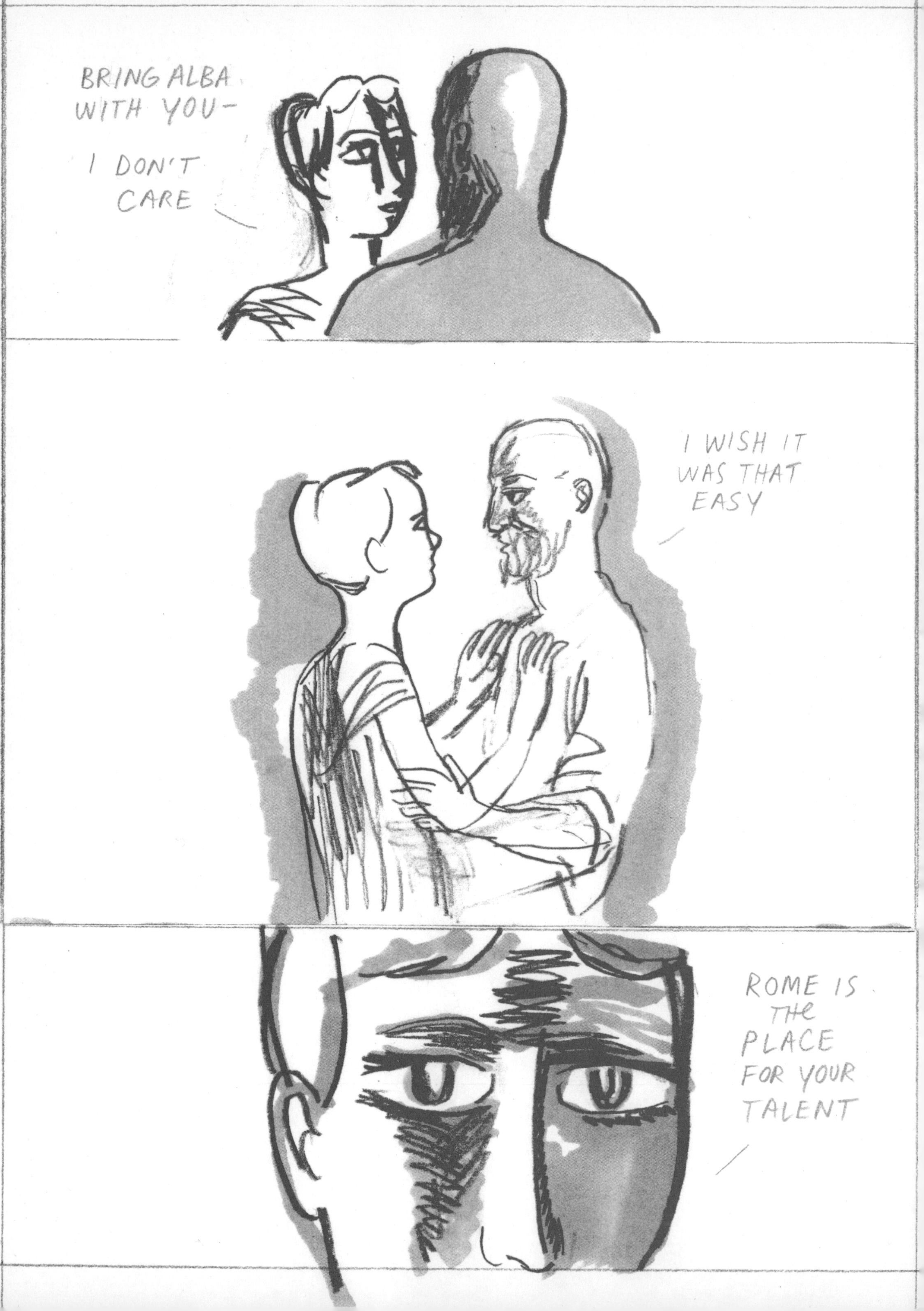
BRING ALBA WITH YOU-
I DON'T CARE
I WISH IT WAS THAT EASY
ROME IS THE PLACE FOR YOUR TALENT

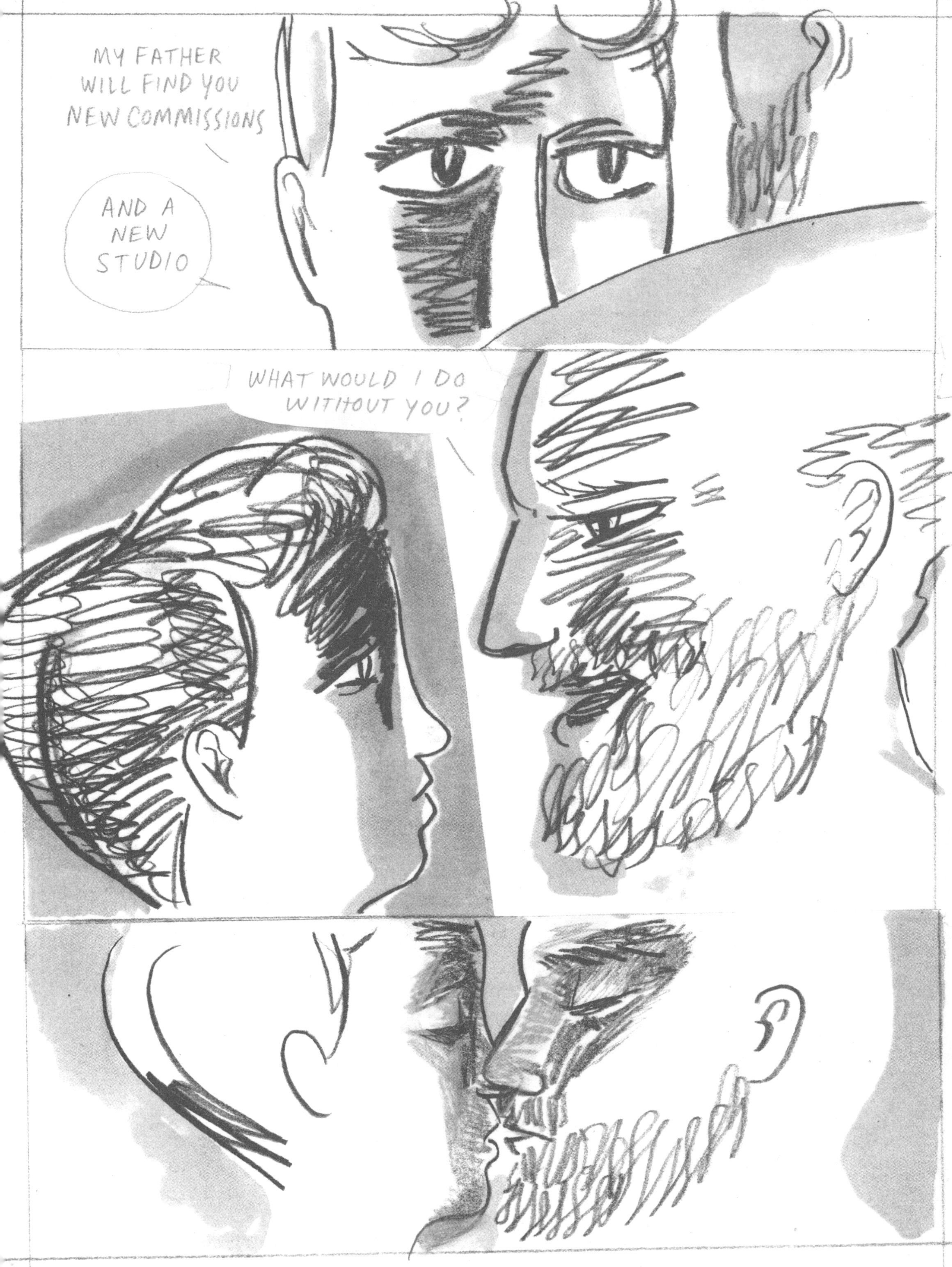
MY FATHER WILL FIND YOU NEW COMMISSIONS
AND A NEW STUDIO
WHAT WOULD I DO WITHOUT YOU?

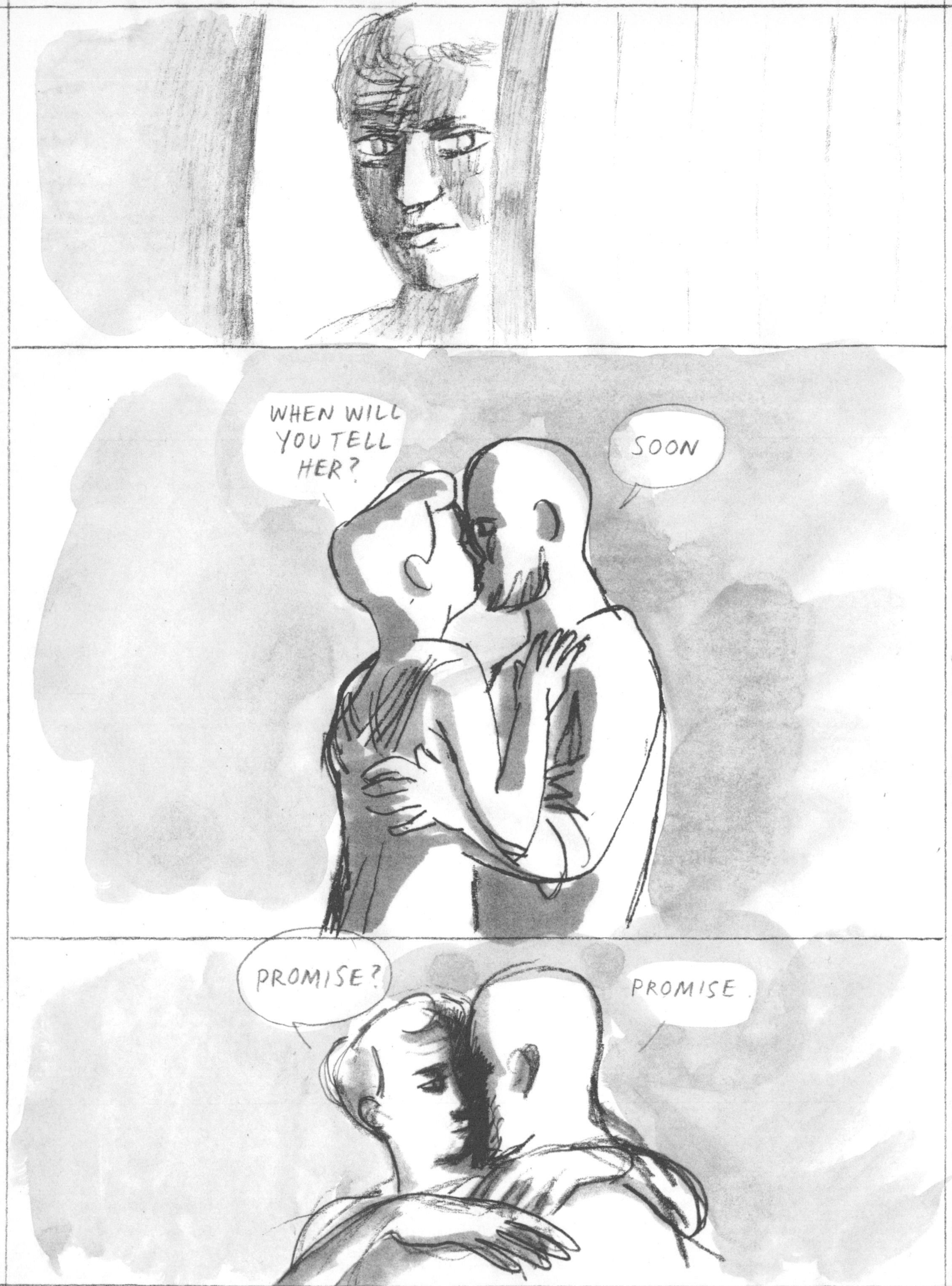
WHEN WILL YOU TELL HER?
SOON
PROMISE?
PROMISE.

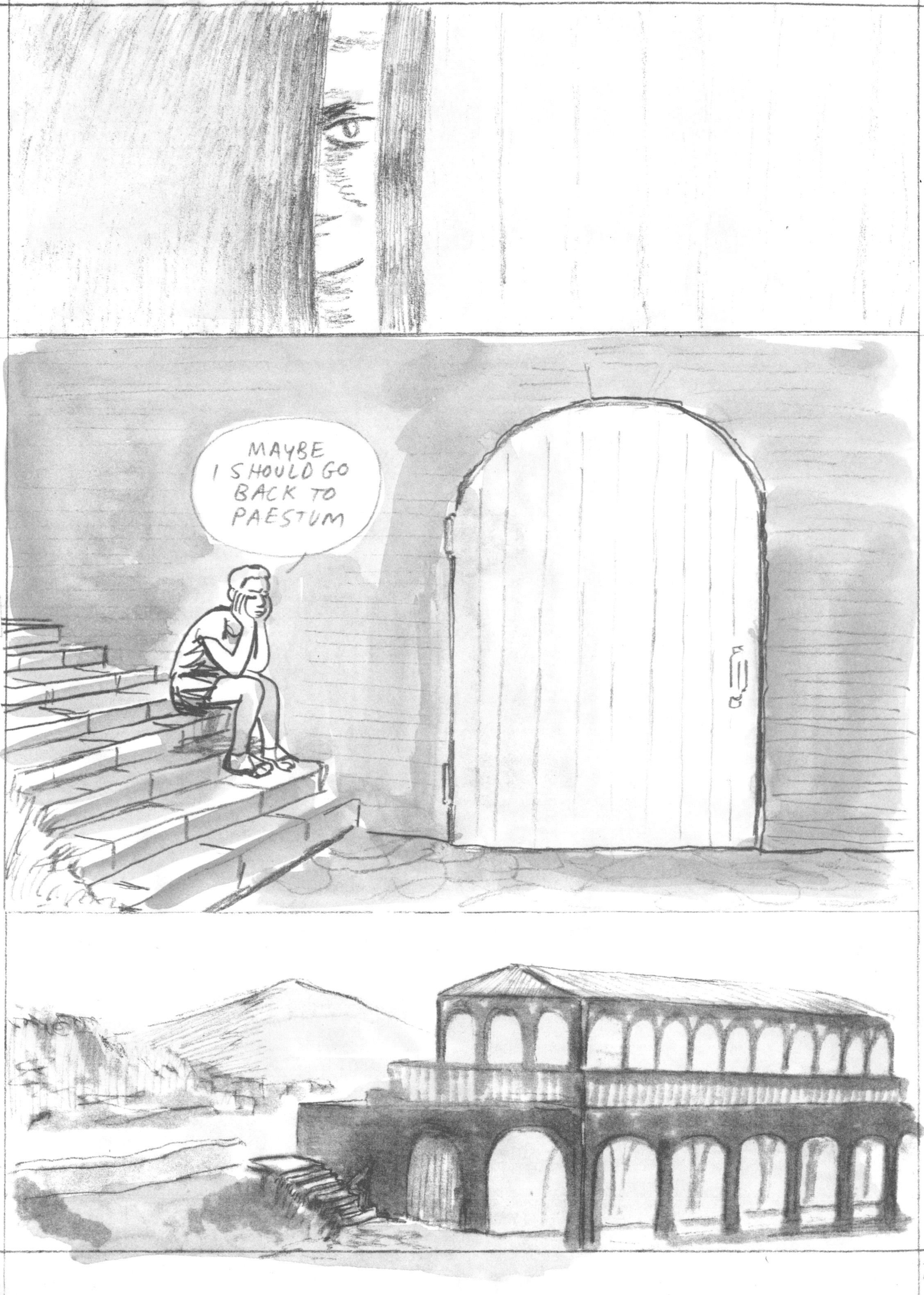
MAYBE I SHOULD GO BACK TO PAESTUM

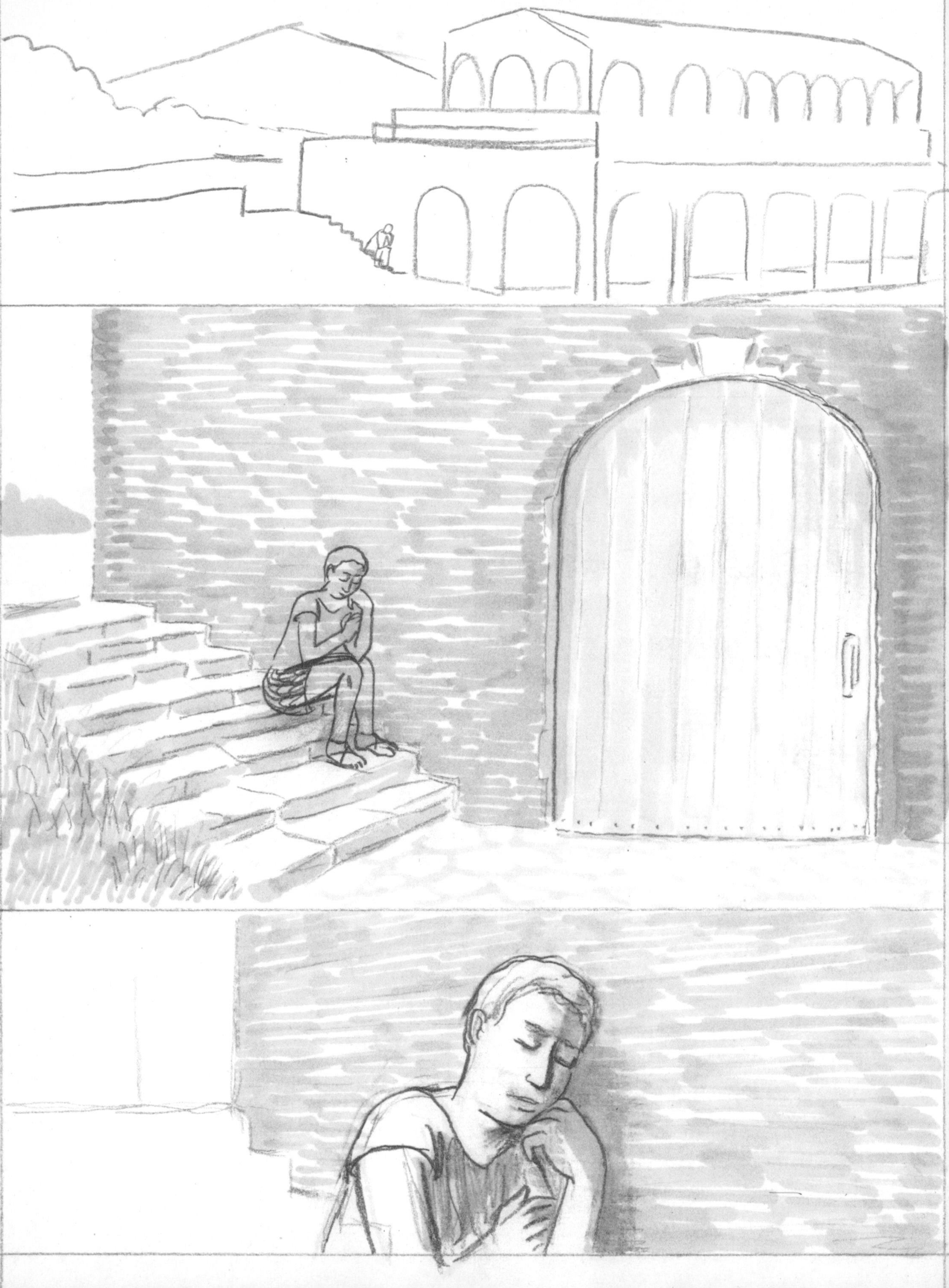

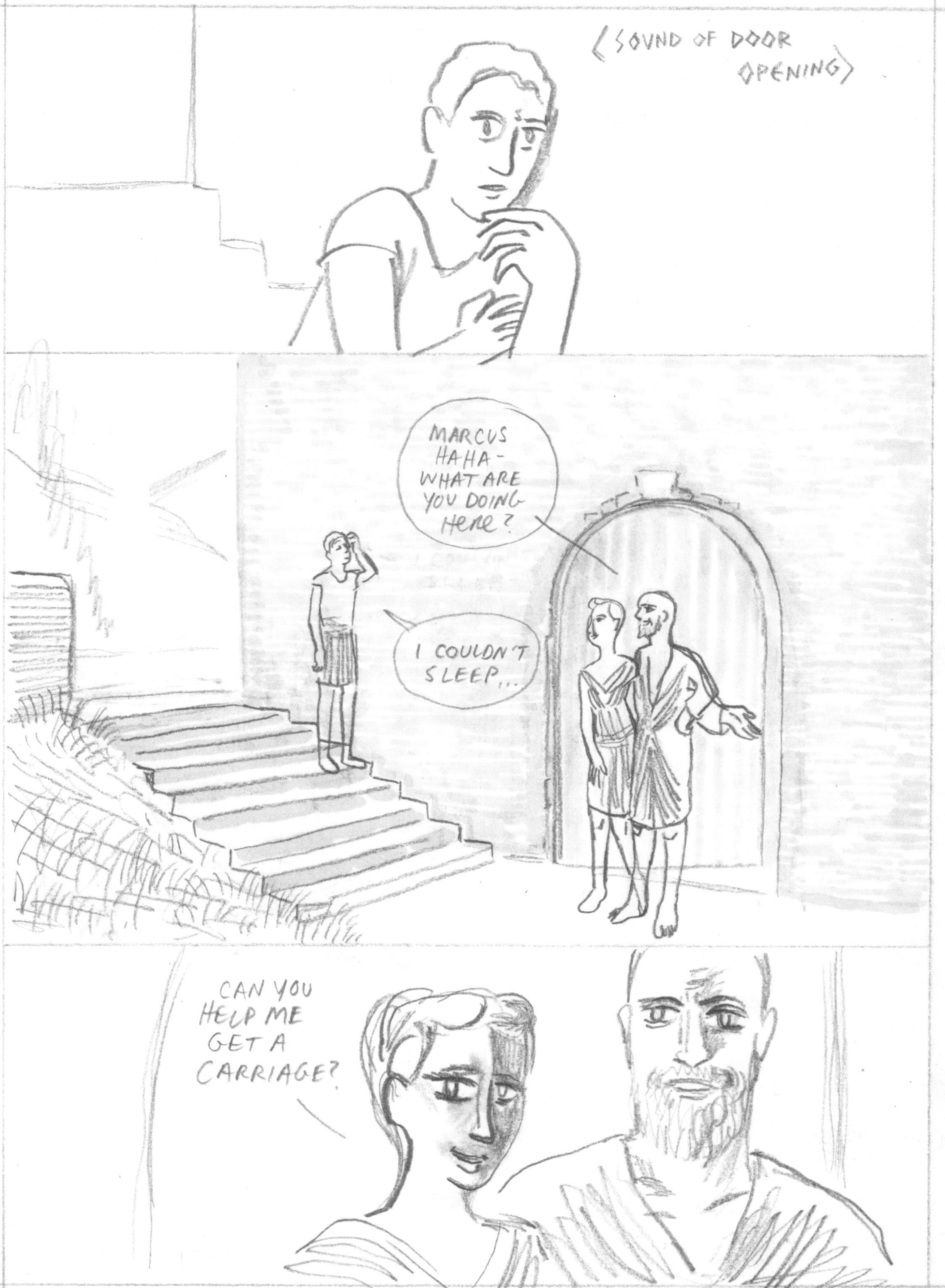

⟨SOUND OF DOOR OPENING⟩
MARCUS HAHA- WHAT ARE YOU DOING HERE?
I COULDN'T SLEEP...
CAN YOU HELP ME GET A CARRIAGE?

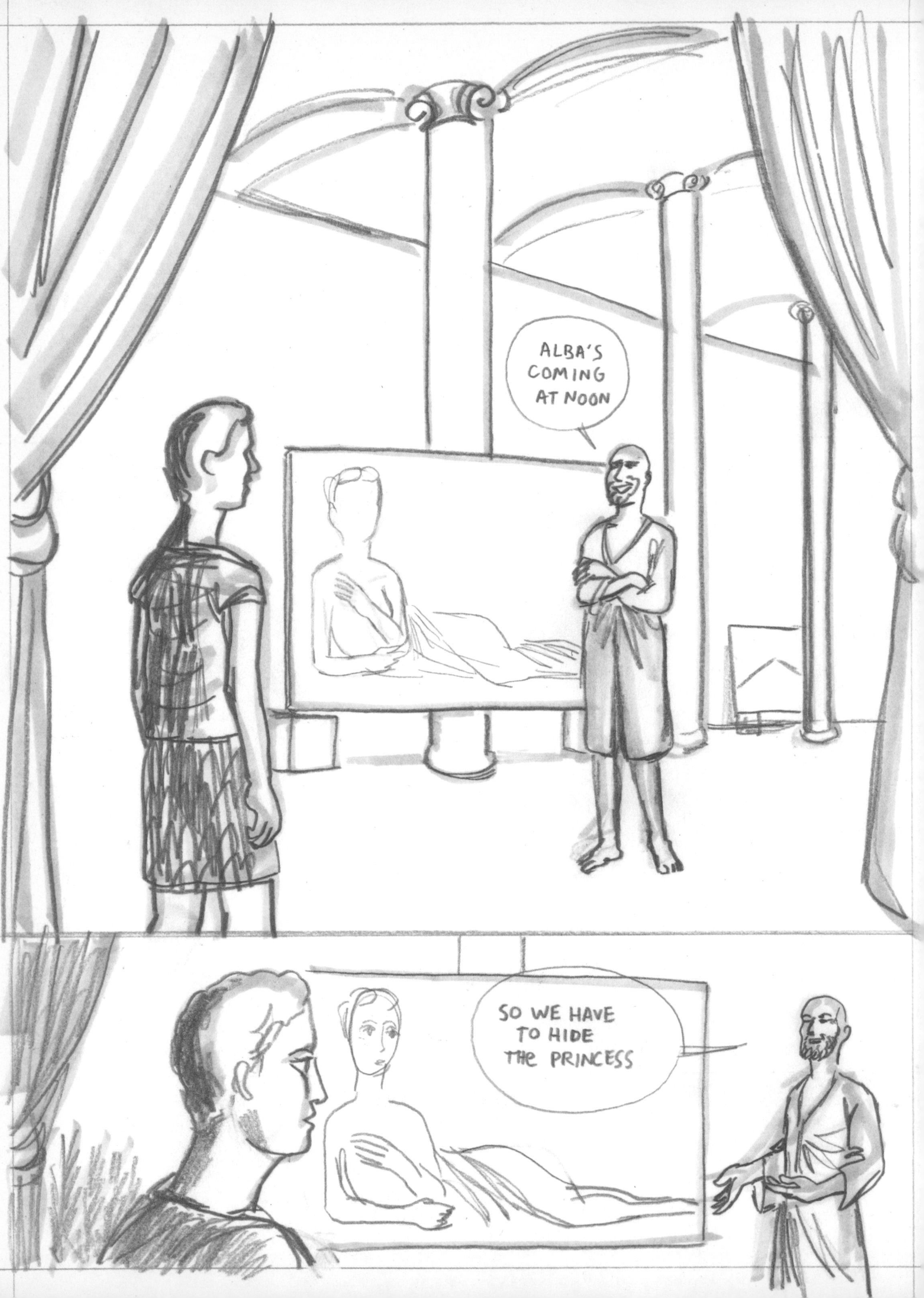
ALBA'S COMING AT NOON
SO WE HAVE TO HIDE THE PRINCESS

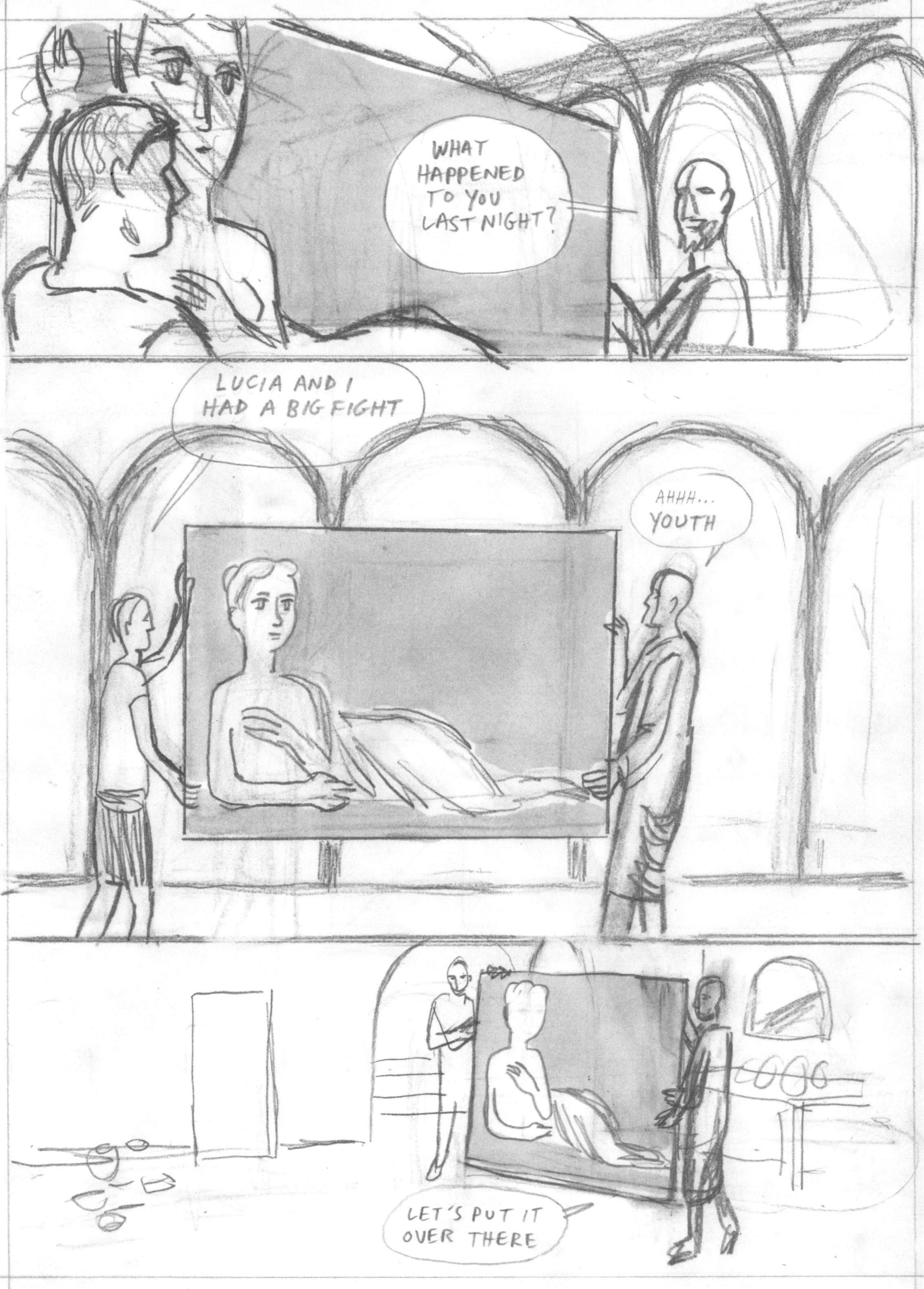
WHAT HAPPENED TO YOU LAST NIGHT?
LUCIA AND I HAD A BIG FIGHT
AHHH... YOUTH
LET'S PUT IT OVER THERE

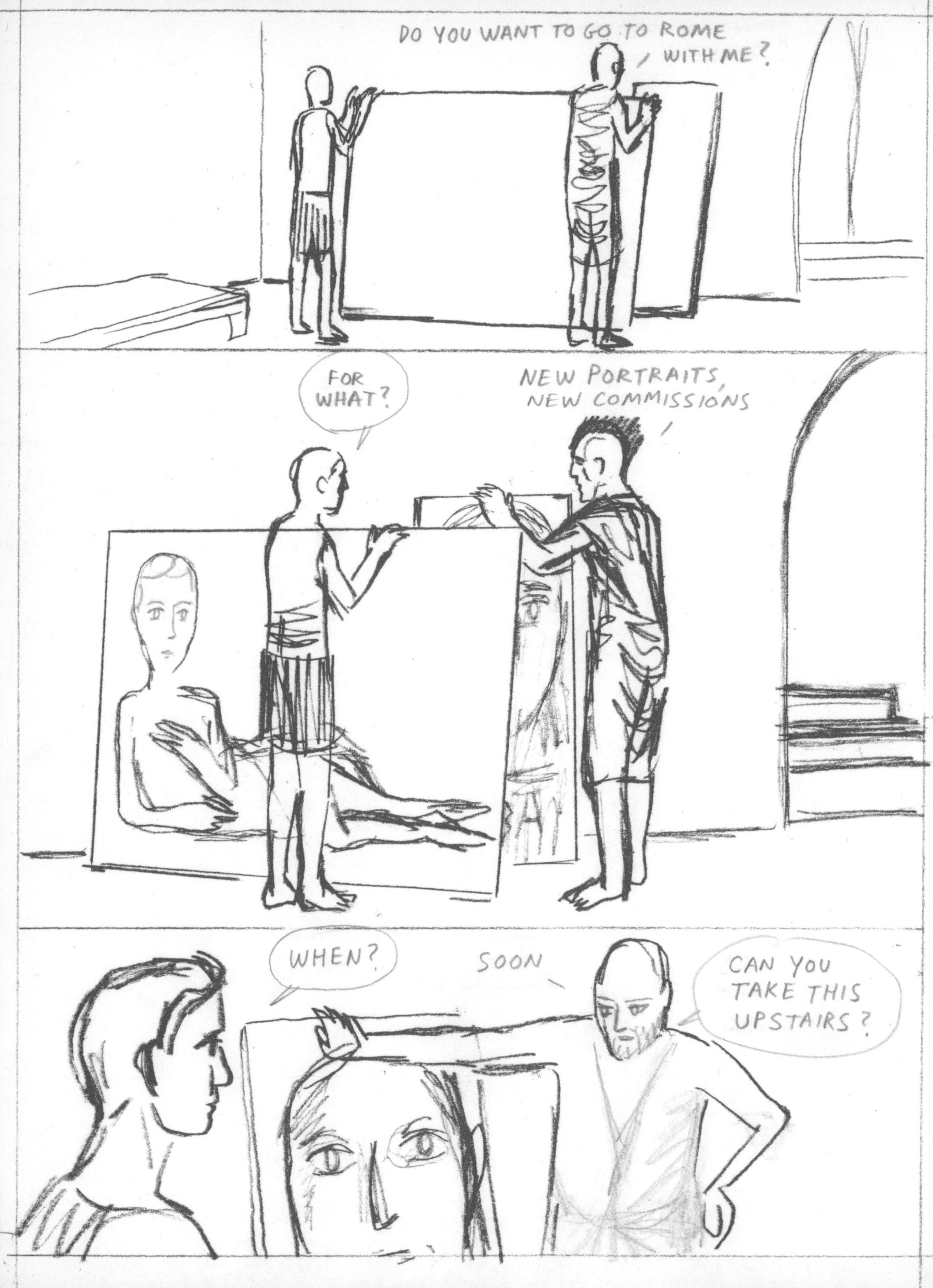
DO YOU WANT TO GO TO ROME WITH ME?
FOR WHAT?
NEW PORTRAITS, NEW COMMISSIONS
WHEN?
SOON
CAN YOU TAKE THIS UPSTAIRS?

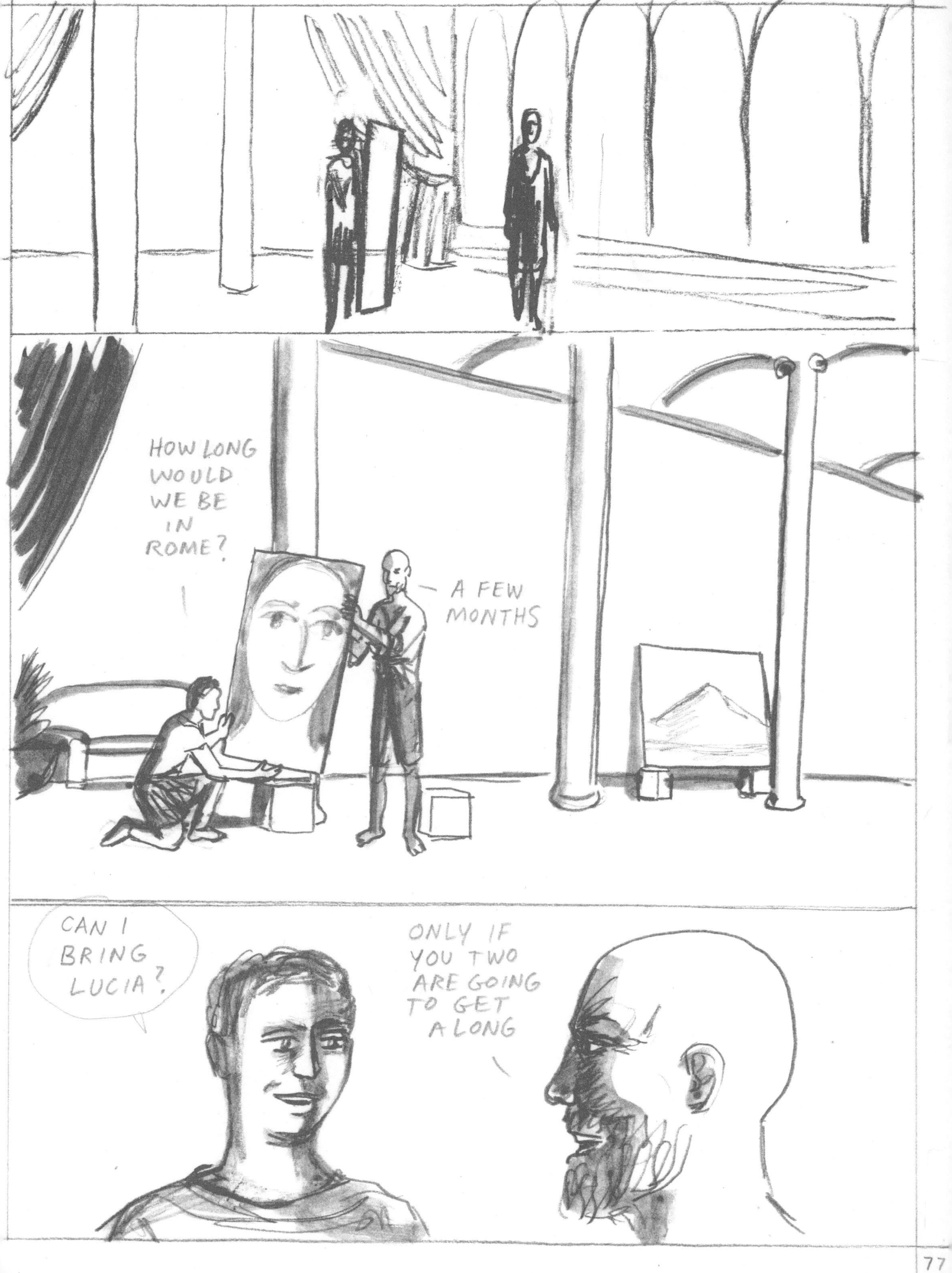
HOW LONG WOULD WE BE IN ROME?
A FEW MONTHS
CAN I BRING LUCIA?
ONLY IF YOU TWO ARE GOING TO GET ALONG

<NOON>

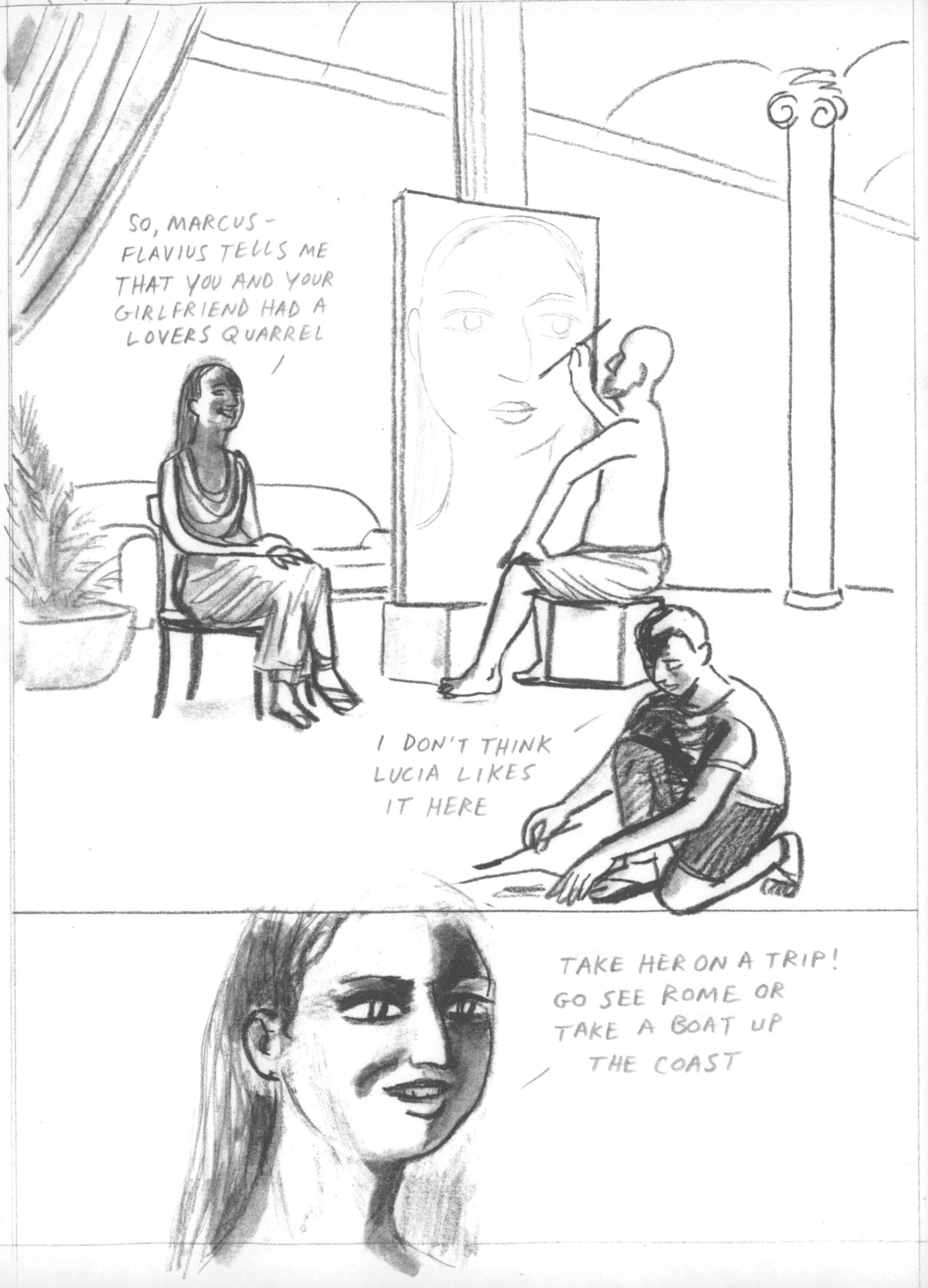
SO, MARCUS-
FLAVIUS TELLS ME
THAT YOU AND YOUR
GIRLFRIEND HAD A
LOVERS QUARREL
I DON'T THINK
LUCIA LIKES
IT HERE
TAKE HER ON A TRIP!
GO SEE ROME OR
TAKE A BOAT UP
THE COAST

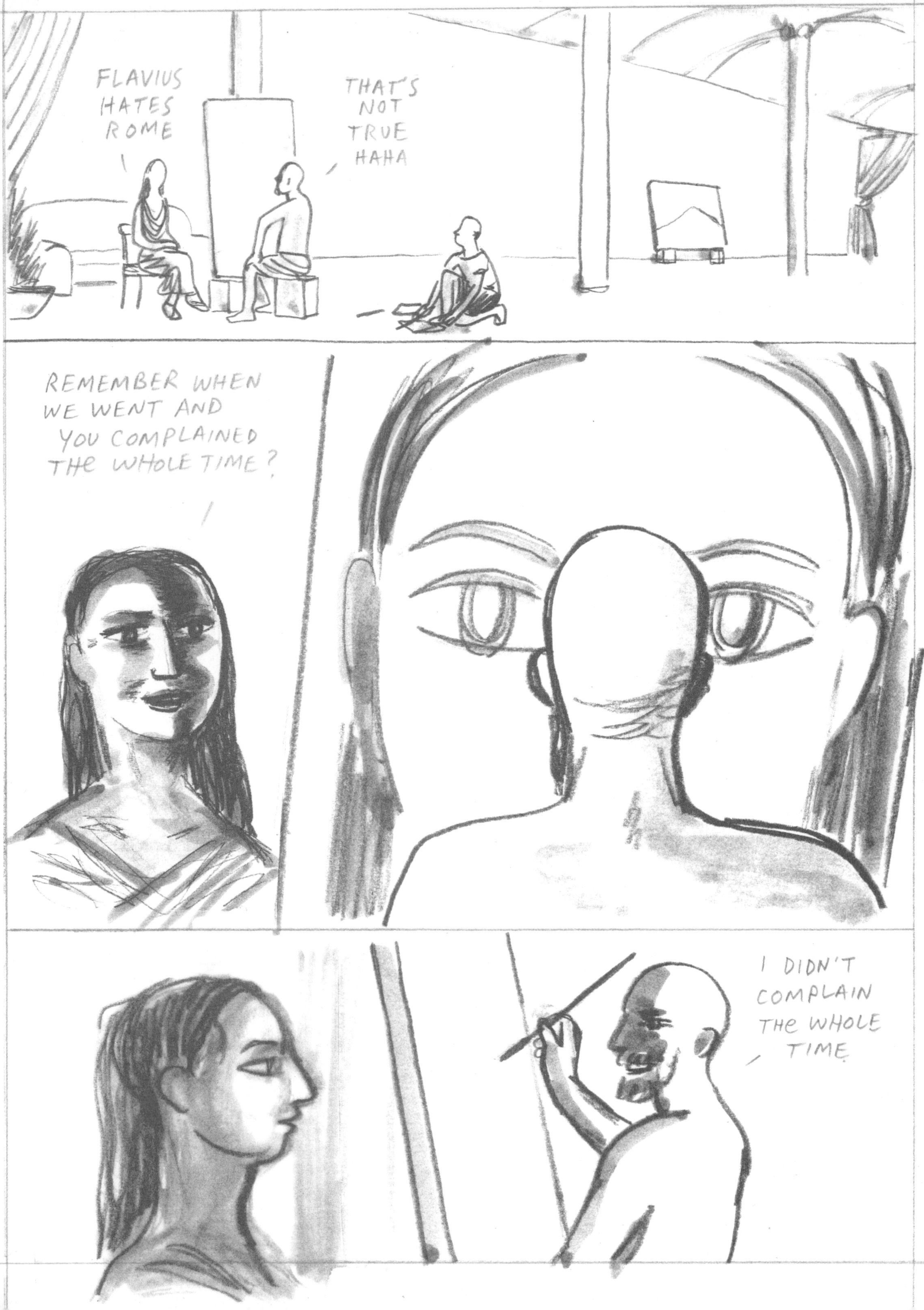
FLAVIUS HATES ROME
THAT'S NOT TRUE HAHA
REMEMBER WHEN WE WENT AND YOU COMPLAINED THE WHOLE TIME?
I DIDN'T COMPLAIN THE WHOLE TIME

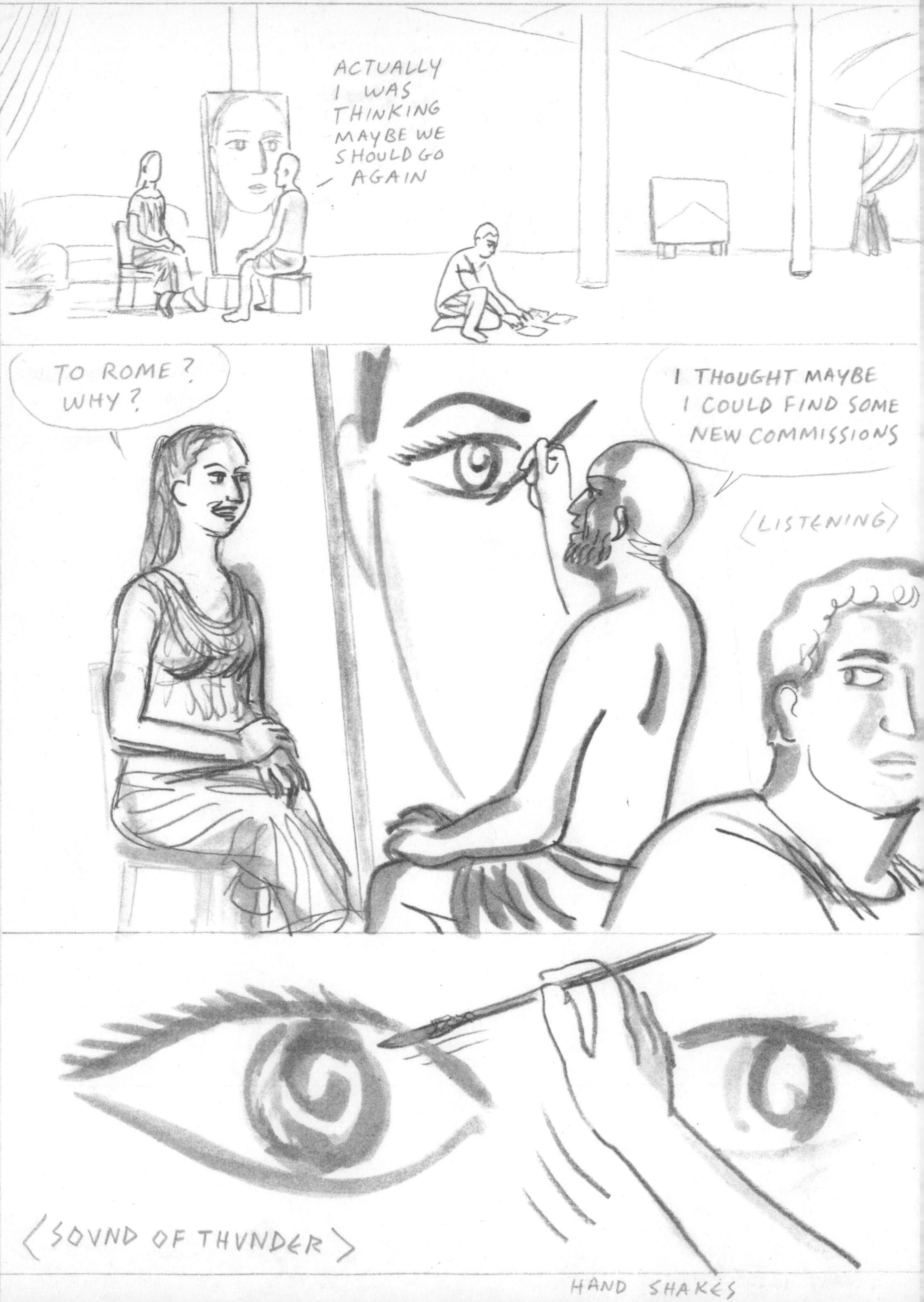
ACTUALLY I WAS THINKING MAYBE WE SHOULD GO AGAIN
TO ROME? WHY?
I THOUGHT MAYBE I COULD FIND SOME NEW COMMISSIONS
<LISTENING>
<SOUND OF THUNDER>
HAND SHAKES

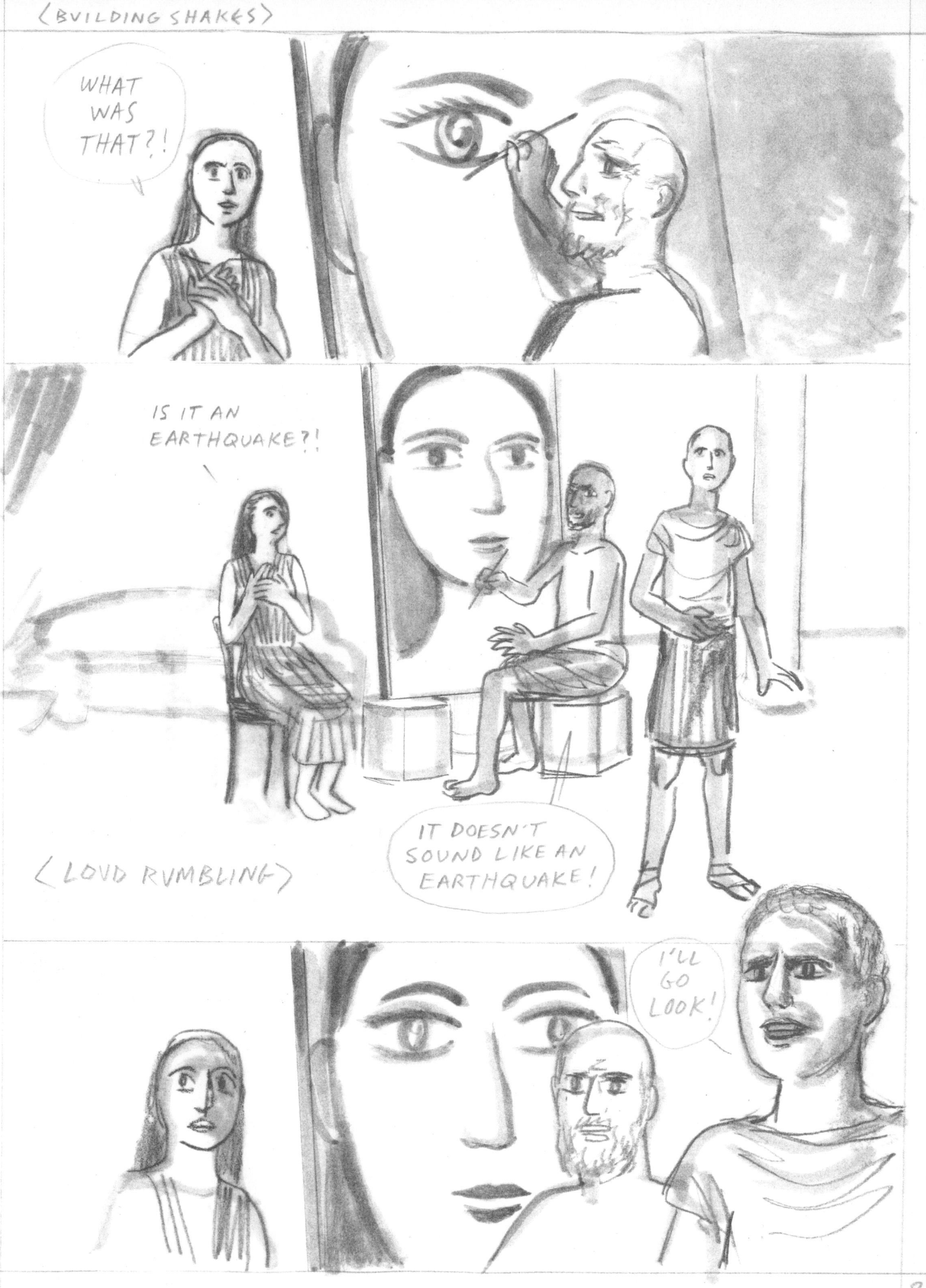
<BUILDING SHAKES>
WHAT WAS THAT?!
IS IT AN EARTHQUAKE?!
<LOUD RUMBLING>
IT DOESN'T SOUND LIKE AN EARTHQUAKE!
I'LL GO LOOK!

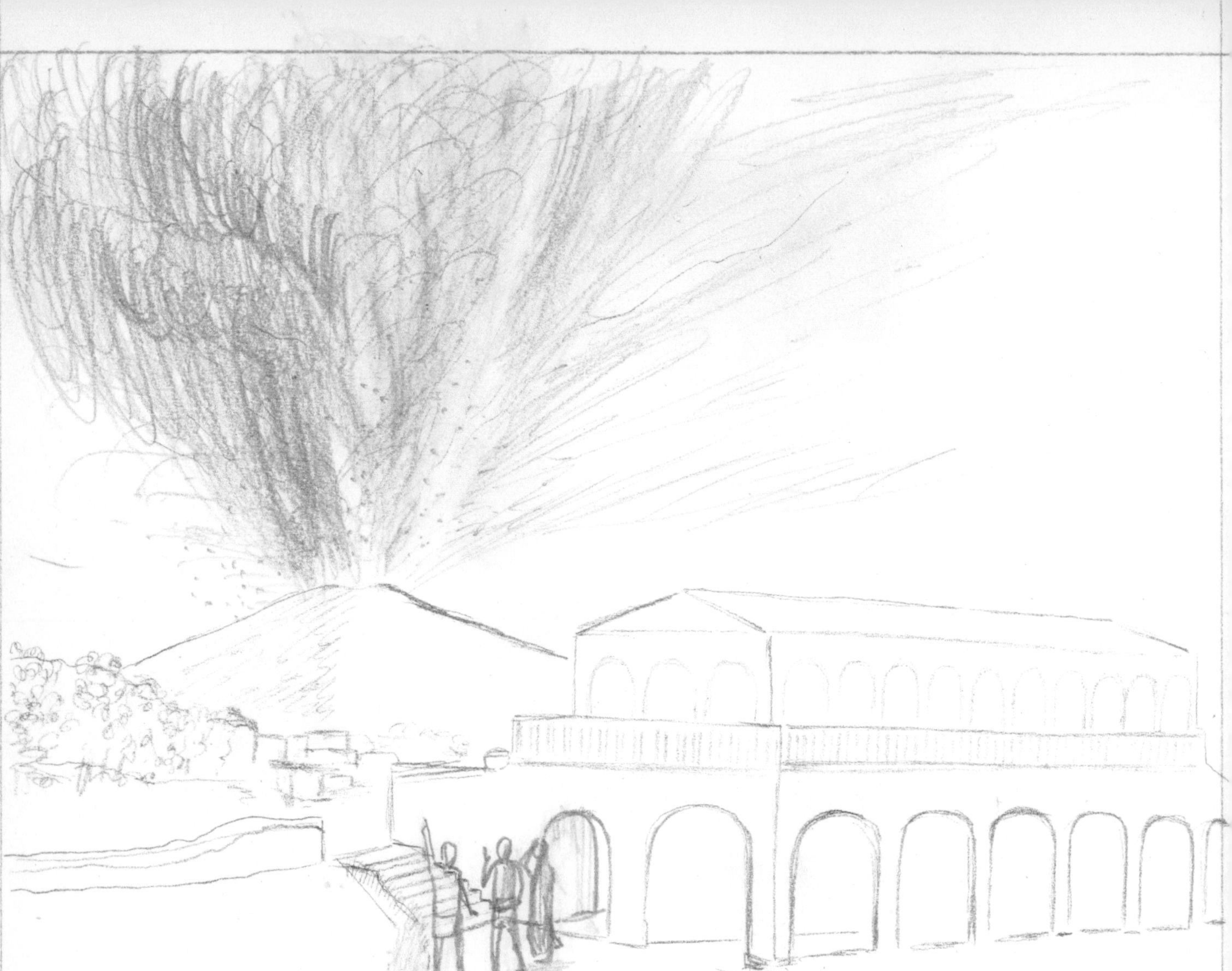
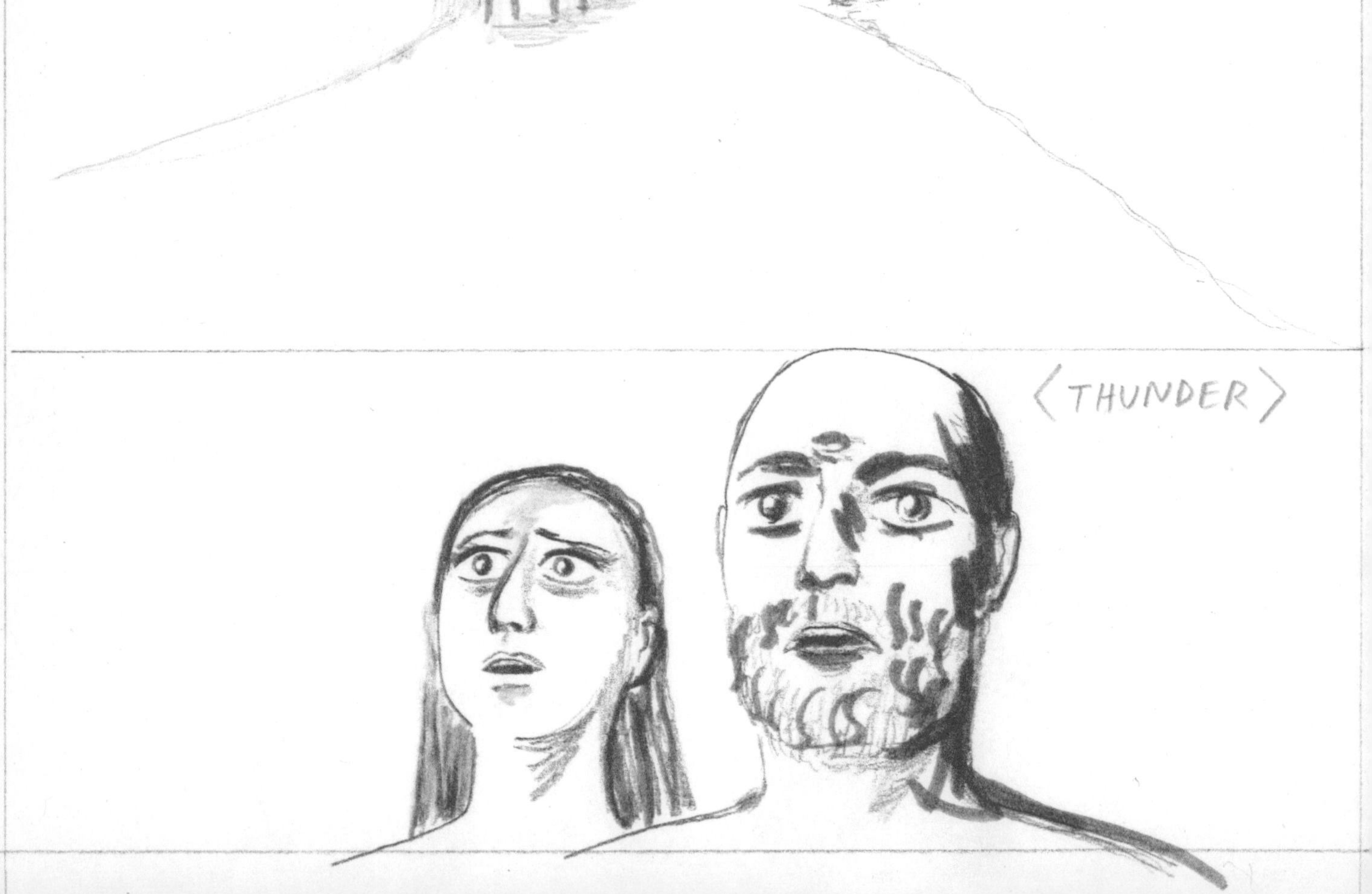
<THUNDER>

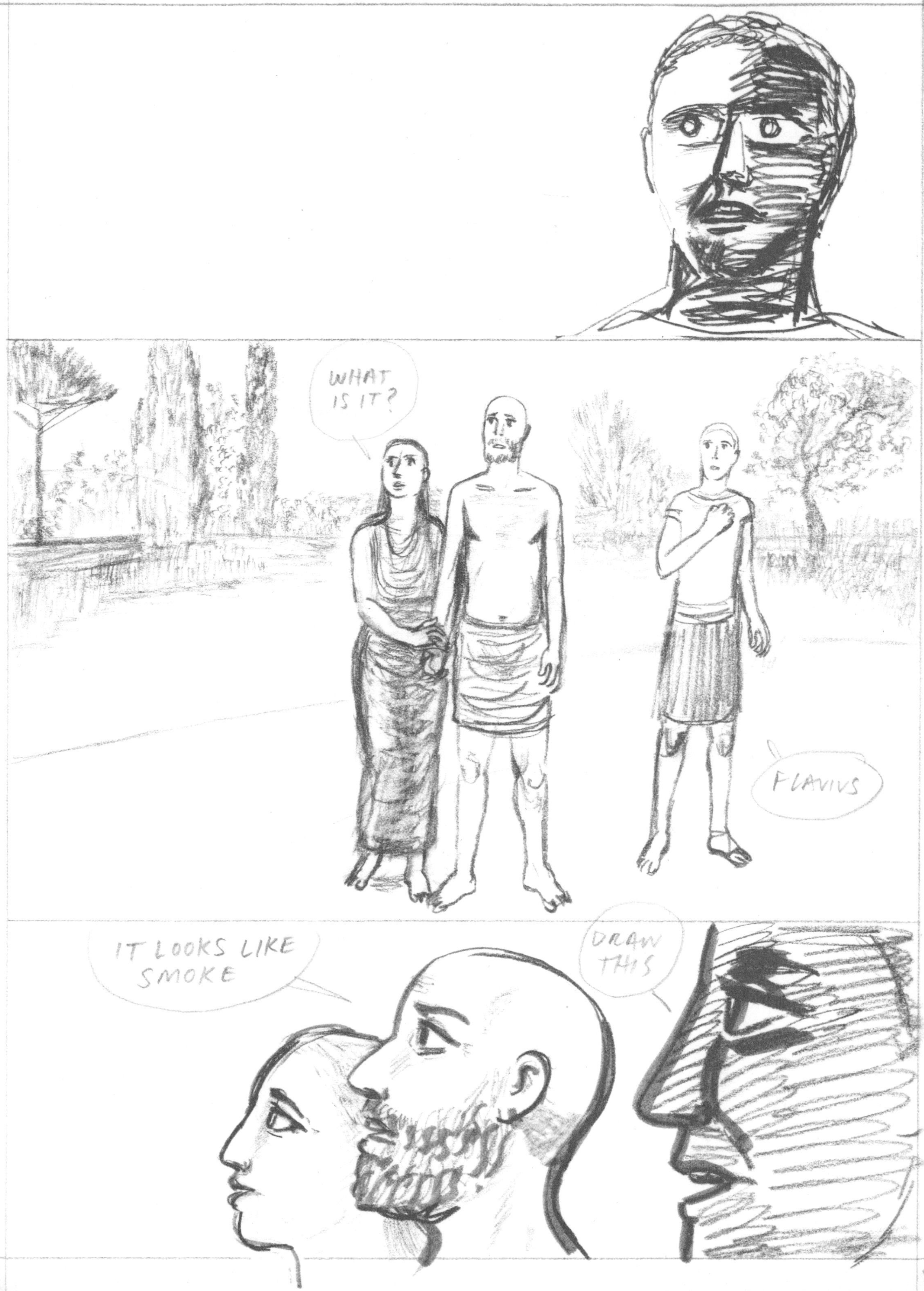
WHAT IS IT?
FLAVIUS
IT LOOKS LIKE SMOKE
DRAW THIS

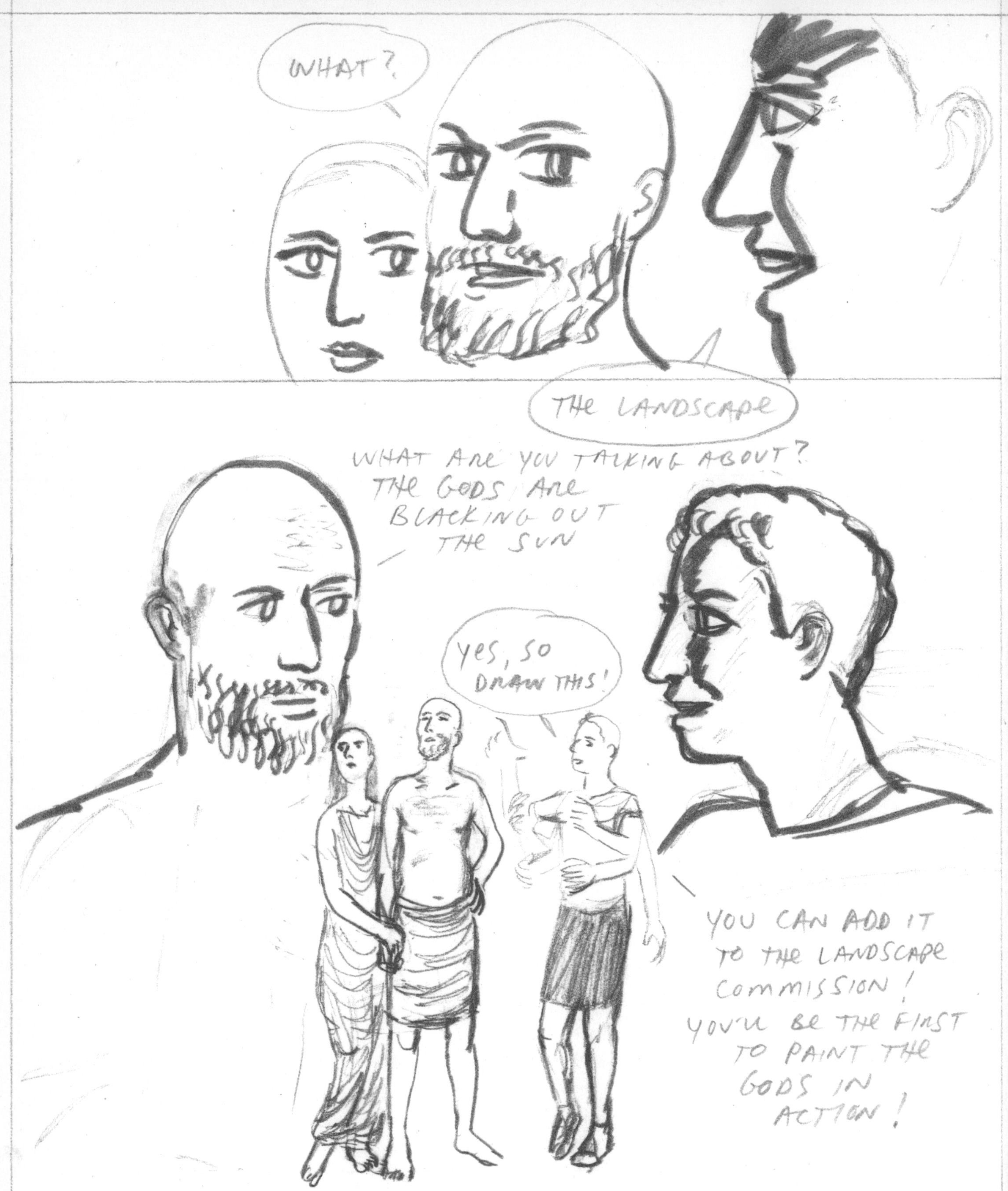

WHAT?
THE LANDSCAPE
WHAT ARE YOU TALKING ABOUT? THE GODS ARE BLACKING OUT THE SUN
YES, SO DRAW THIS!
YOU CAN ADD IT TO THE LANDSCAPE COMMISSION! YOU'LL BE THE FIRST TO PAINT THE GODS IN ACTION!

(TEN MINUTES LATER)

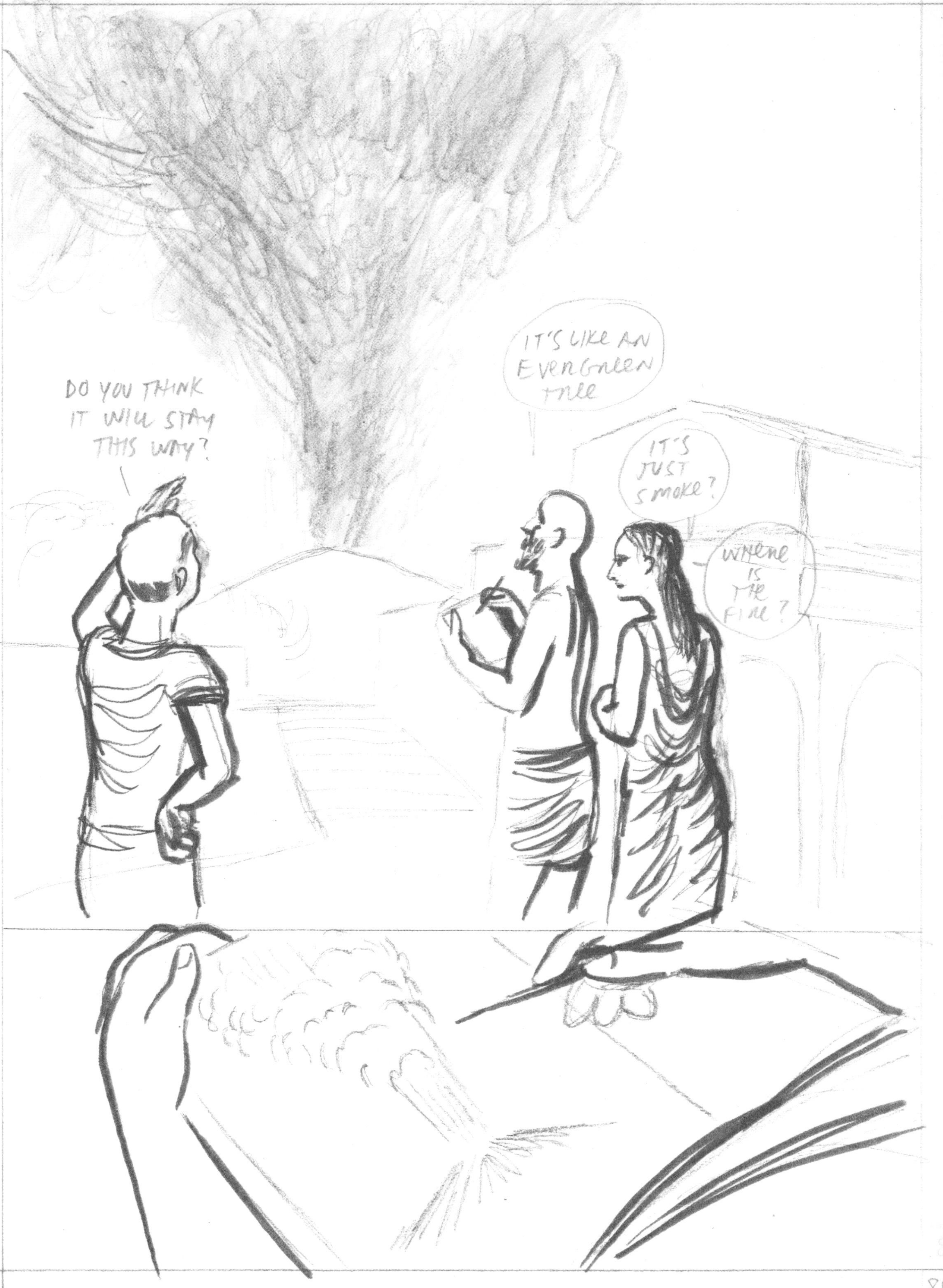
DO YOU THINK IT WILL STAY THIS WAY?
IT'S LIKE AN EVERGREEN TREE
IT'S JUST SMOKE?
WHERE IS THE FIRE?

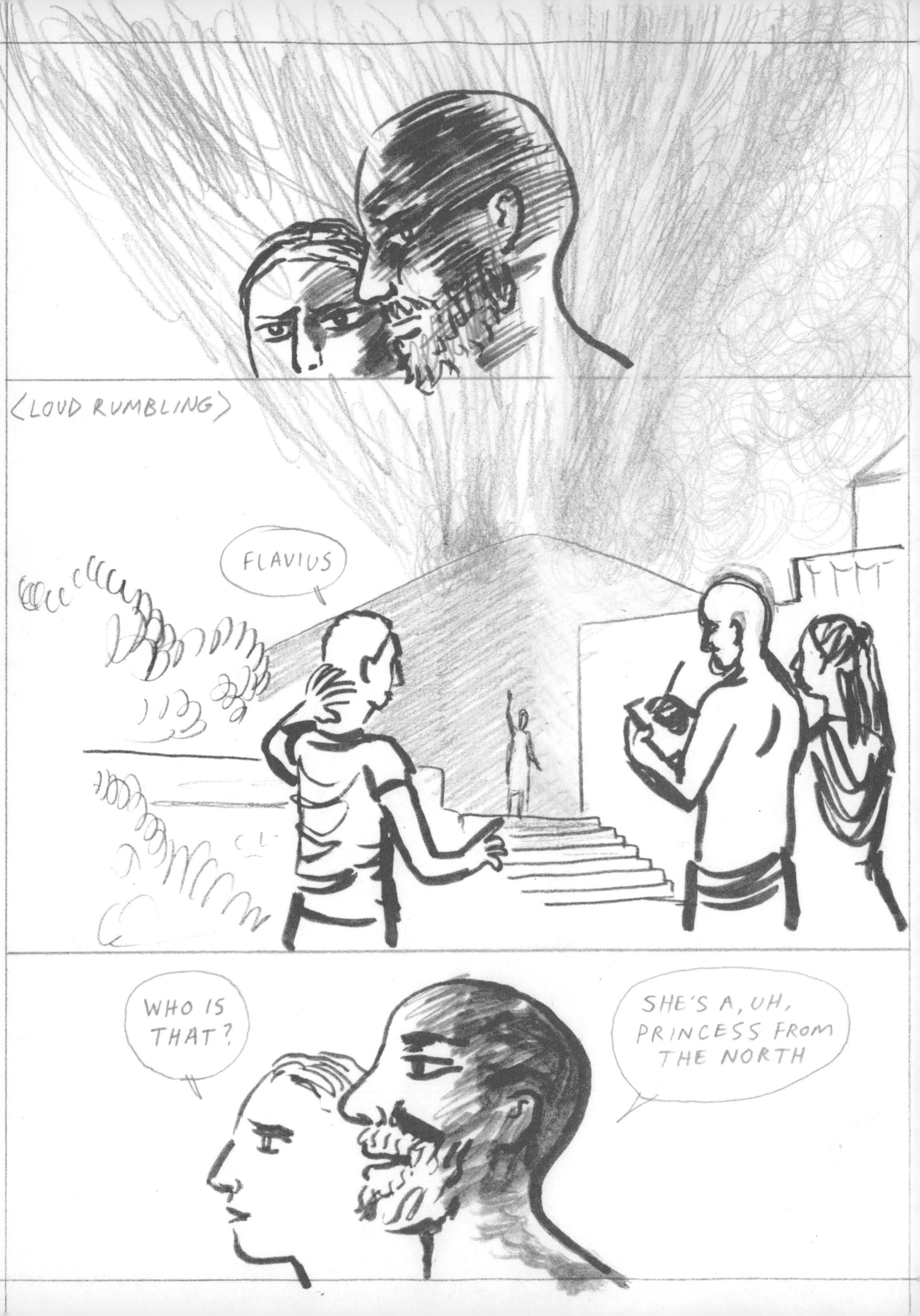
<LOUD RUMBLING>
FLAVIUS
WHO IS THAT?
SHE'S A, UH, PRINCESS FROM THE NORTH

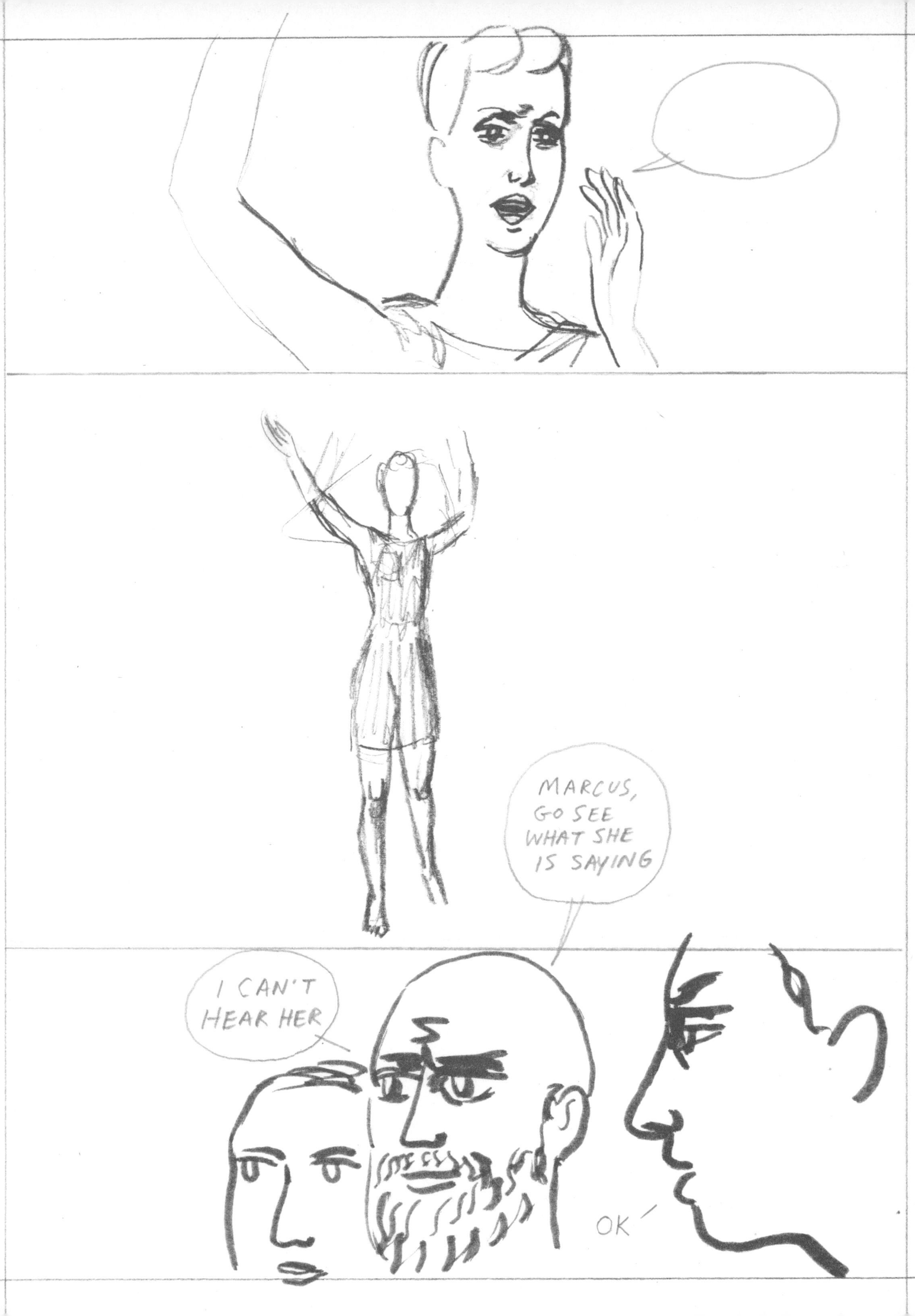
MARCUS, GO SEE WHAT SHE IS SAYING
I CAN'T HEAR HER
OK

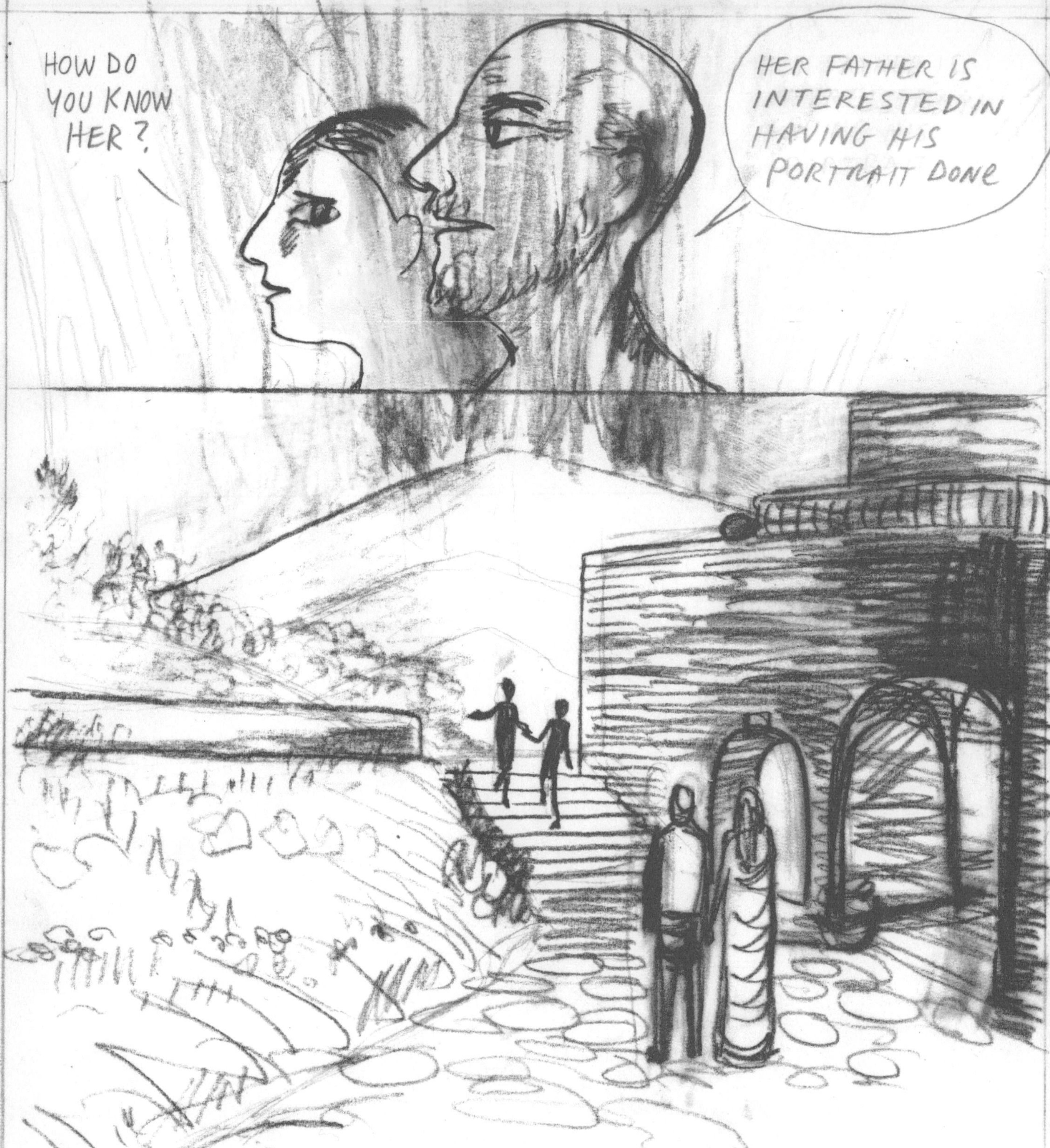
HOW DO YOU KNOW HER?
HER FATHER IS INTERESTED IN HAVING HIS PORTRAIT DONE

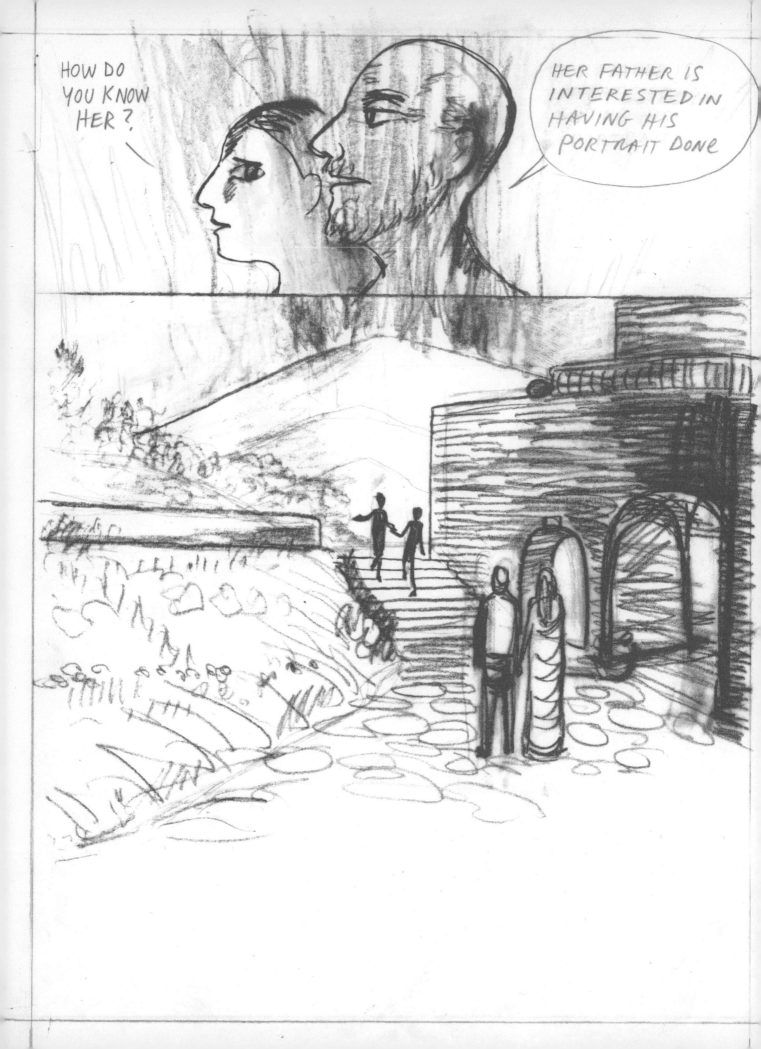

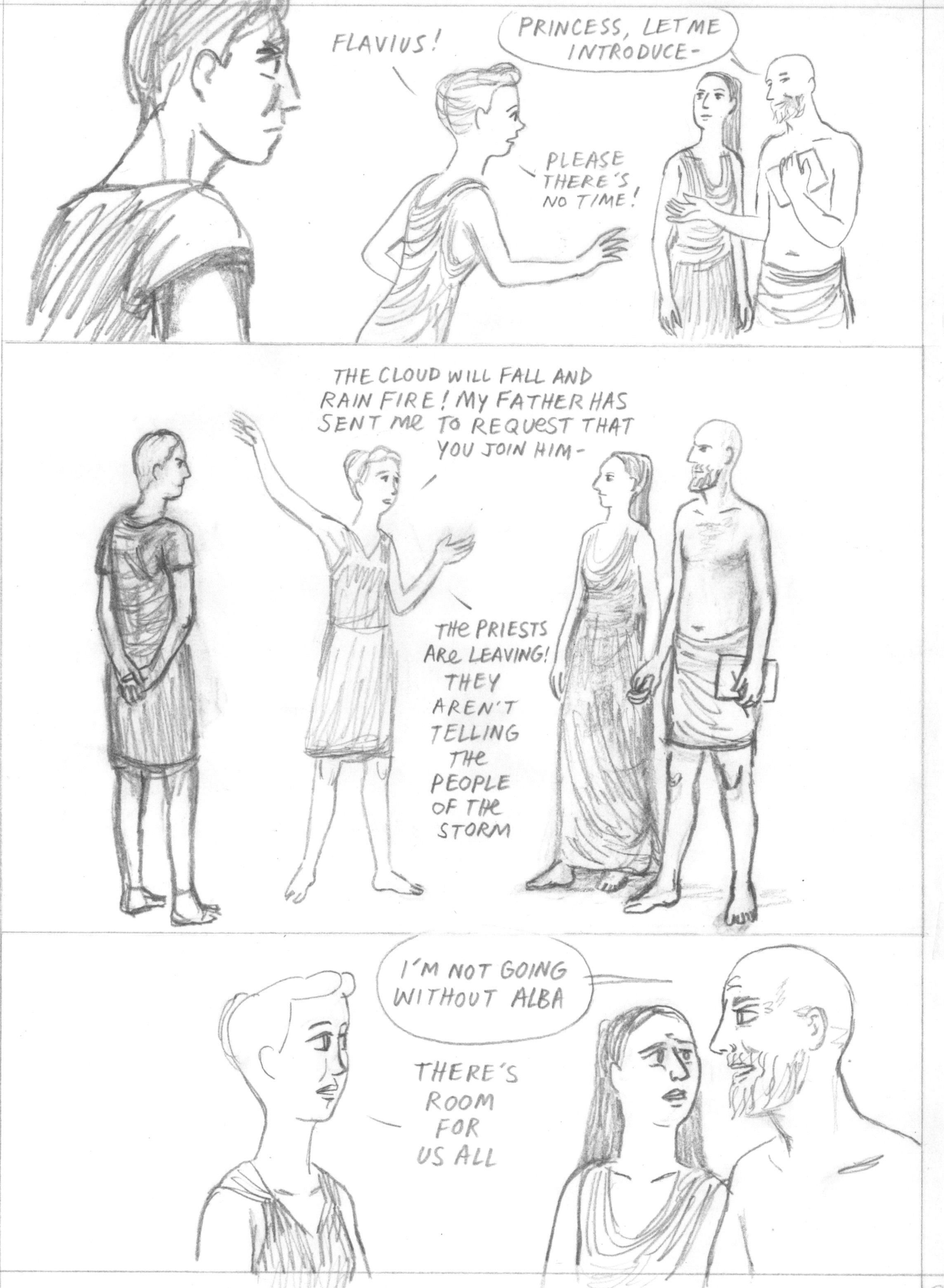
FLAVIUS!
PRINCESS, LETME INTRODUCE-
PLEASE THERE'S NO TIME!
THE CLOUD WILL FALL AND RAIN FIRE! MY FATHER HAS SENT ME TO REQUEST THAT YOU JOIN HIM-
THE PRIESTS ARE LEAVING! THEY AREN'T TELLING THE PEOPLE OF THE STORM
I'M NOT GOING WITHOUT ALBA
THERE'S ROOM FOR US ALL

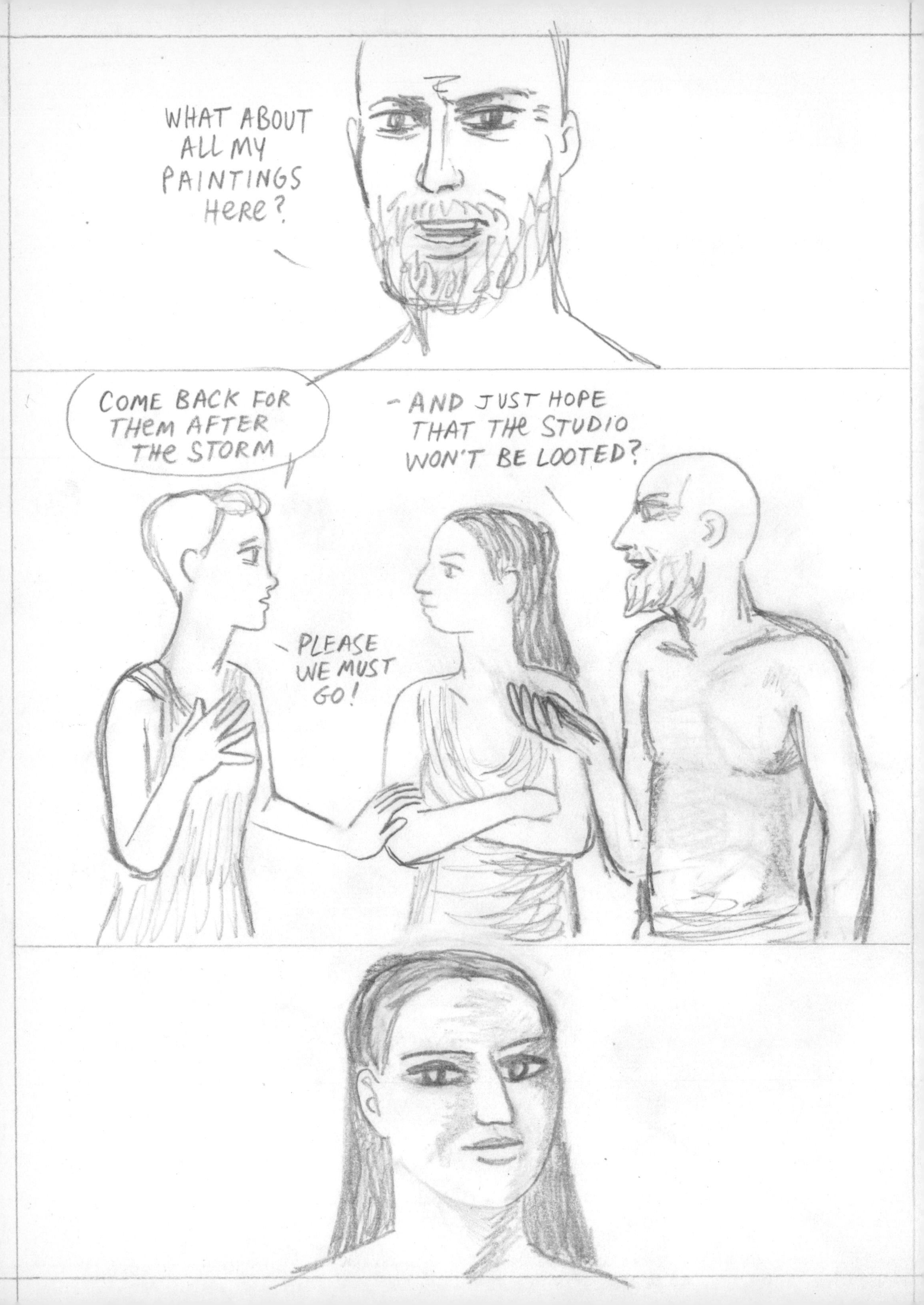
WHAT ABOUT ALL MY PAINTINGS HERE?
COME BACK FOR THEM AFTER THE STORM
- AND JUST HOPE THAT THE STUDIO WON'T BE LOOTED?
PLEASE WE MUST GO!

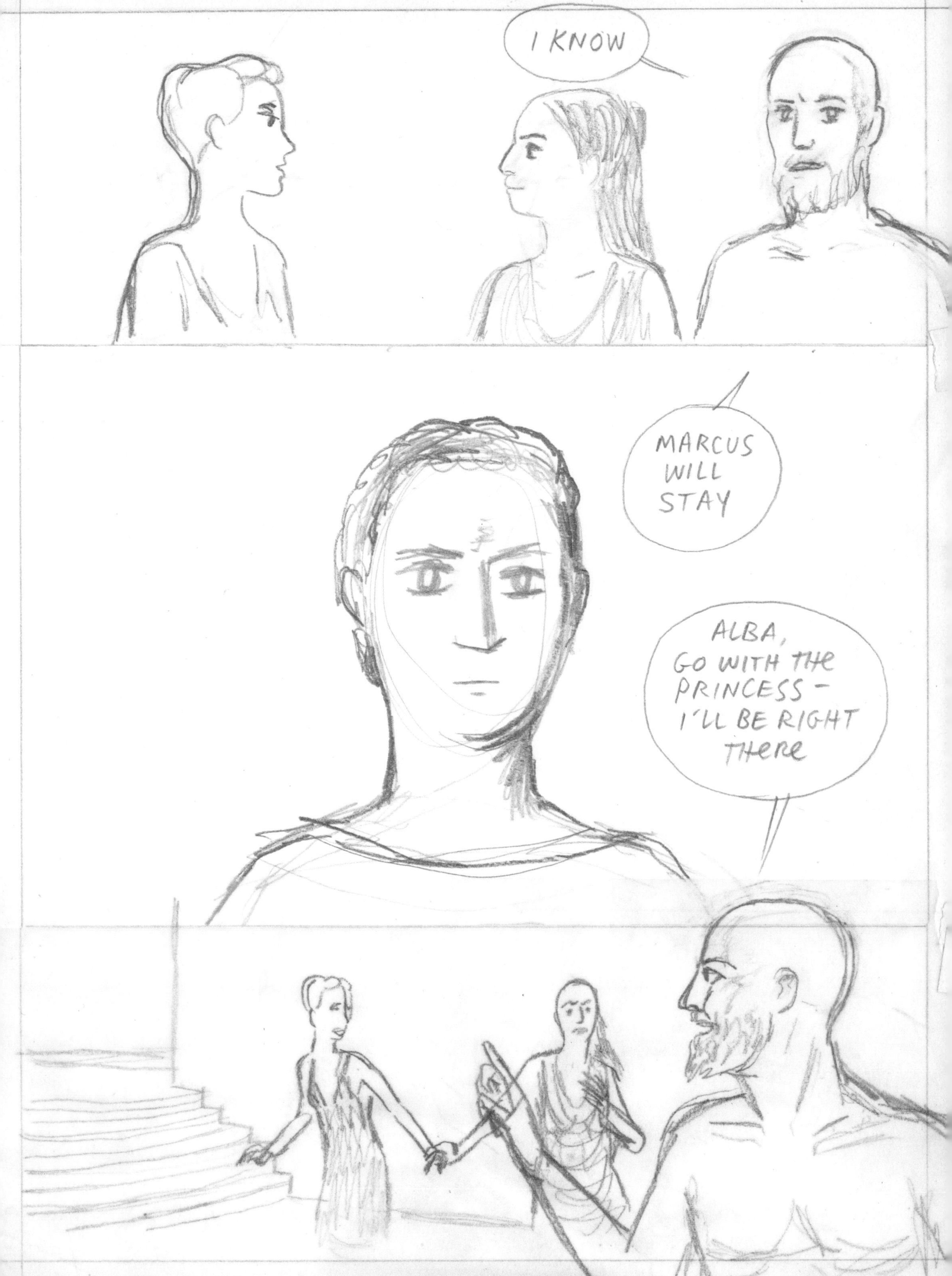
I KNOW
MARCUS WILL STAY
ALBA, GO WITH THE PRINCESS - I'LL BE RIGHT THERE

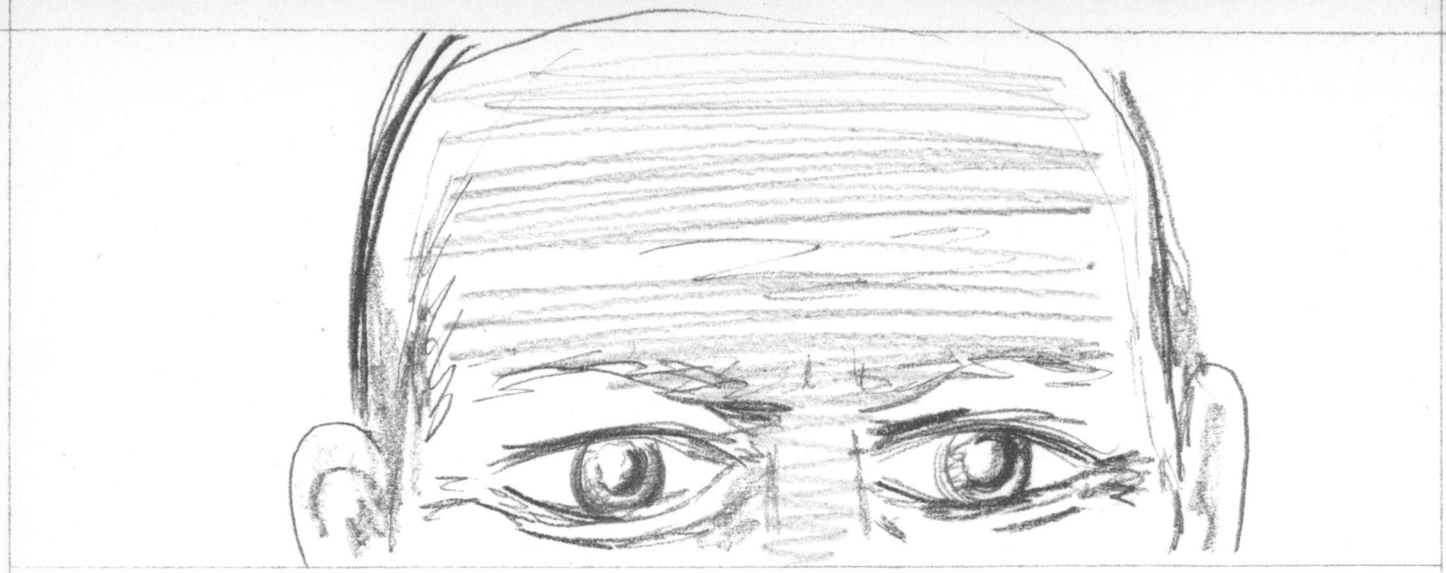

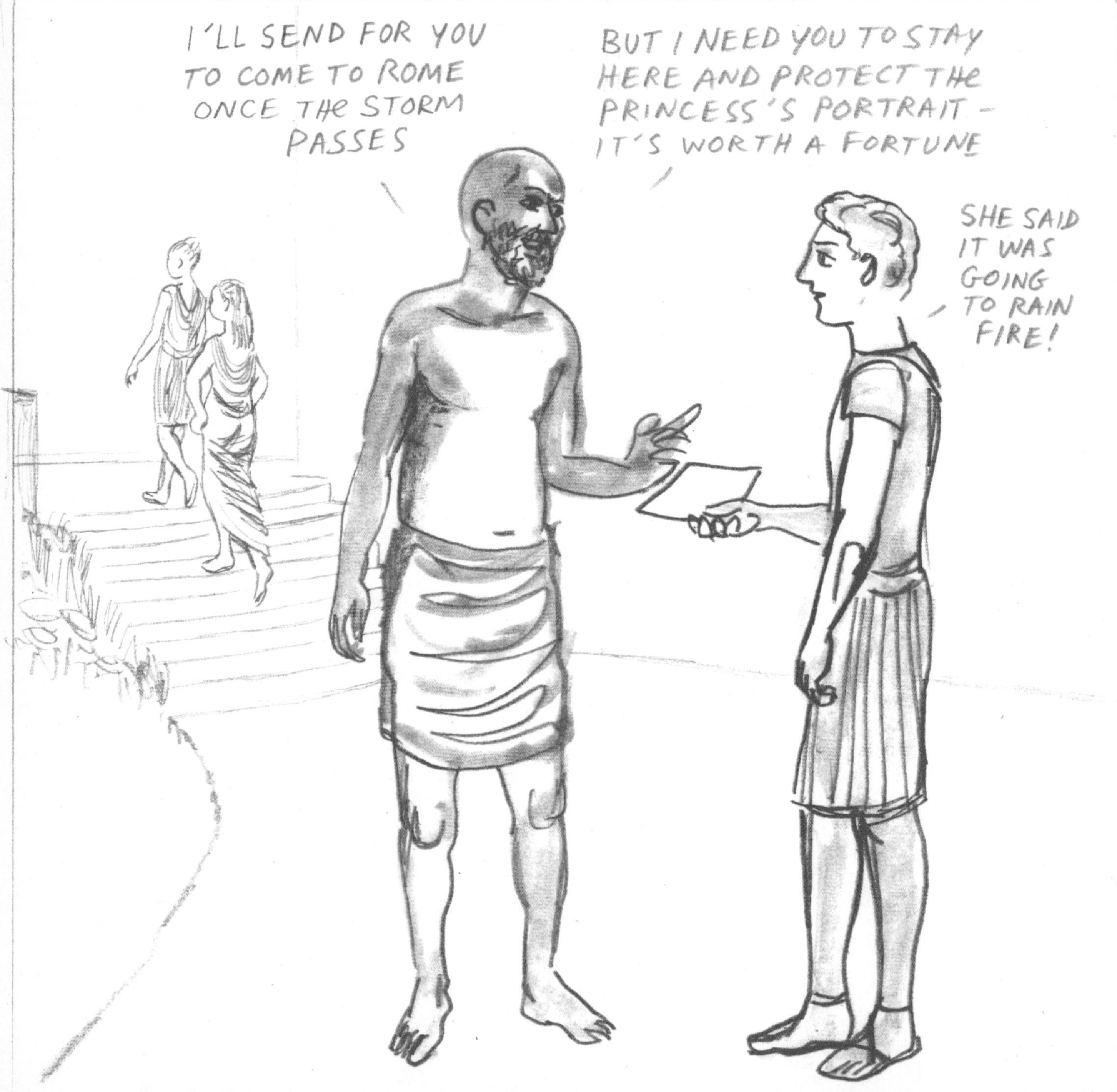
I'LL SEND FOR YOU TO COME TO ROME ONCE THE STORM PASSES
BUT I NEED YOU TO STAY HERE AND PROTECT THE PRINCESS'S PORTRAIT - IT'S WORTH A FORTUNE
SHE SAID IT WAS GOING TO RAIN FIRE!

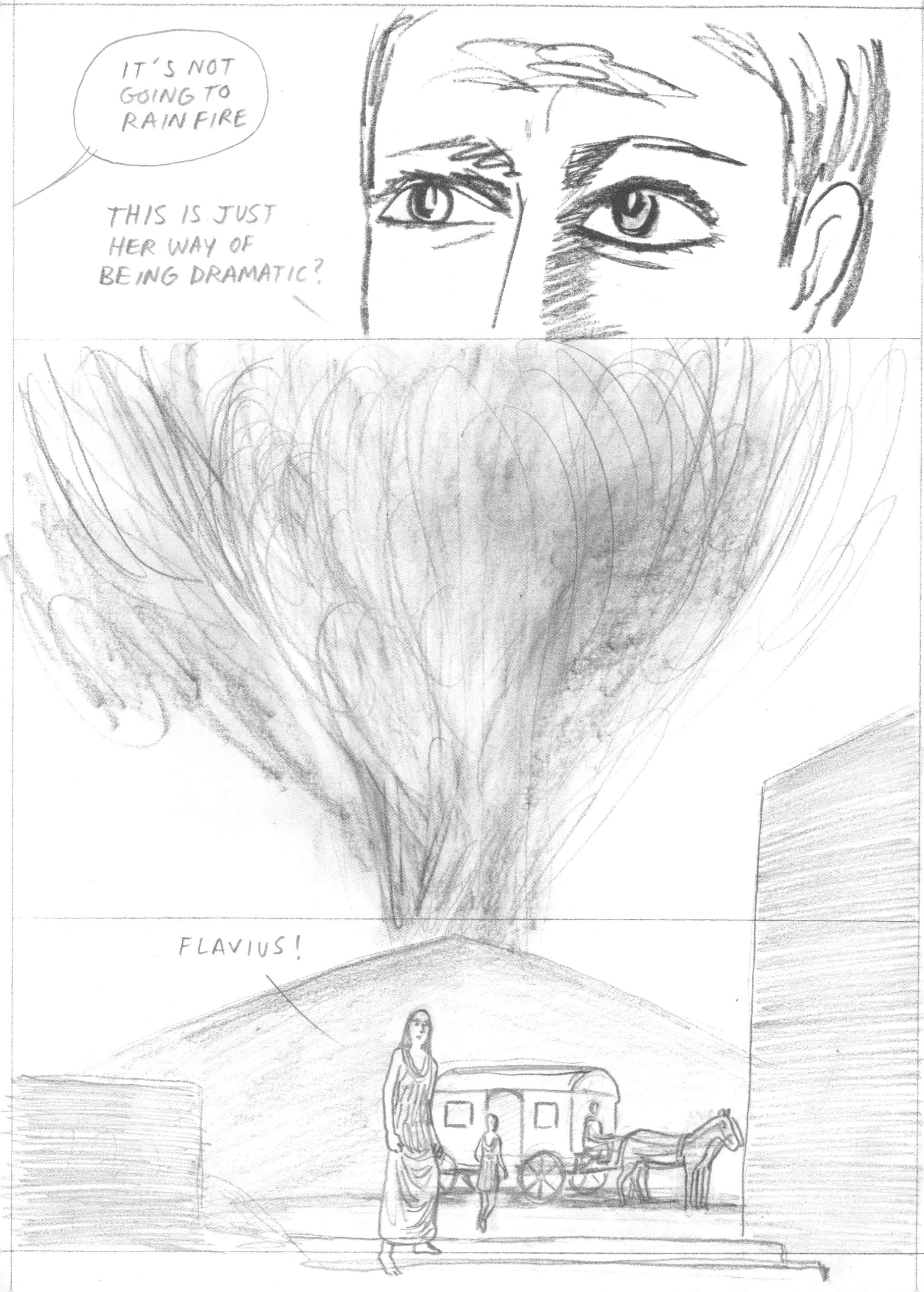
IT'S NOT GOING TO RAIN FIRE
THIS IS JUST HER WAY OF BEING DRAMATIC?
FLAVIUS!

93

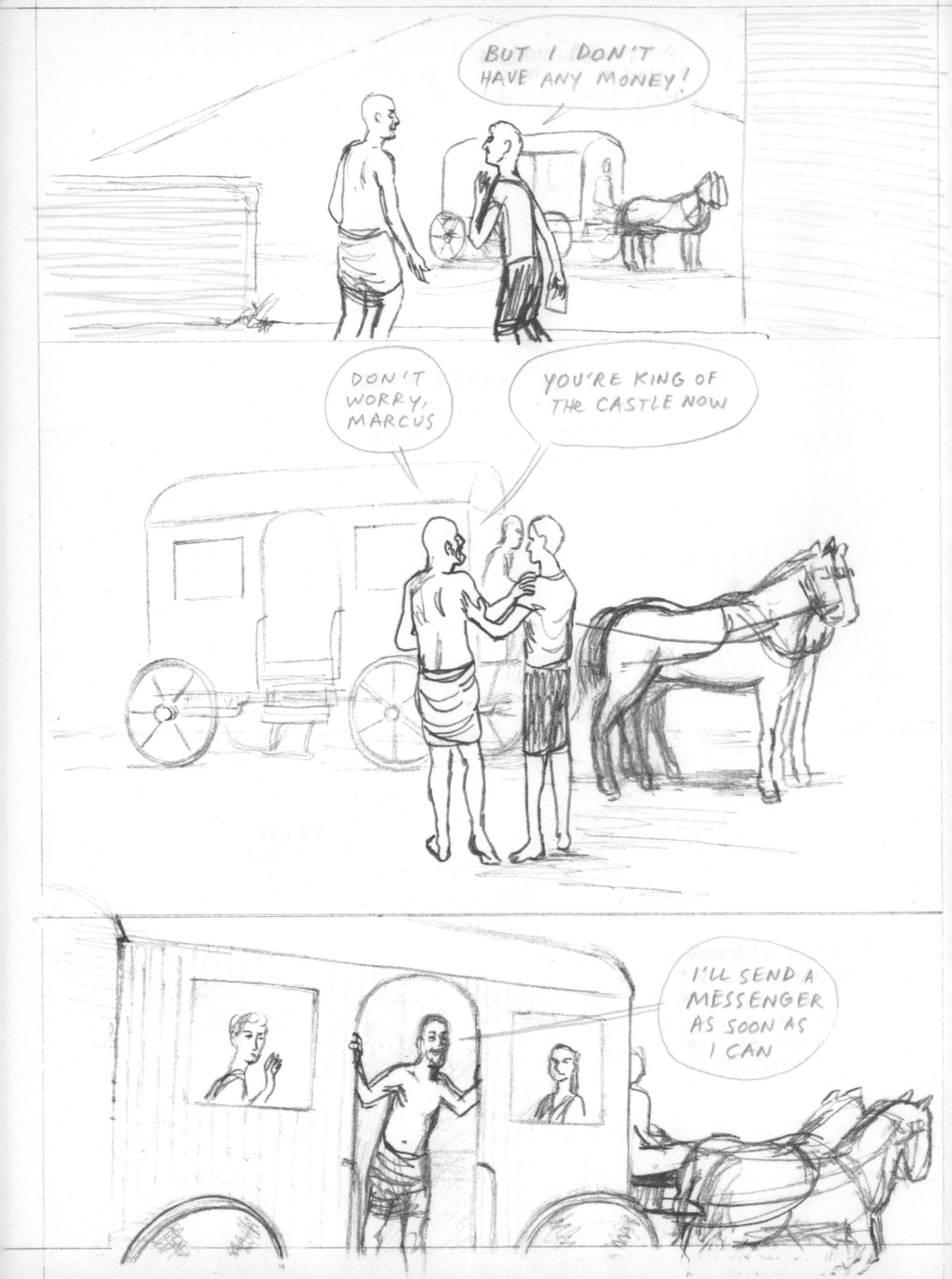
BUT I DON'T HAVE ANY MONEY!
DON'T WORRY, MARCUS
YOU'RE KING OF THE CASTLE NOW
I'LL SEND A MESSENGER AS SOON AS I CAN

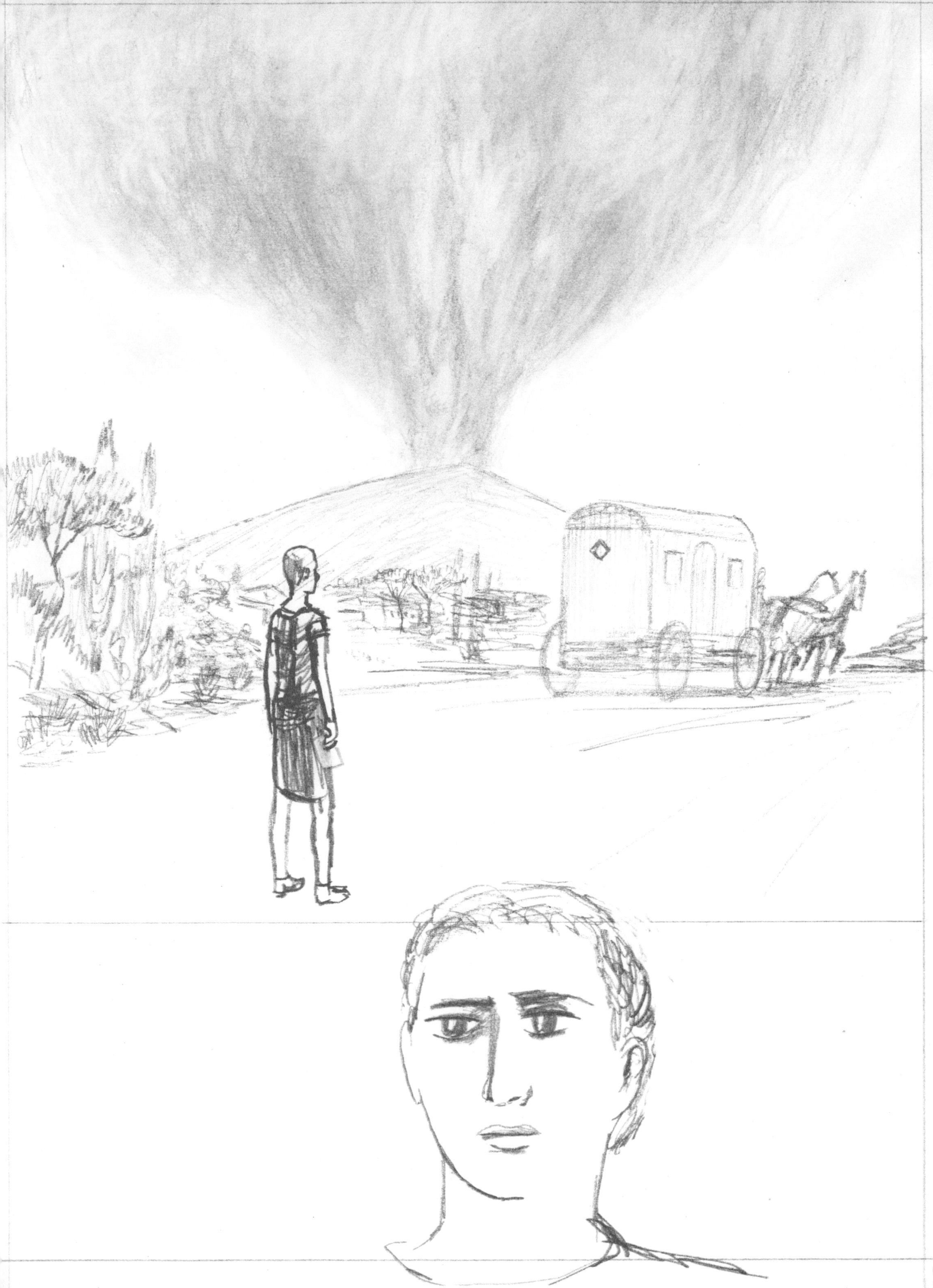

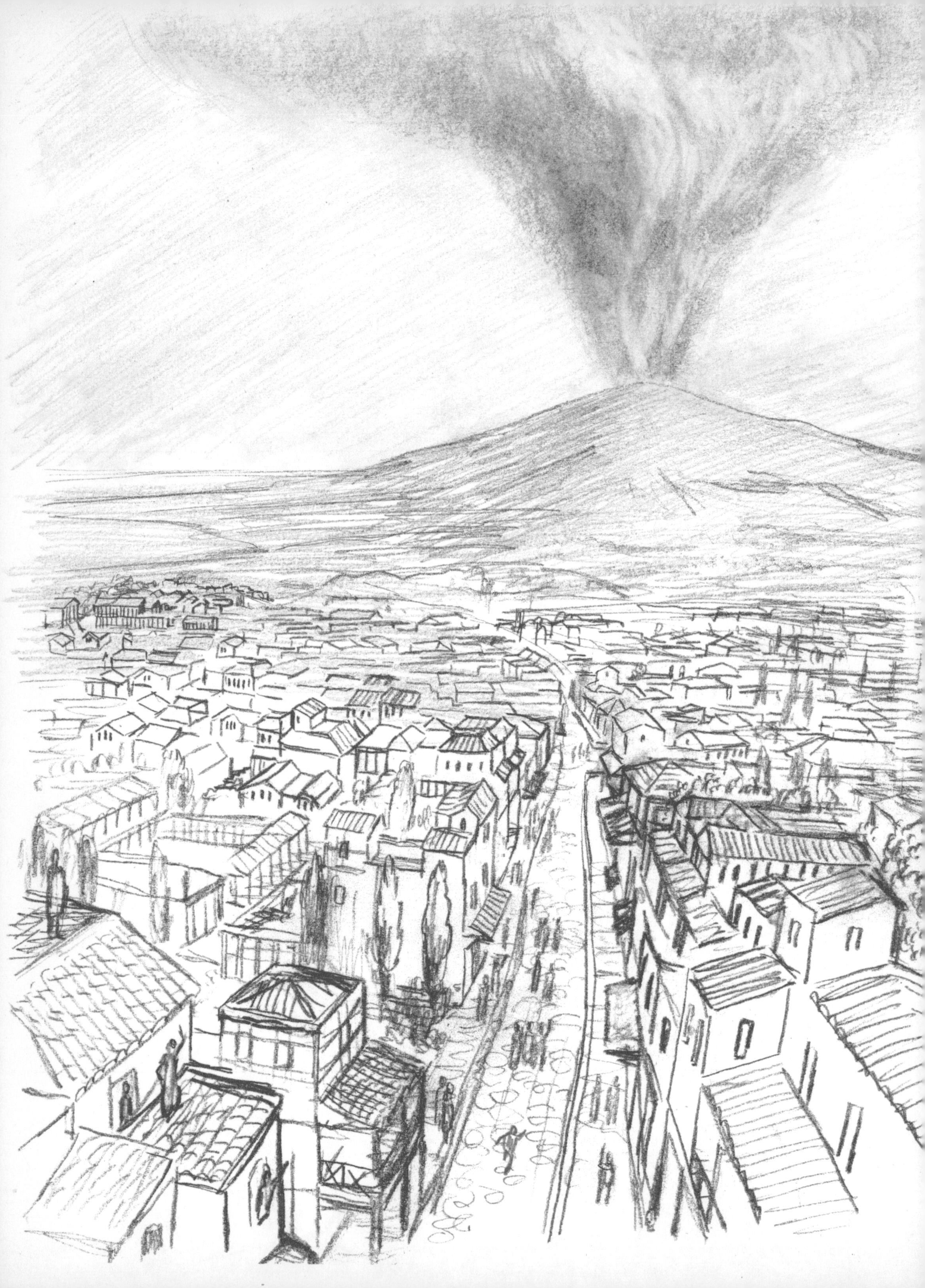

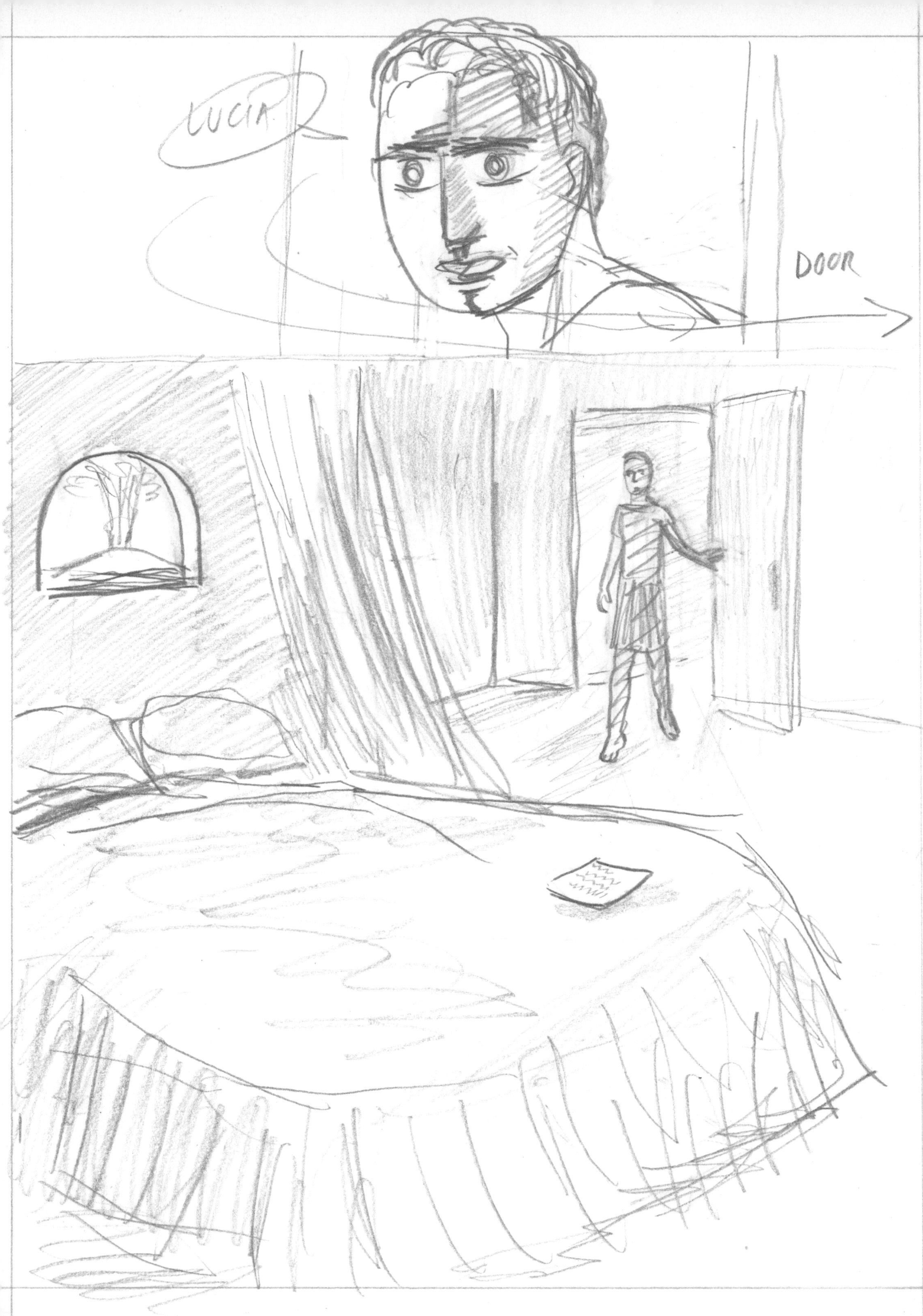
LUCIA
DOOR

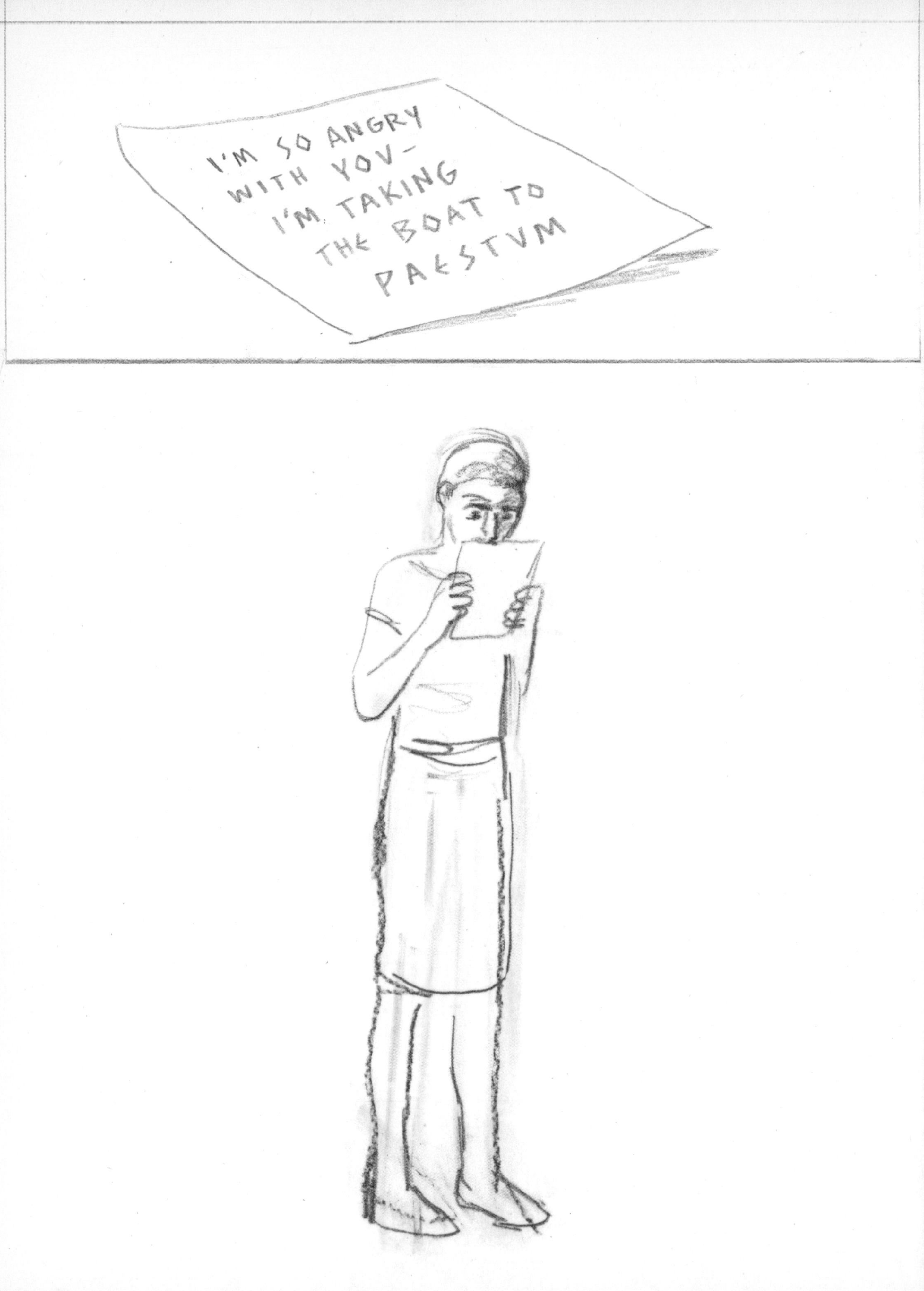
I'M SO ANGRY WITH YOU— I'M TAKING THE BOAT TO PAESTUM

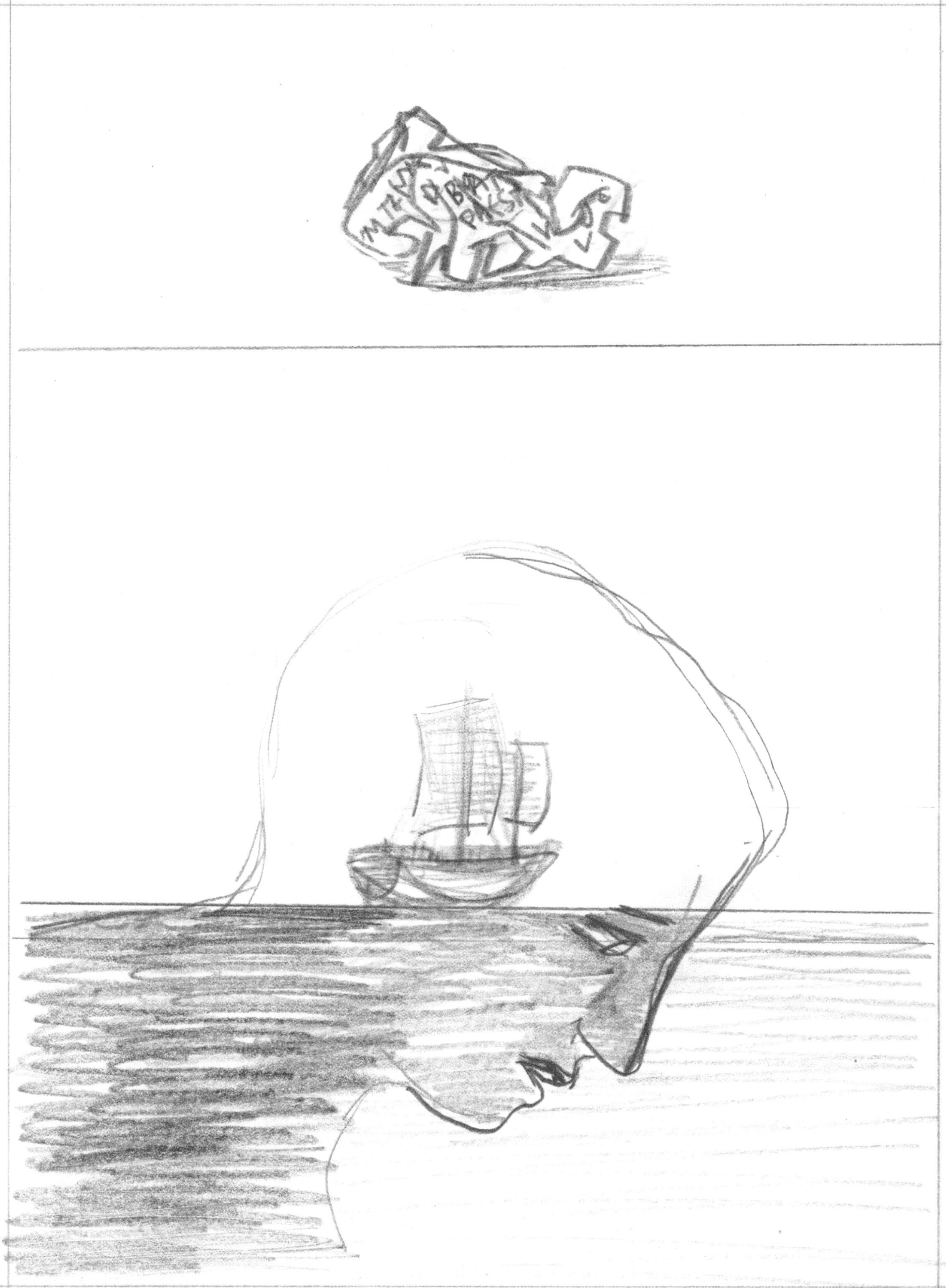

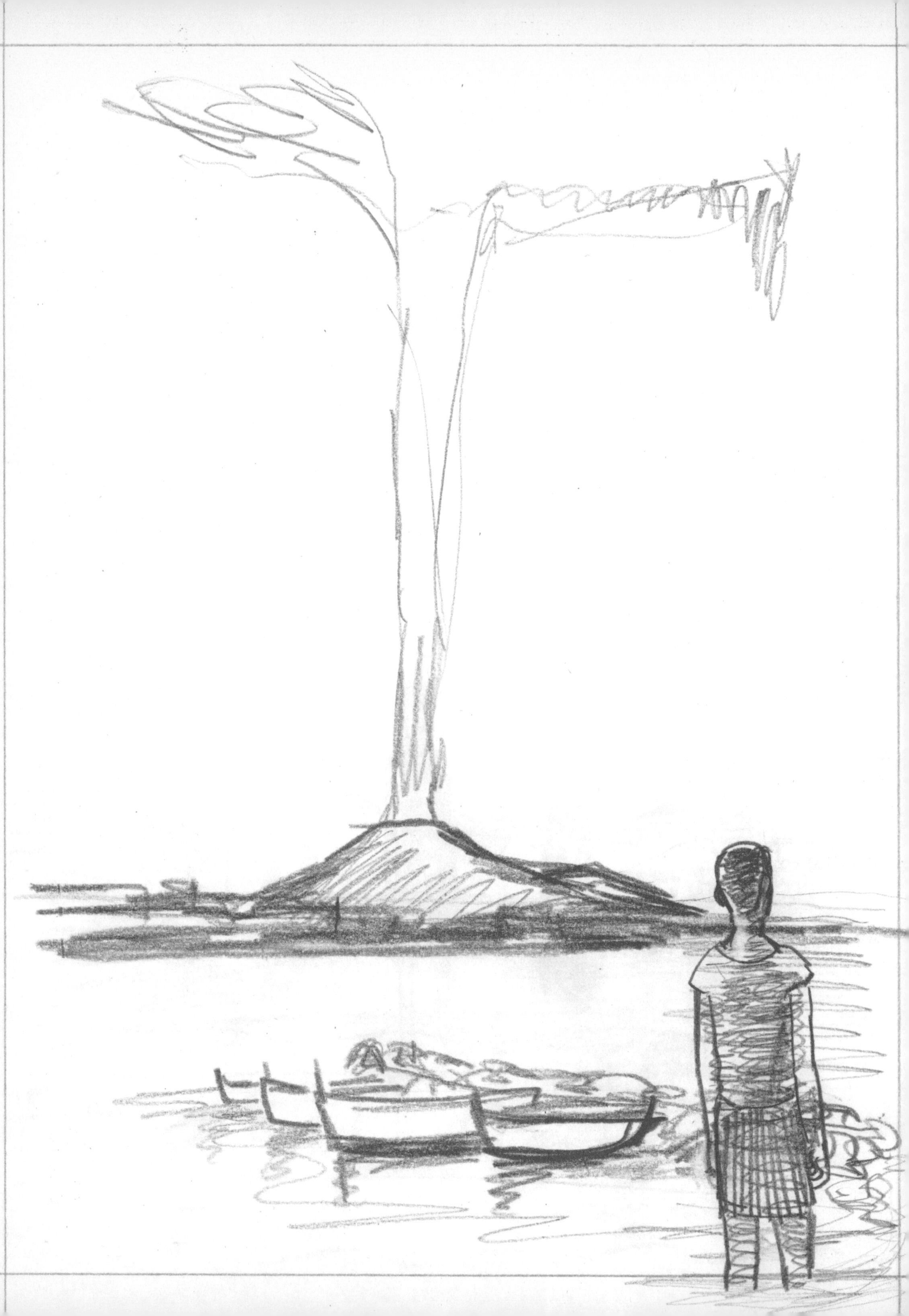

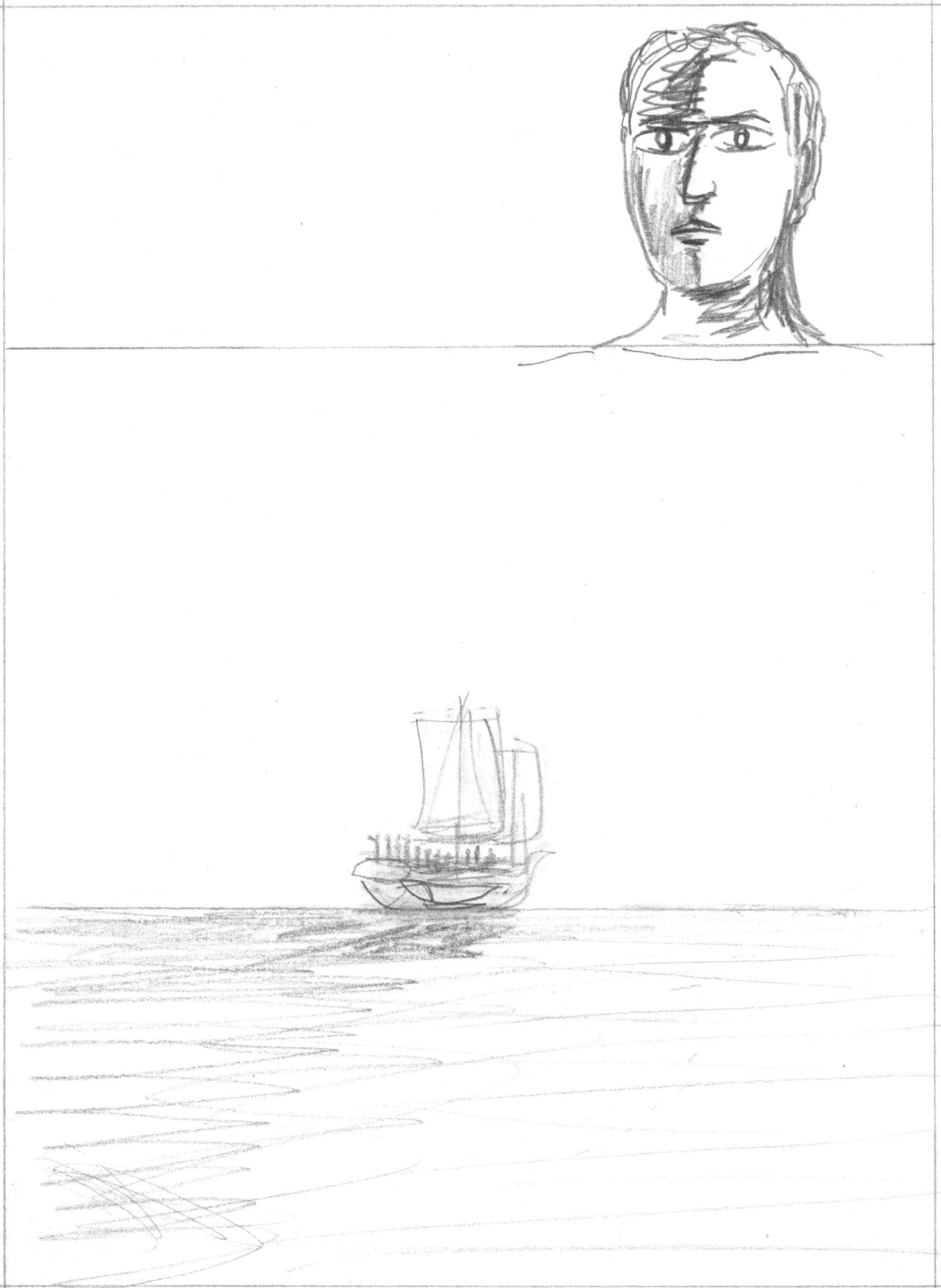

(SOUNDS OF CROWD)

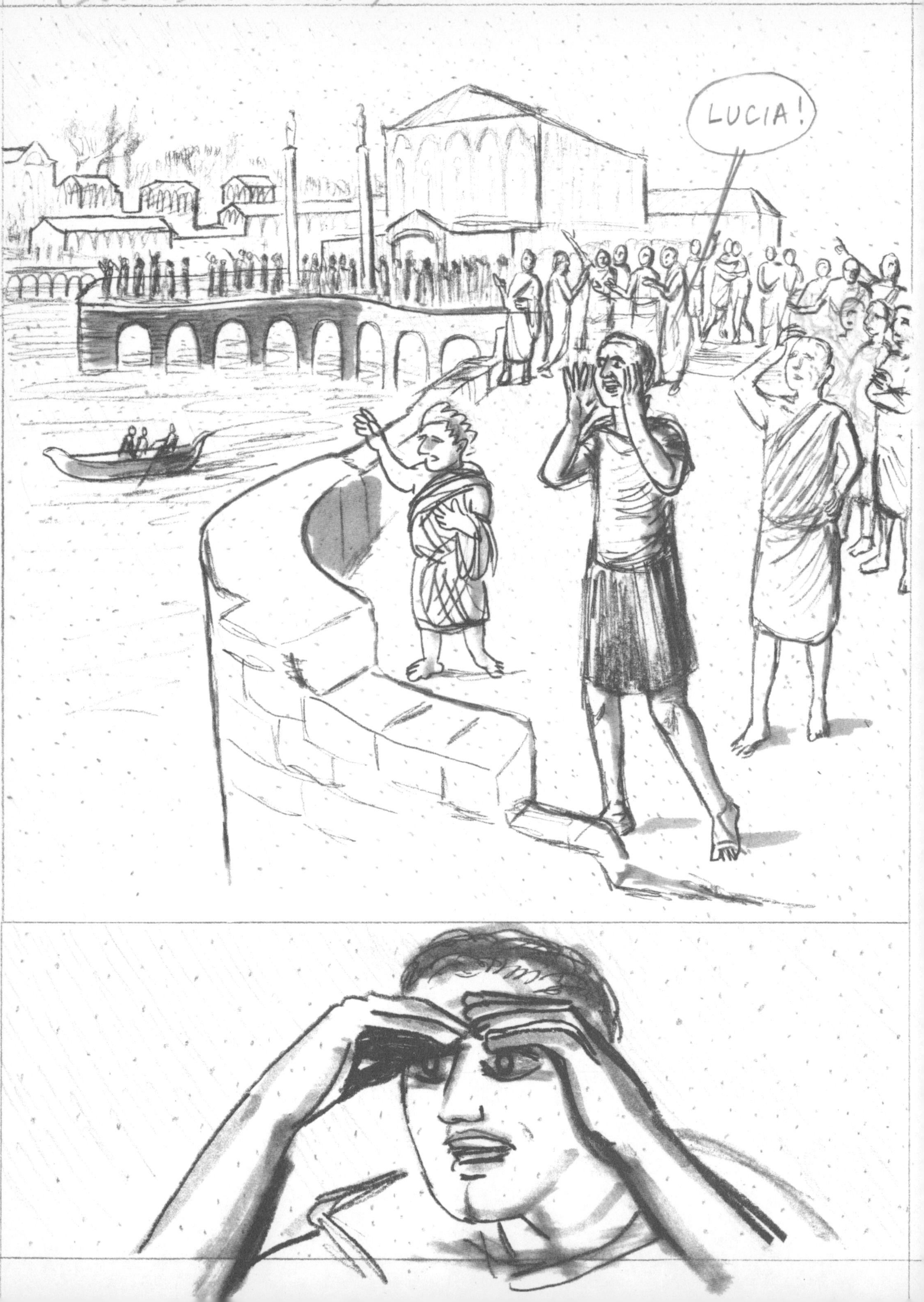
LUCIA!

(FALLING ASH)

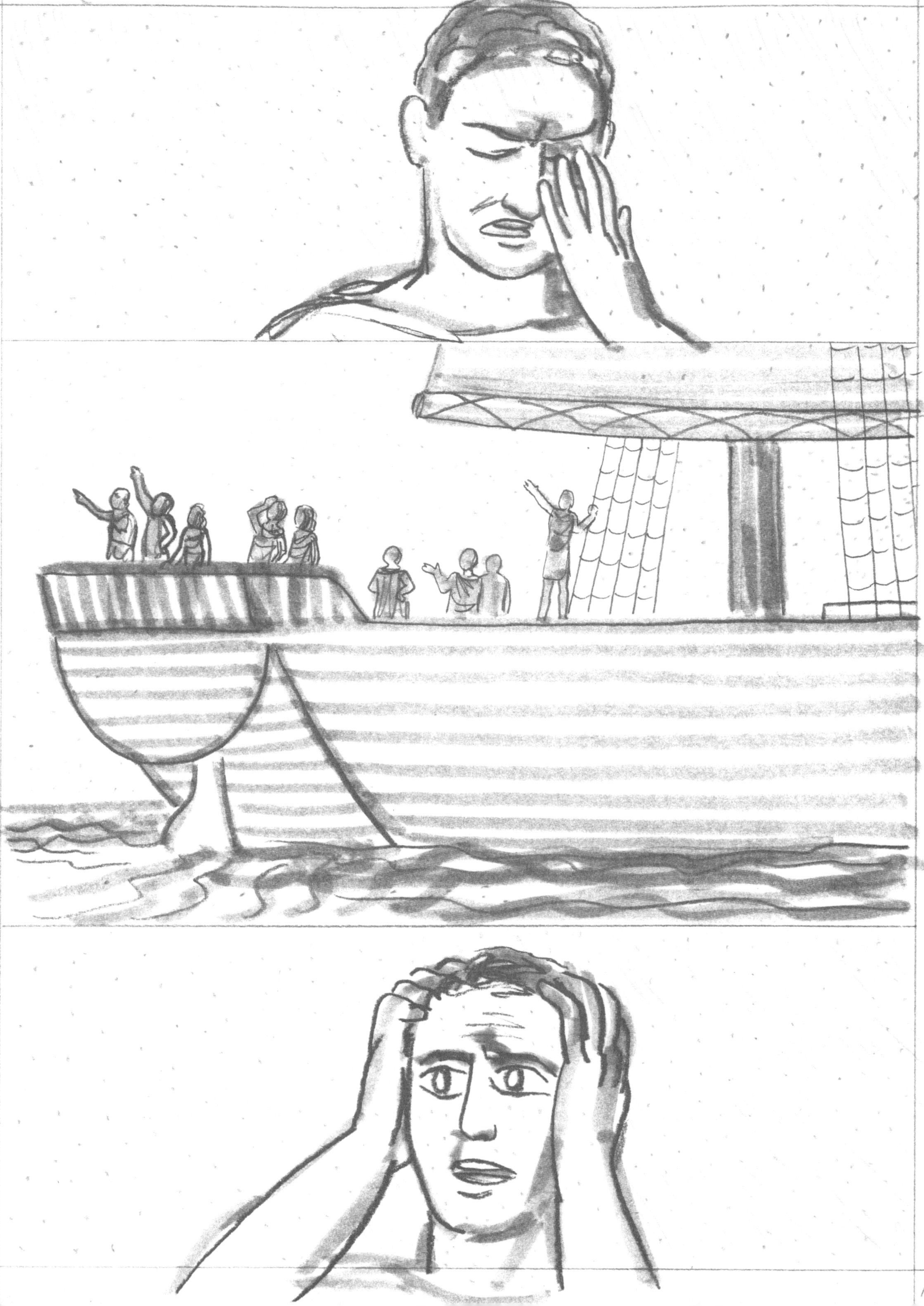

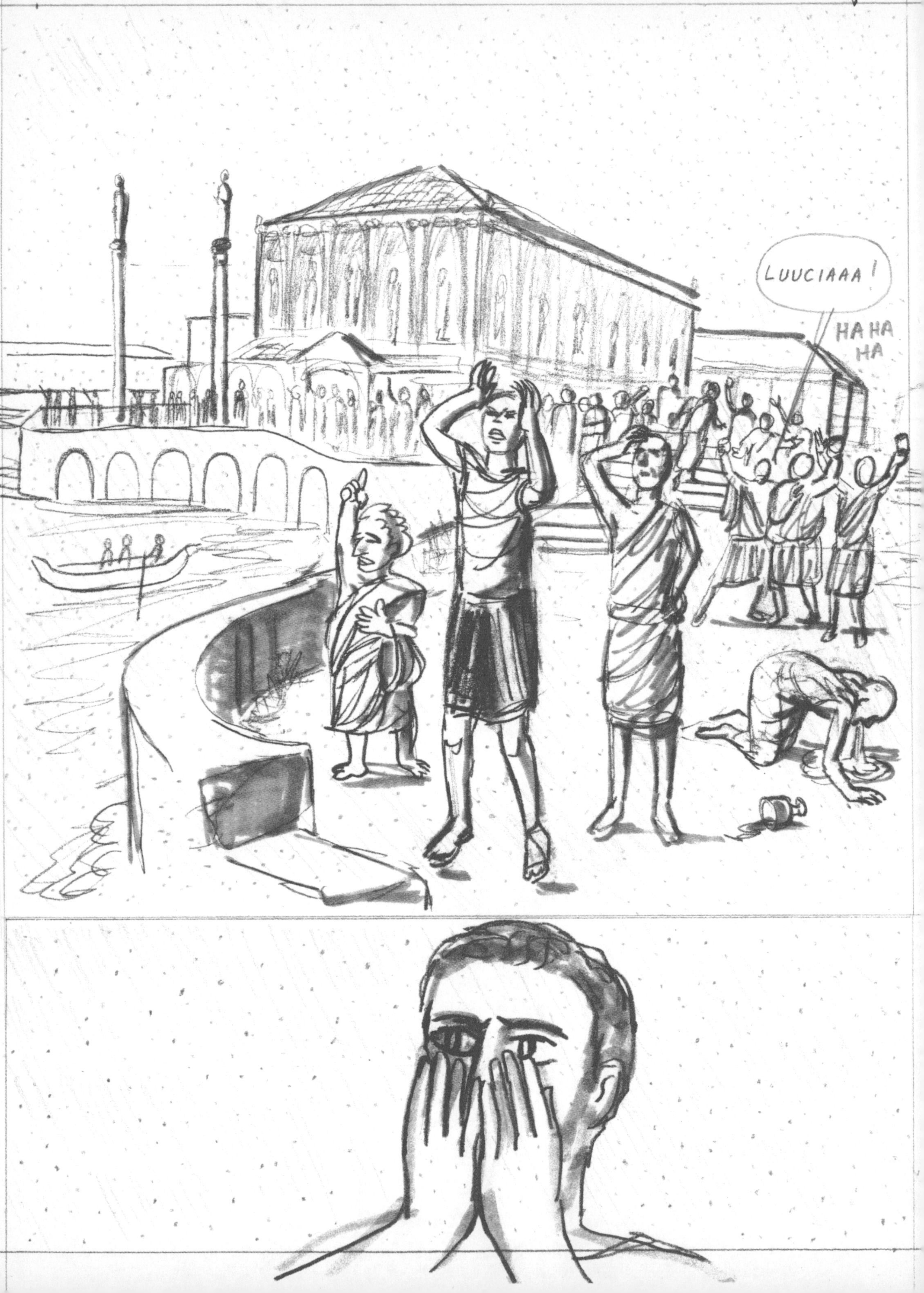
LUUCIAAA!
HA HA
HA

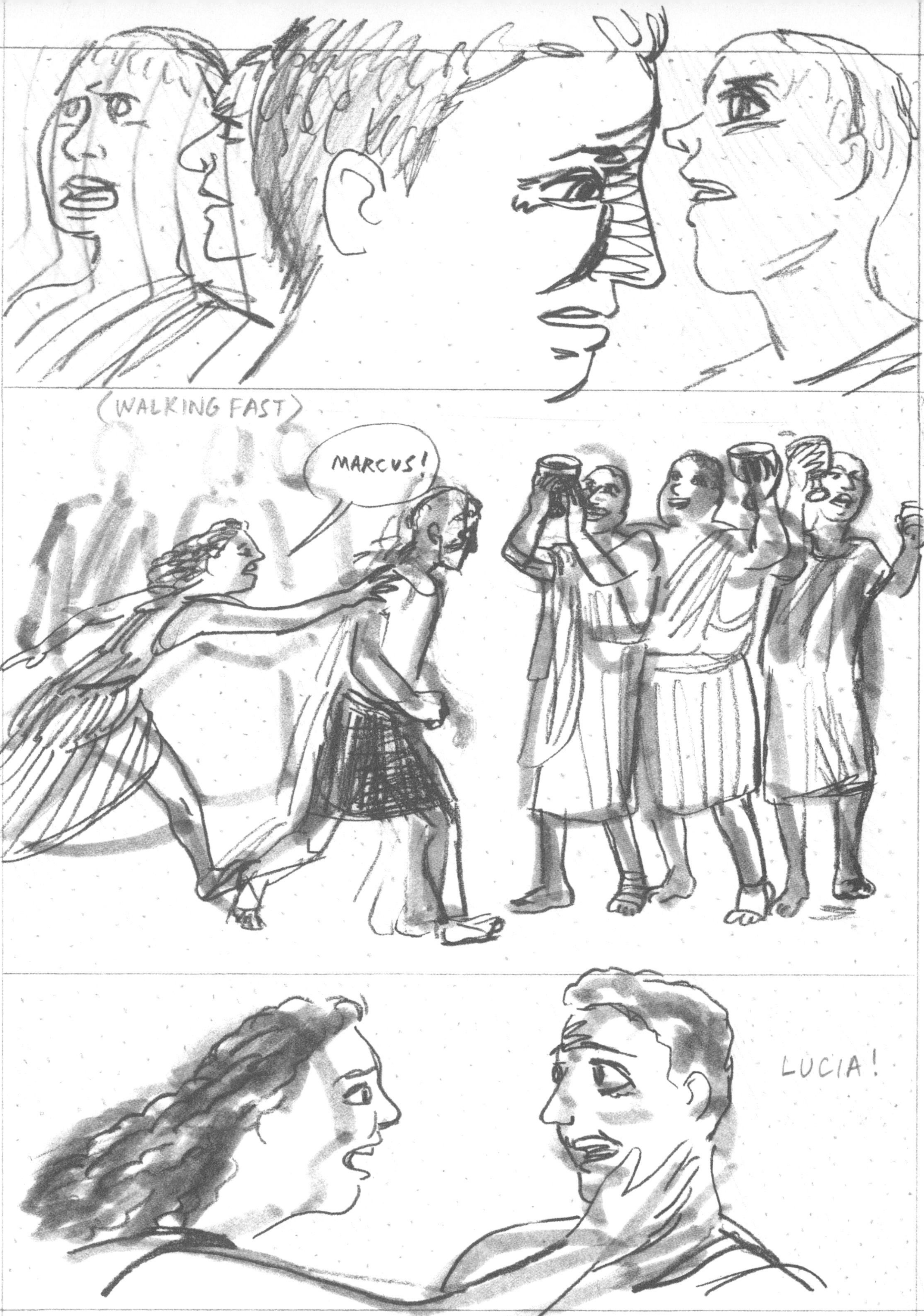
(WALKING FAST)
MARCUS!
LUCIA!

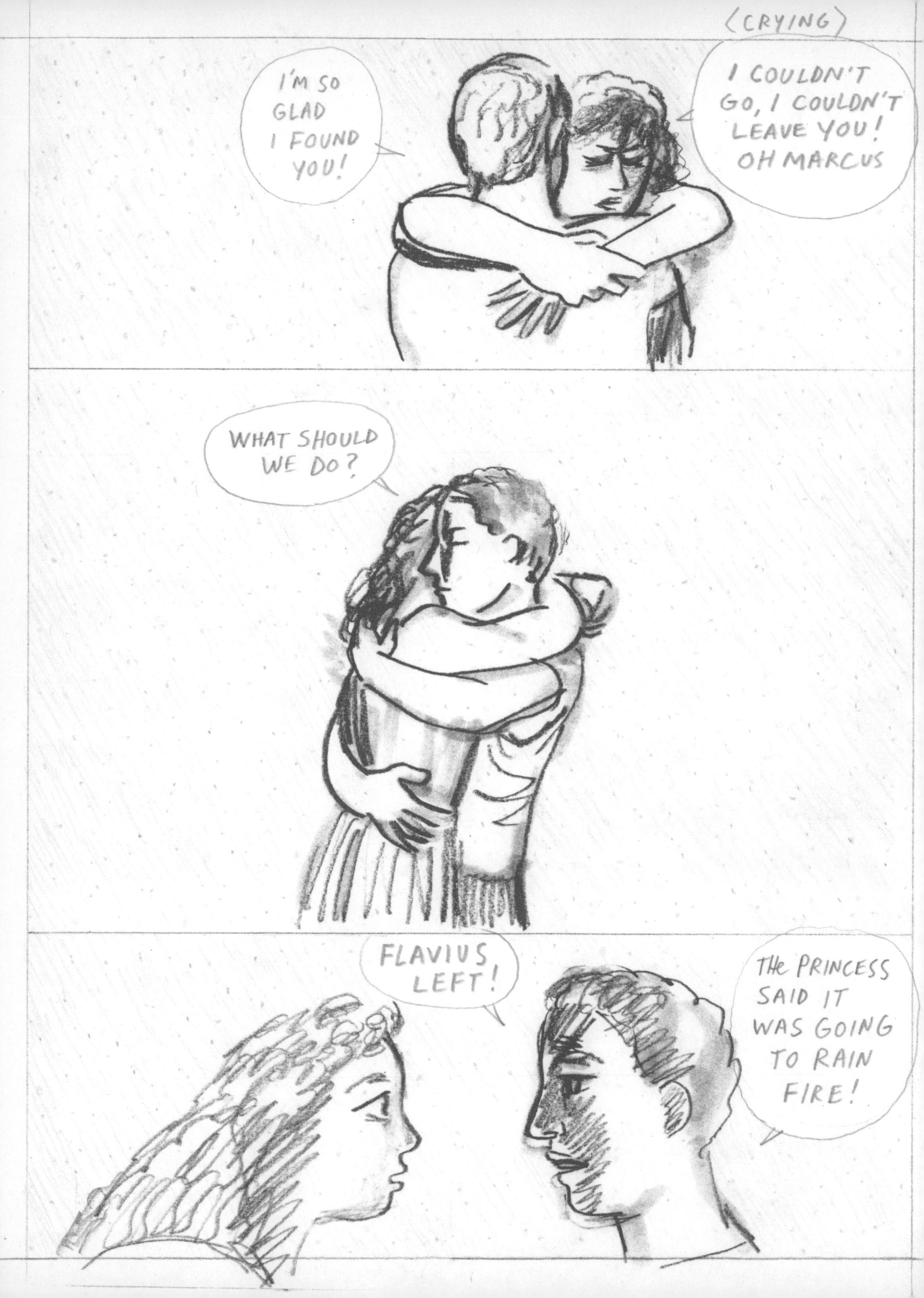

⟨CRYING⟩
I'M SO GLAD I FOUND YOU!
I COULDN'T GO, I COULDN'T LEAVE YOU! OH MARCUS
WHAT SHOULD WE DO?
FLAVIUS LEFT!
THE PRINCESS SAID IT WAS GOING TO RAIN FIRE!

<SOON>

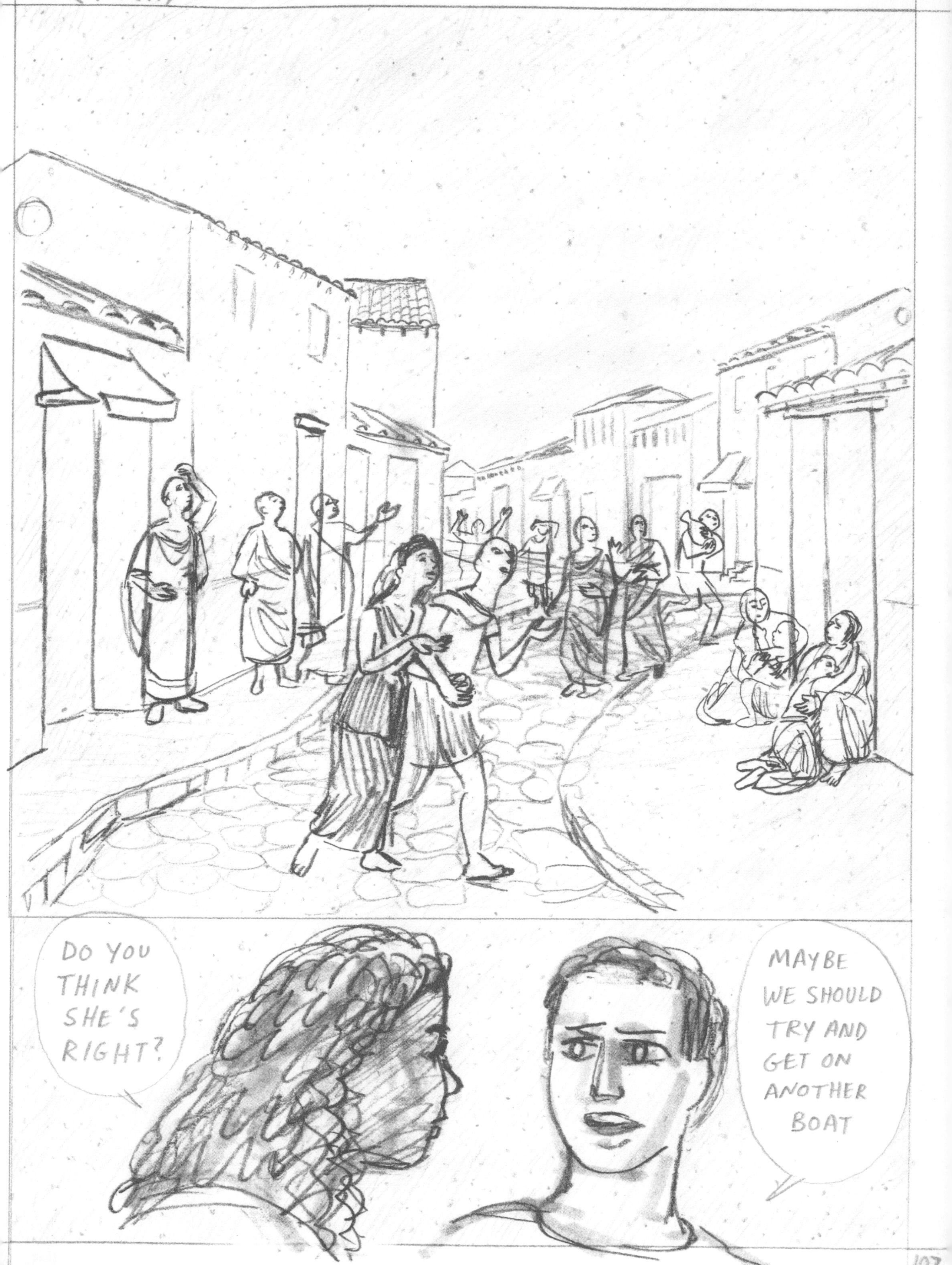
DO YOU THINK SHE'S RIGHT?
MAYBE WE SHOULD TRY AND GET ON ANOTHER BOAT

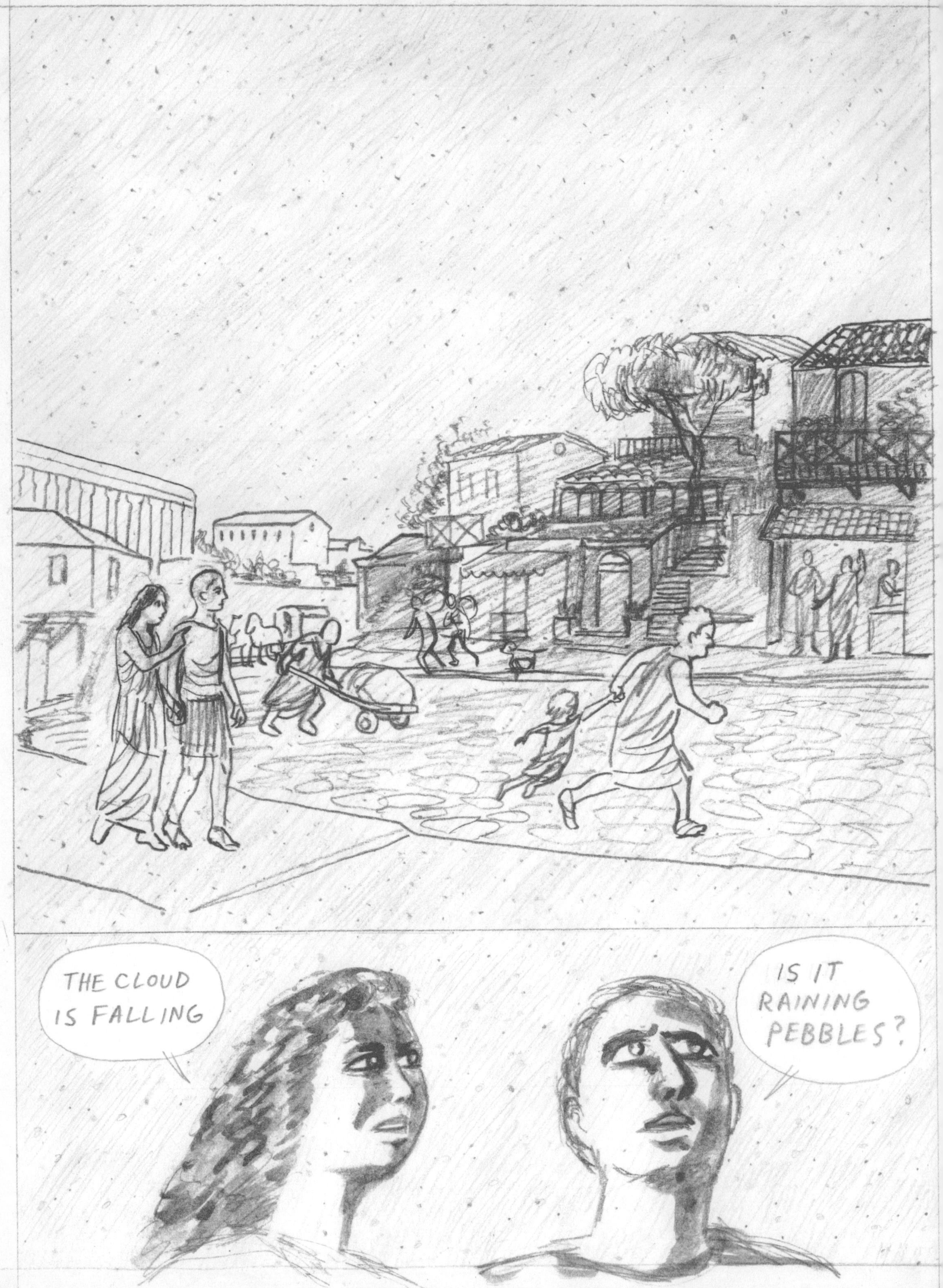
THE CLOUD IS FALLING
IS IT RAINING PEBBLES?

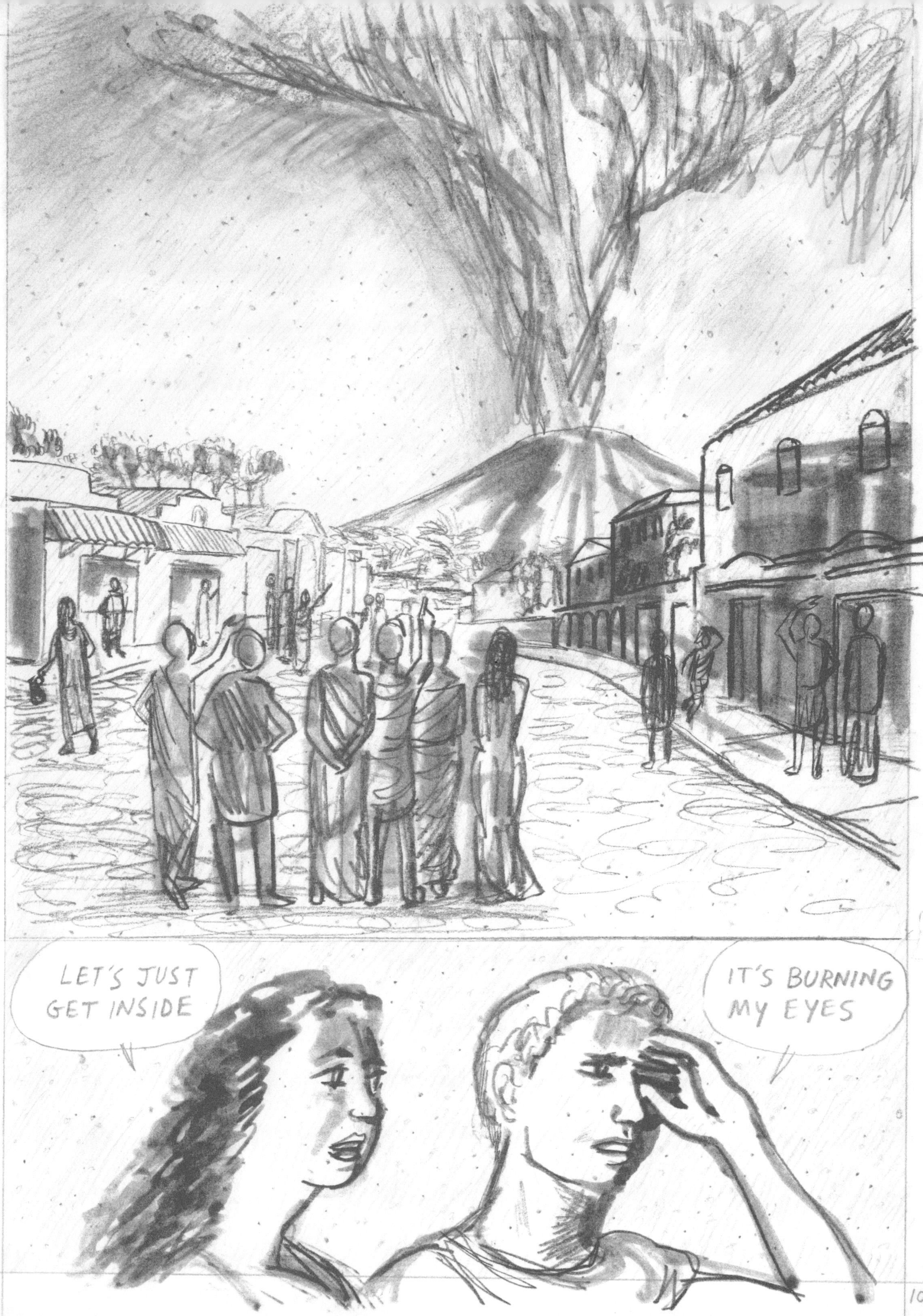
LET'S JUST GET INSIDE
IT'S BURNING MY EYES

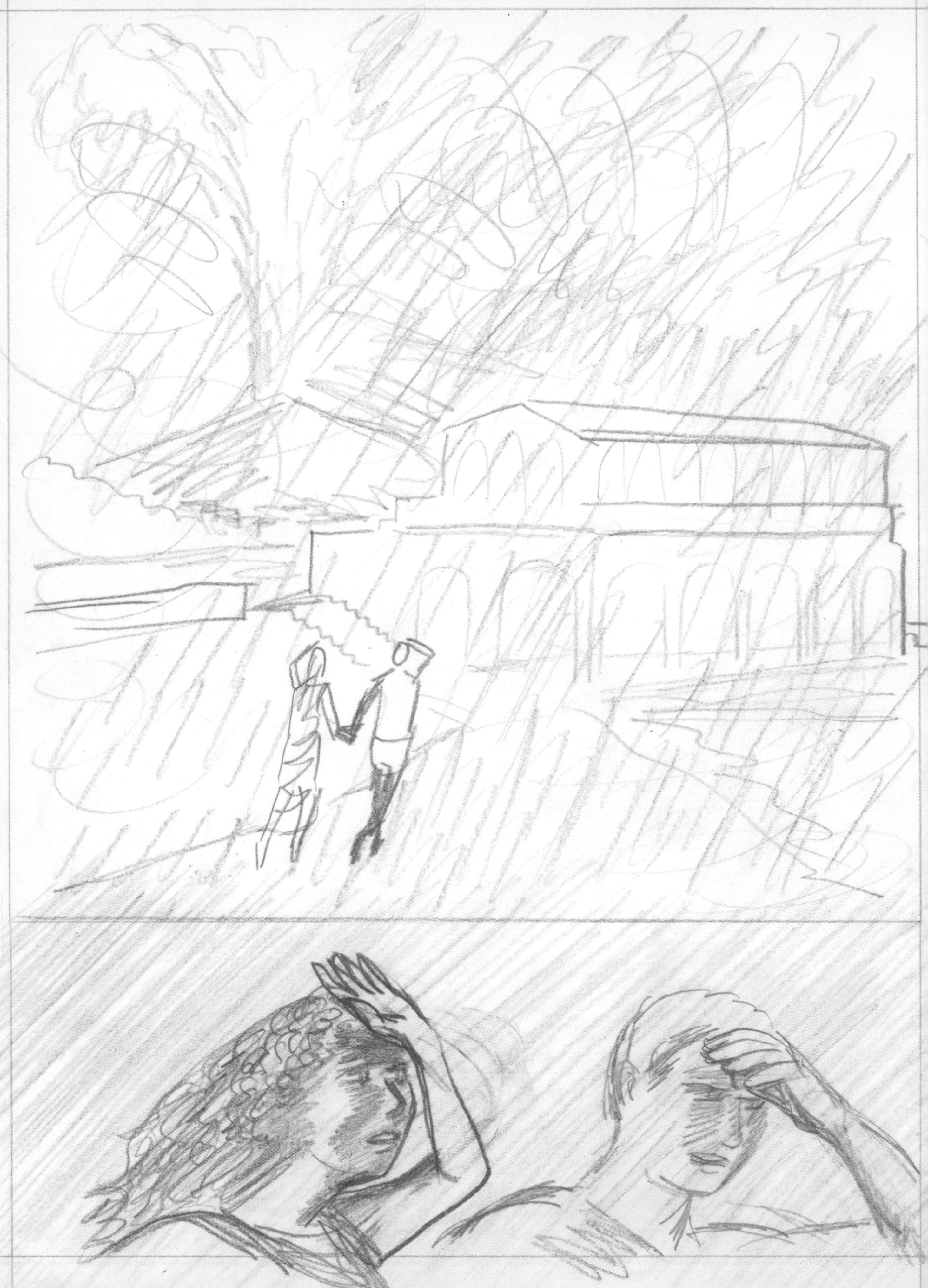

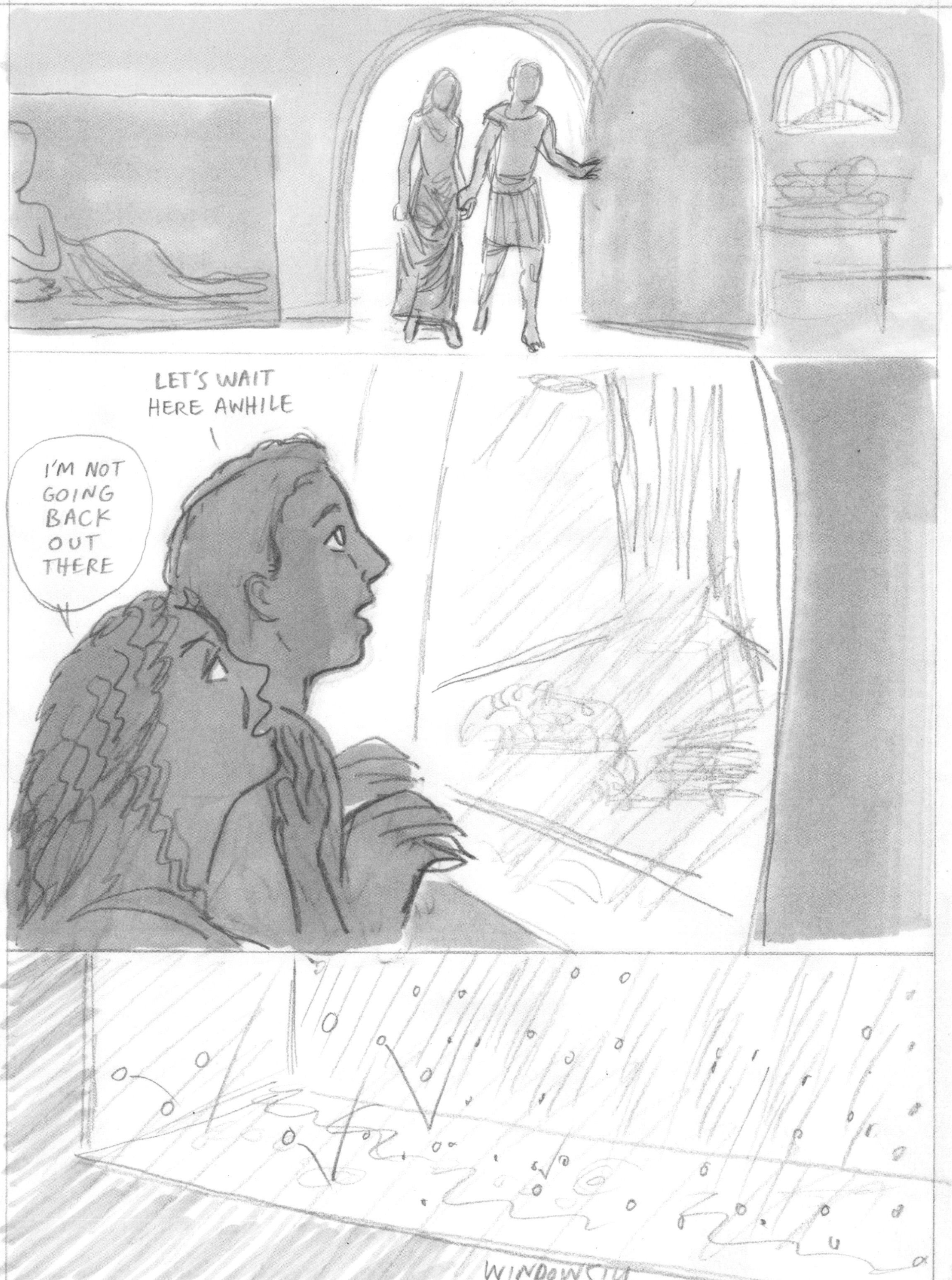
LET'S WAIT HERE AWHILE
I'M NOT GOING BACK OUT THERE
WINDOWSILL

PEBBLES/ROCKS/ASH

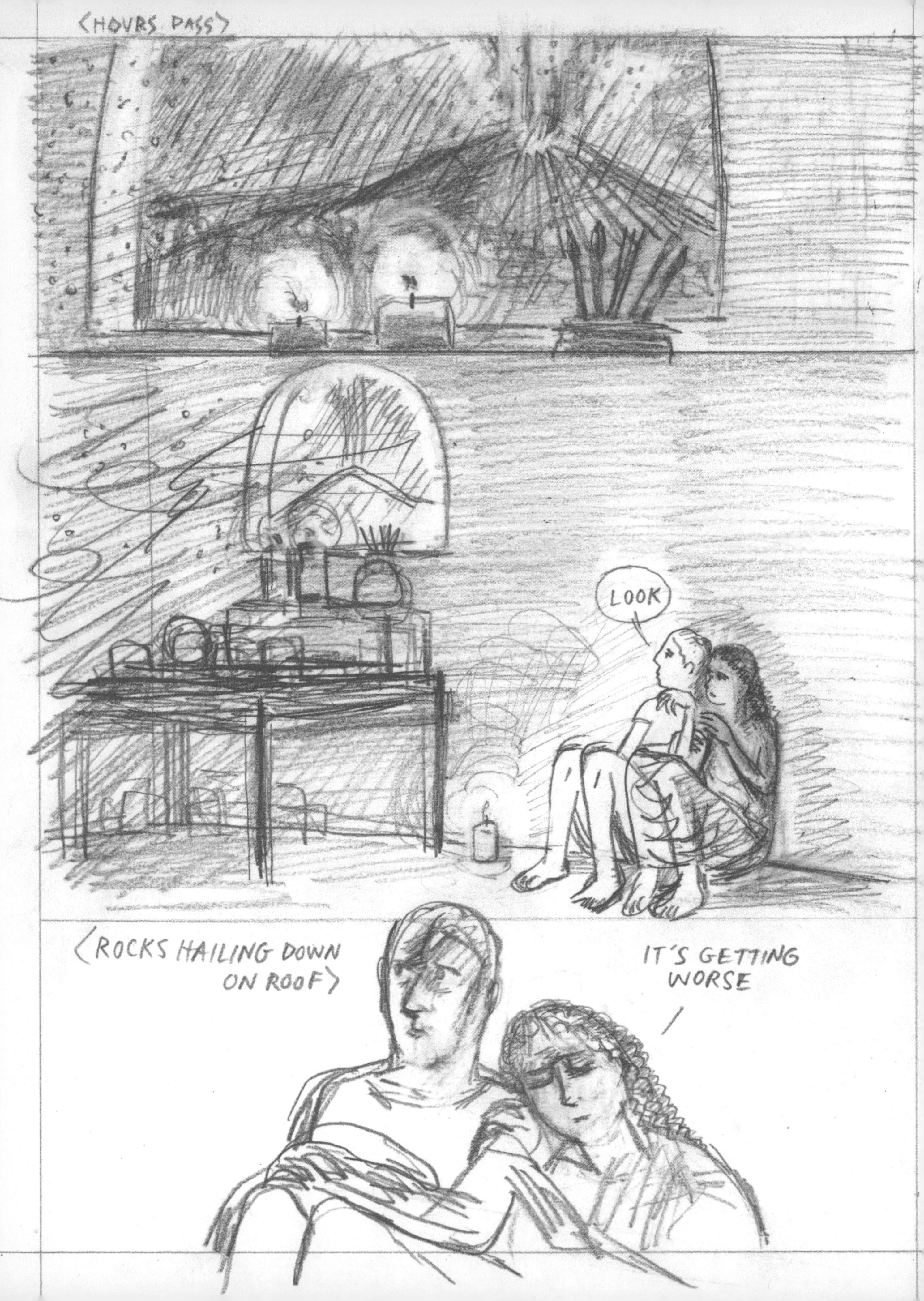
<HOURS PASS>
LOOK
<ROCKS HAILING DOWN ON ROOF>
IT'S GETTING WORSE

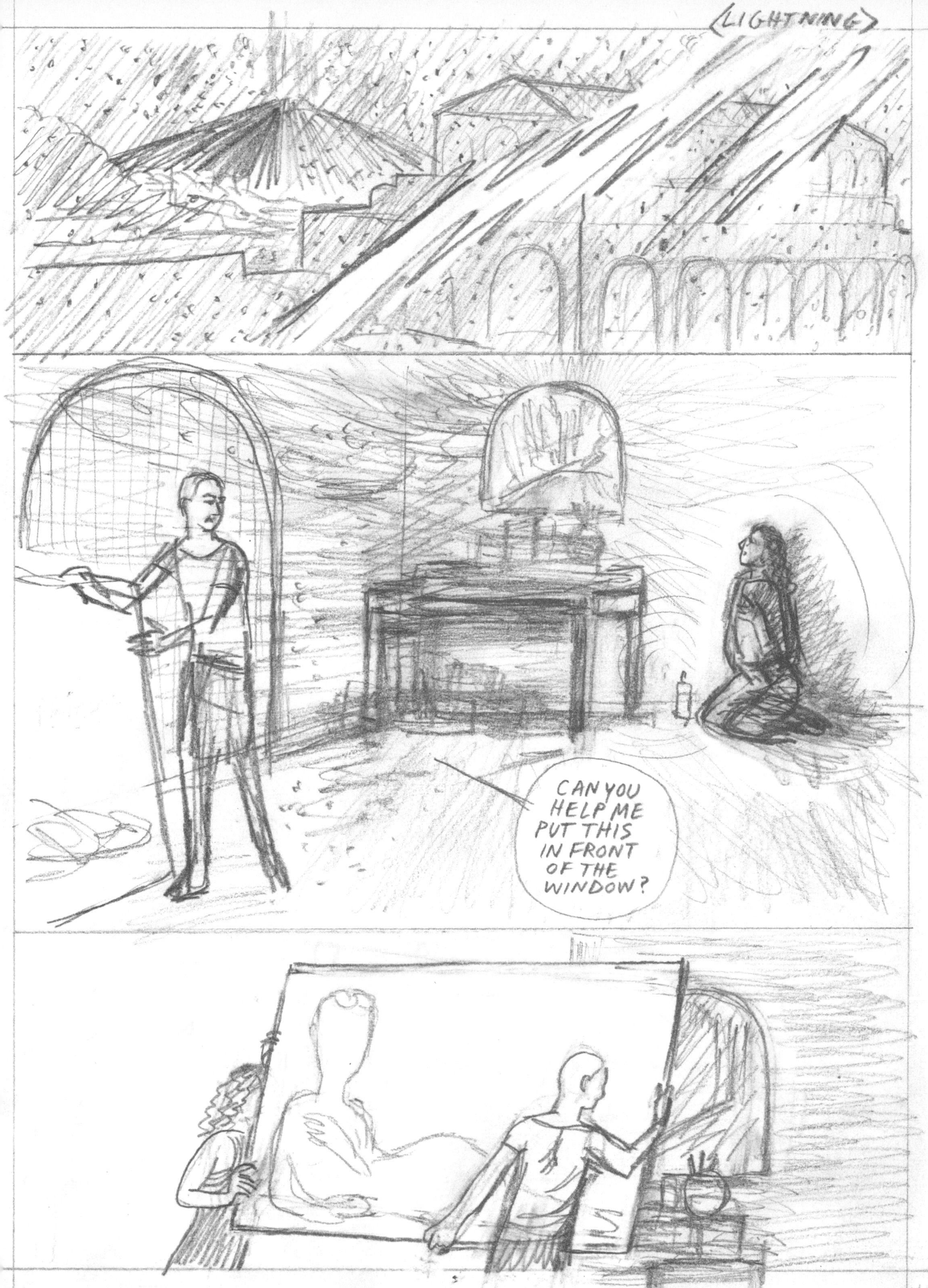
<LIGHTNING>
CAN YOU HELP ME PUT THIS IN FRONT OF THE WINDOW?

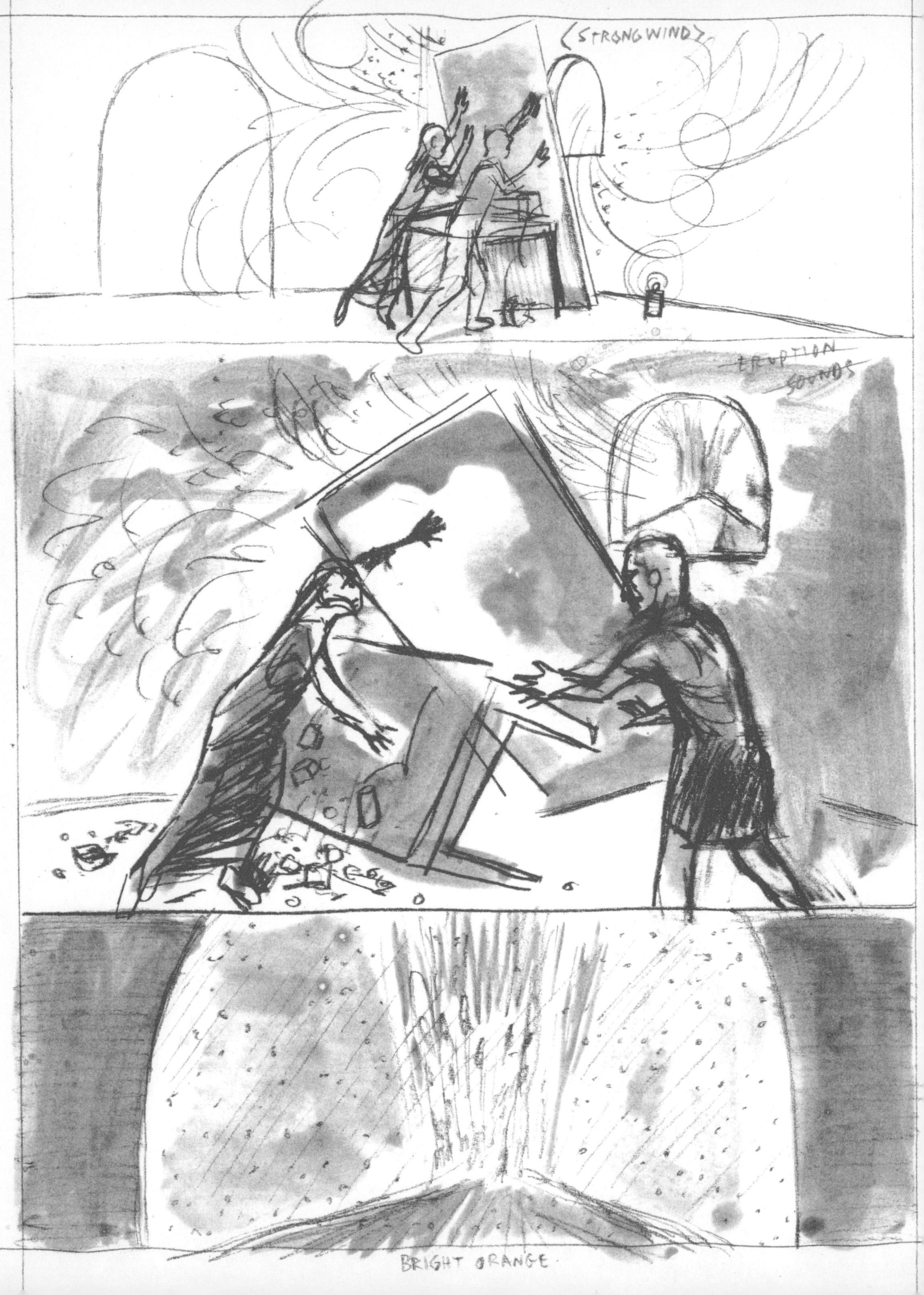
<STRONG WIND>
ERUPTION SOUNDS
BRIGHT ORANGE

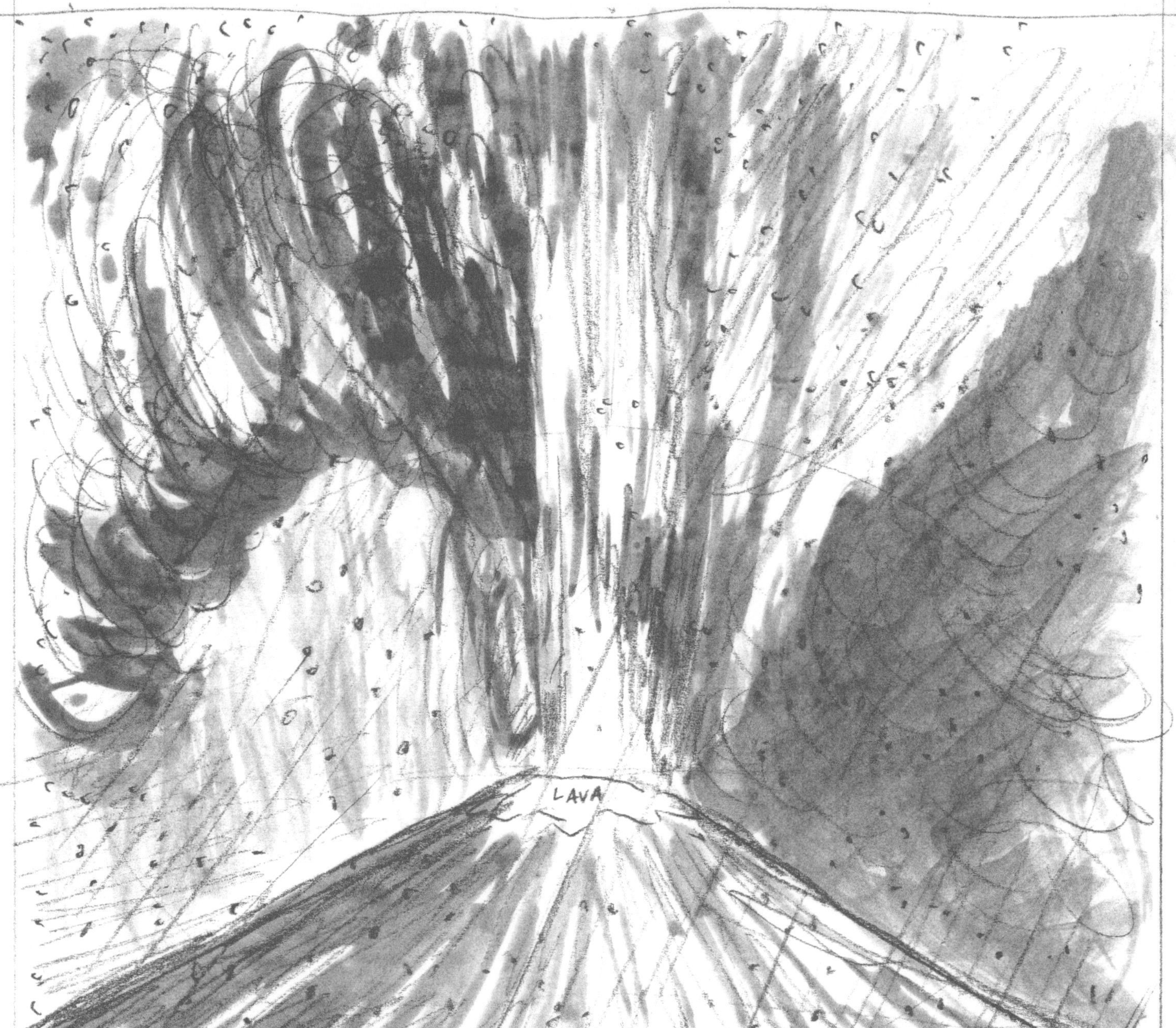
LAVA

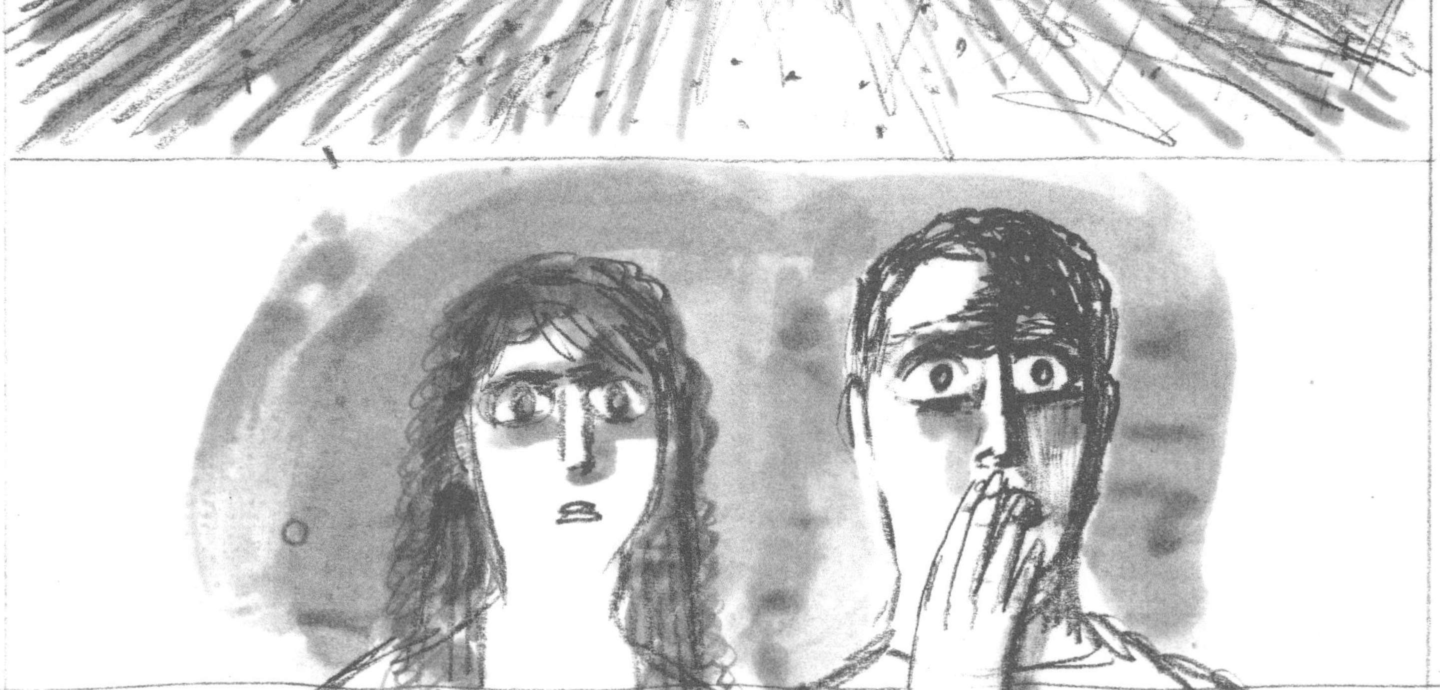

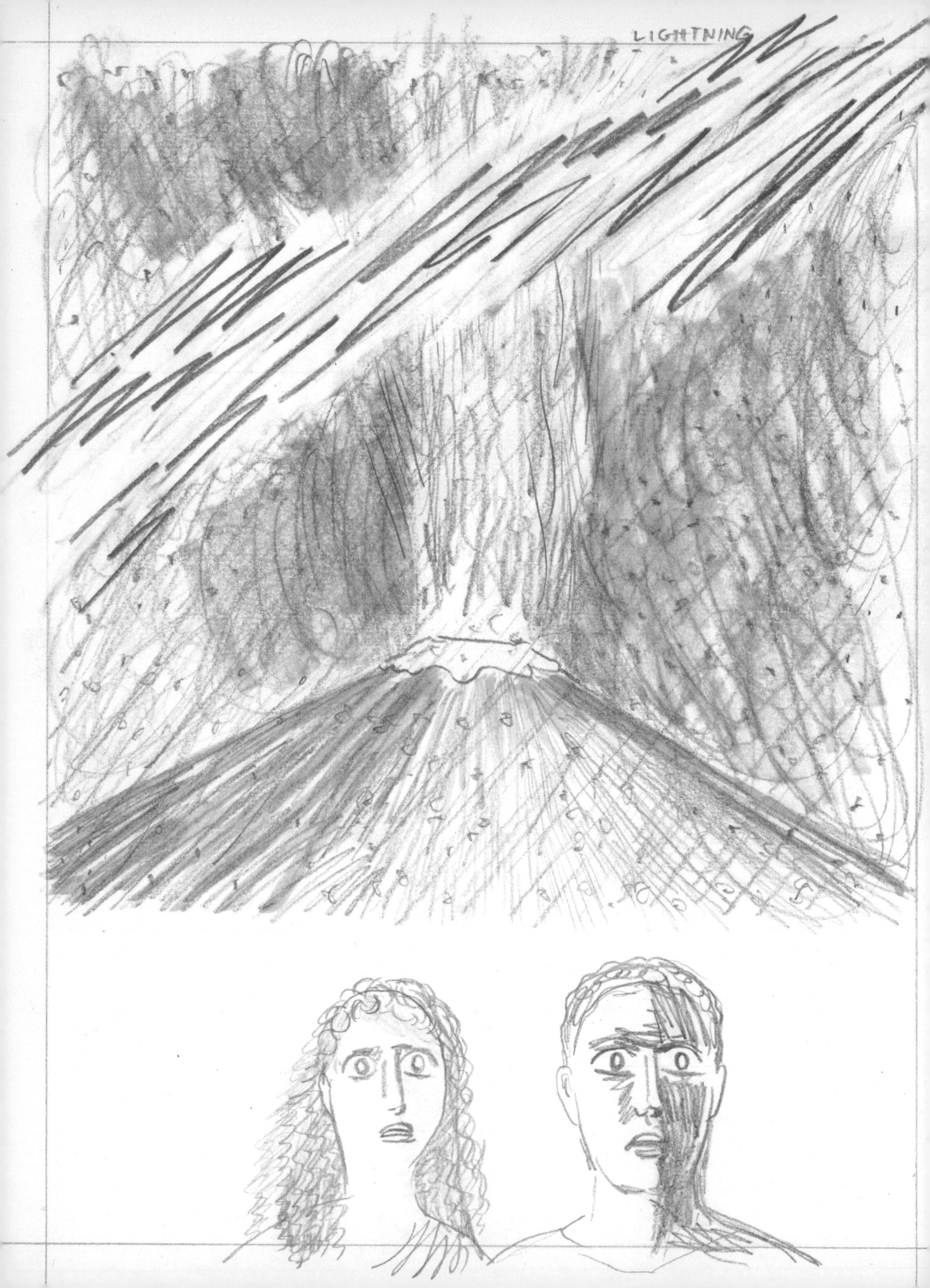
LIGHTNING

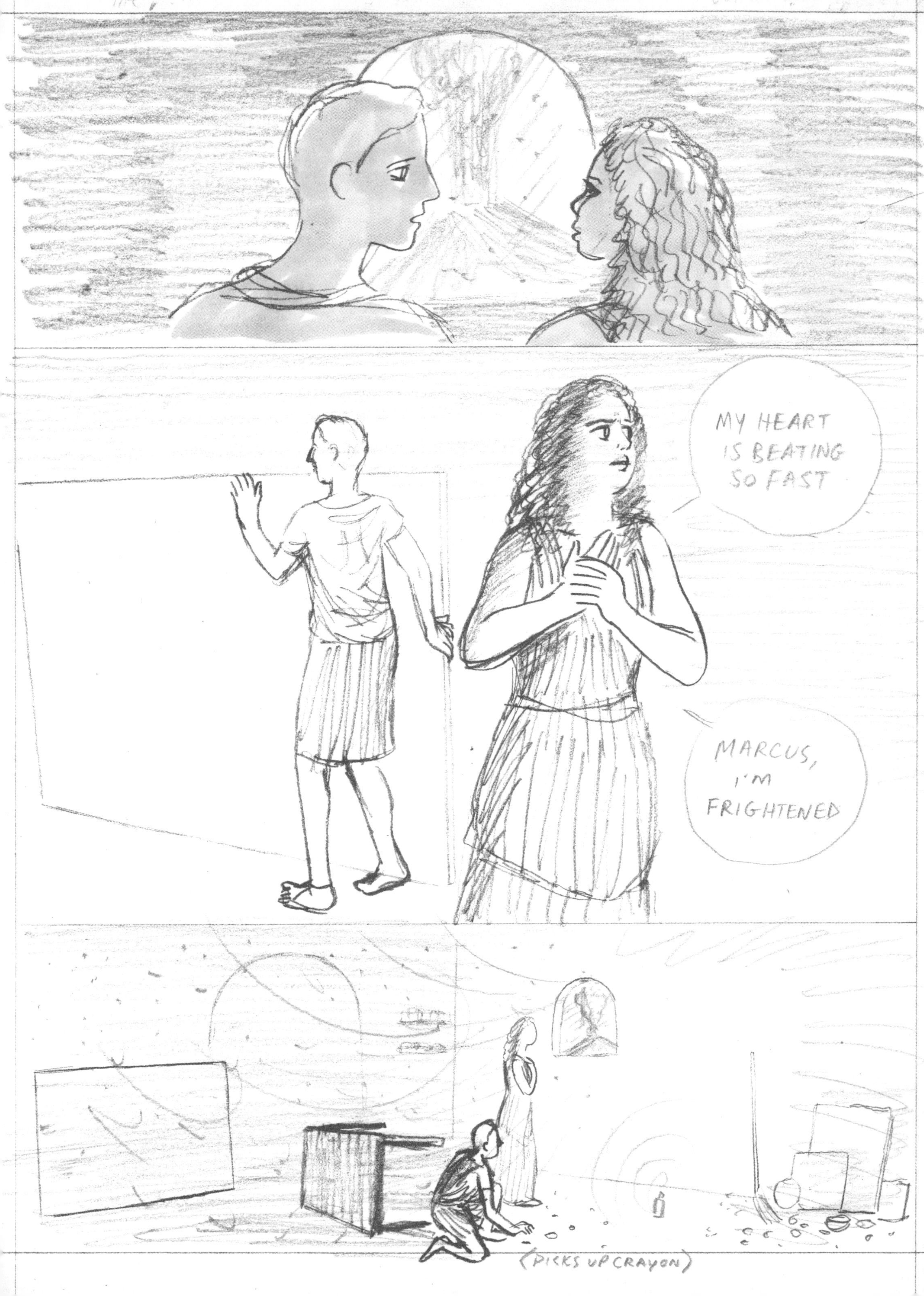
MY HEART IS BEATING SO FAST
MARCUS, I'M FRIGHTENED
(PICKS UP CRAYON)

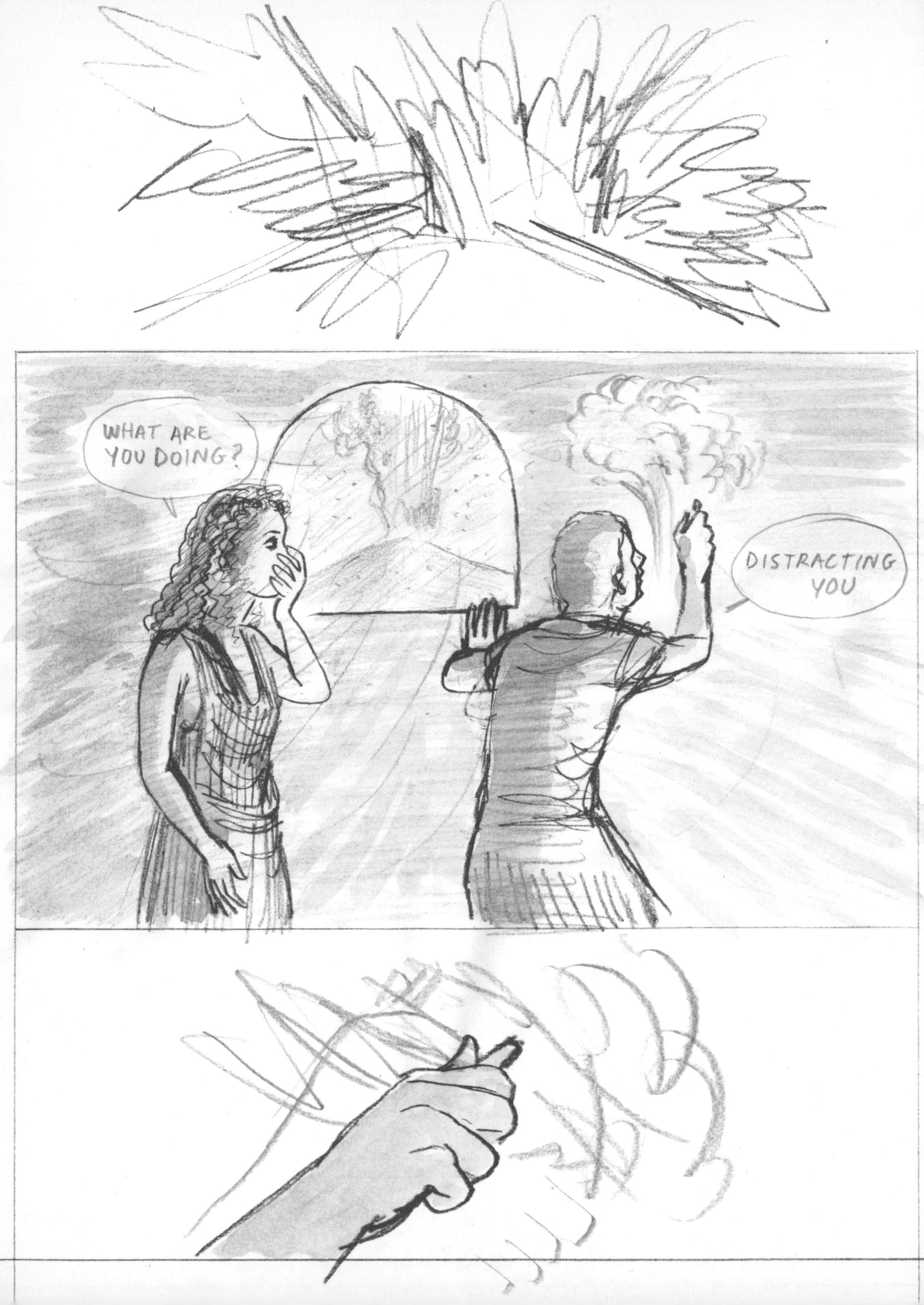
WHAT ARE YOU DOING?
DISTRACTING YOU

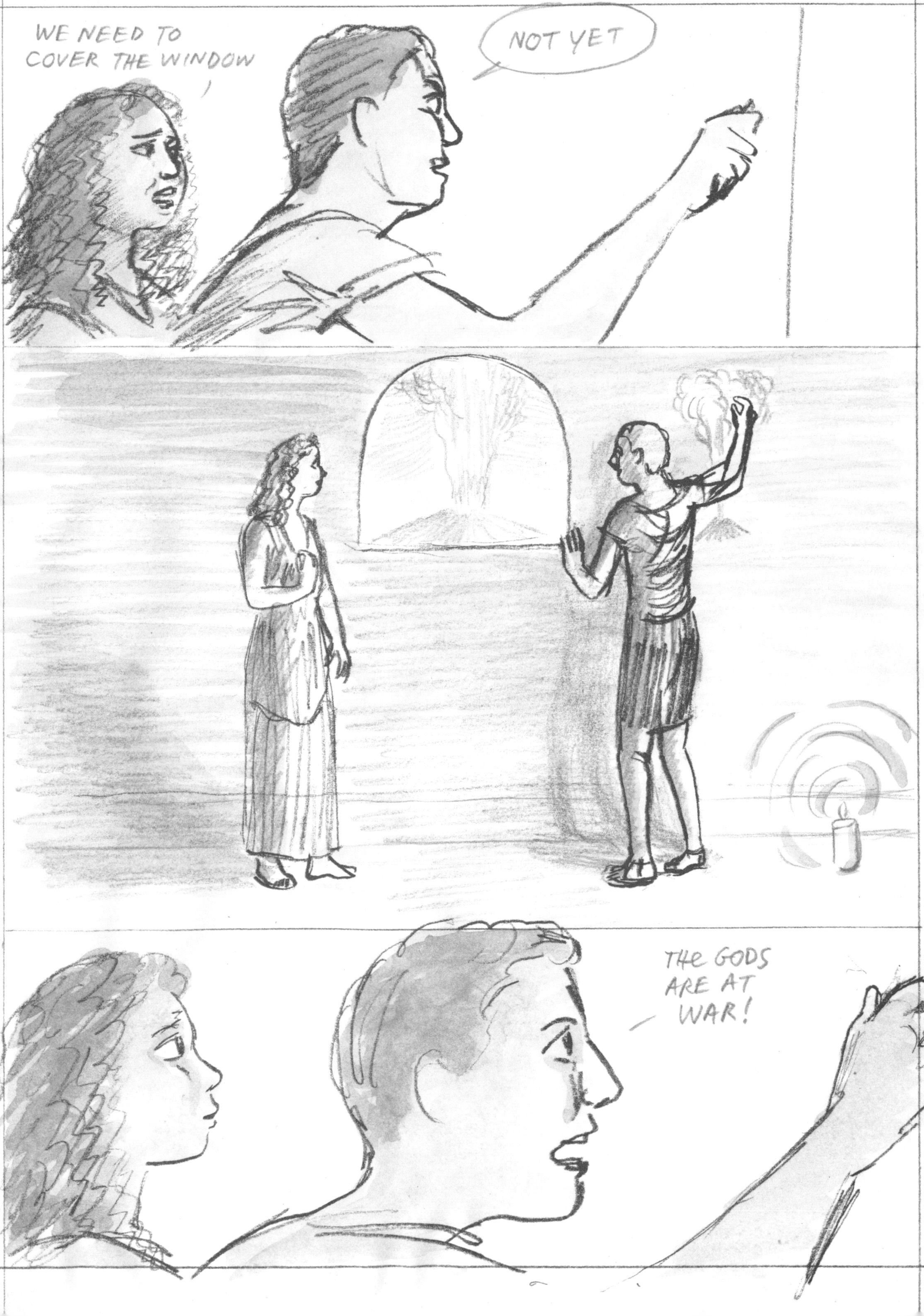
WE NEED TO COVER THE WINDOW
NOT YET
THE GODS ARE AT WAR!

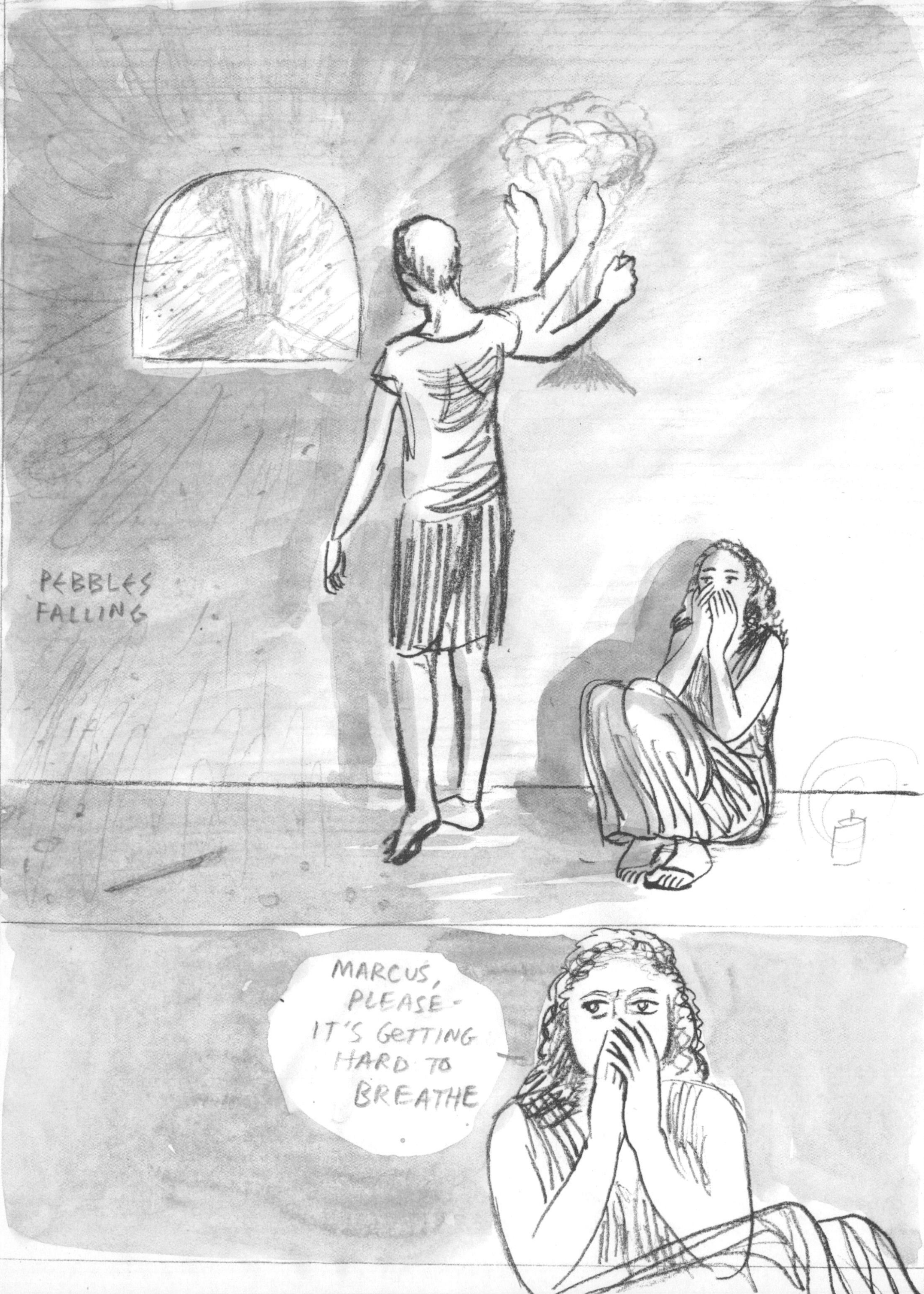
PEBBLES FALLING
MARCUS, PLEASE - IT'S GETTING HARD TO BREATHE

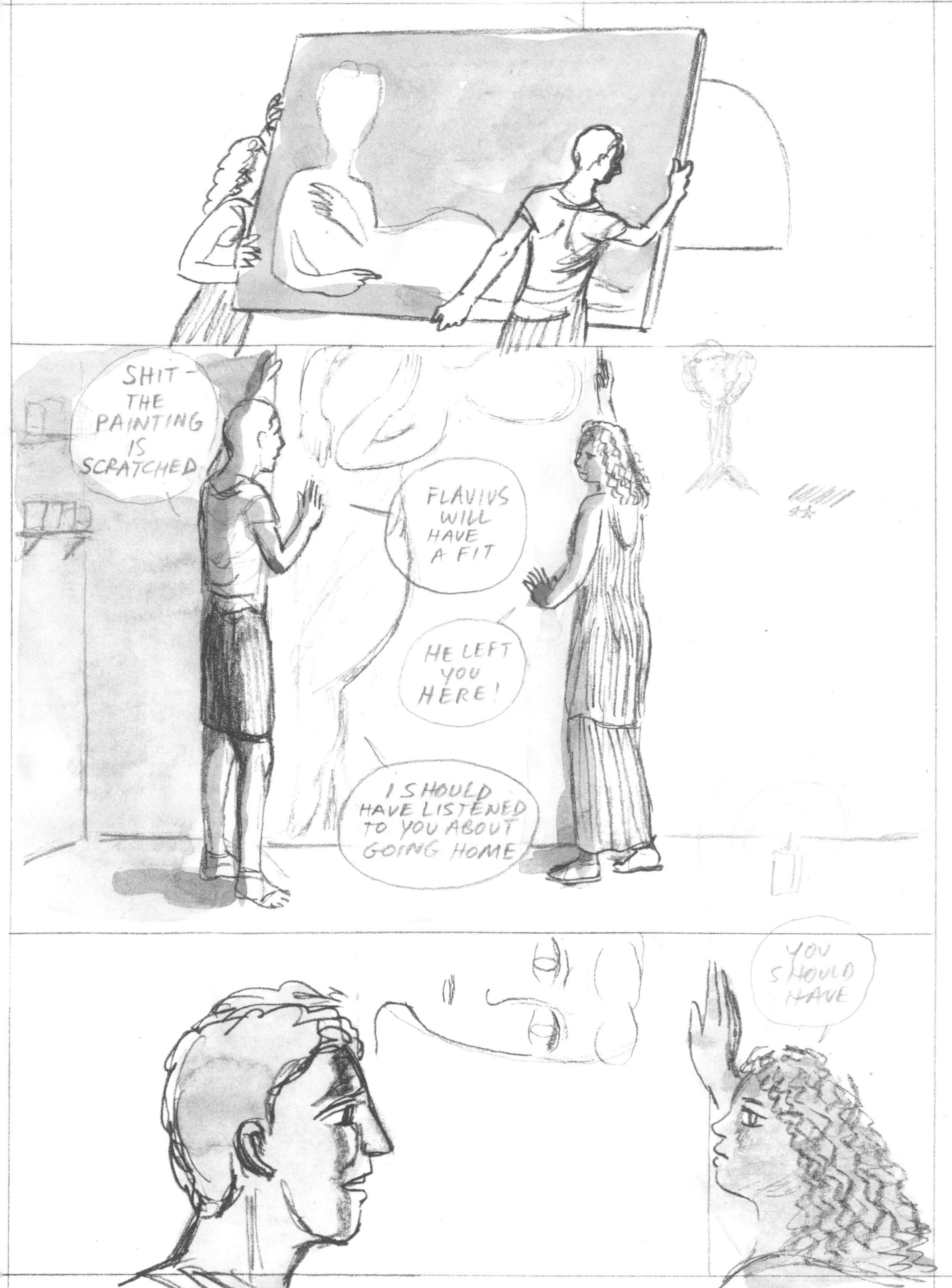
SHIT- THE PAINTING IS SCRATCHED
FLAVIUS WILL HAVE A FIT
HE LEFT YOU HERE!
I SHOULD HAVE LISTENED TO YOU ABOUT GOING HOME
YOU SHOULD HAVE

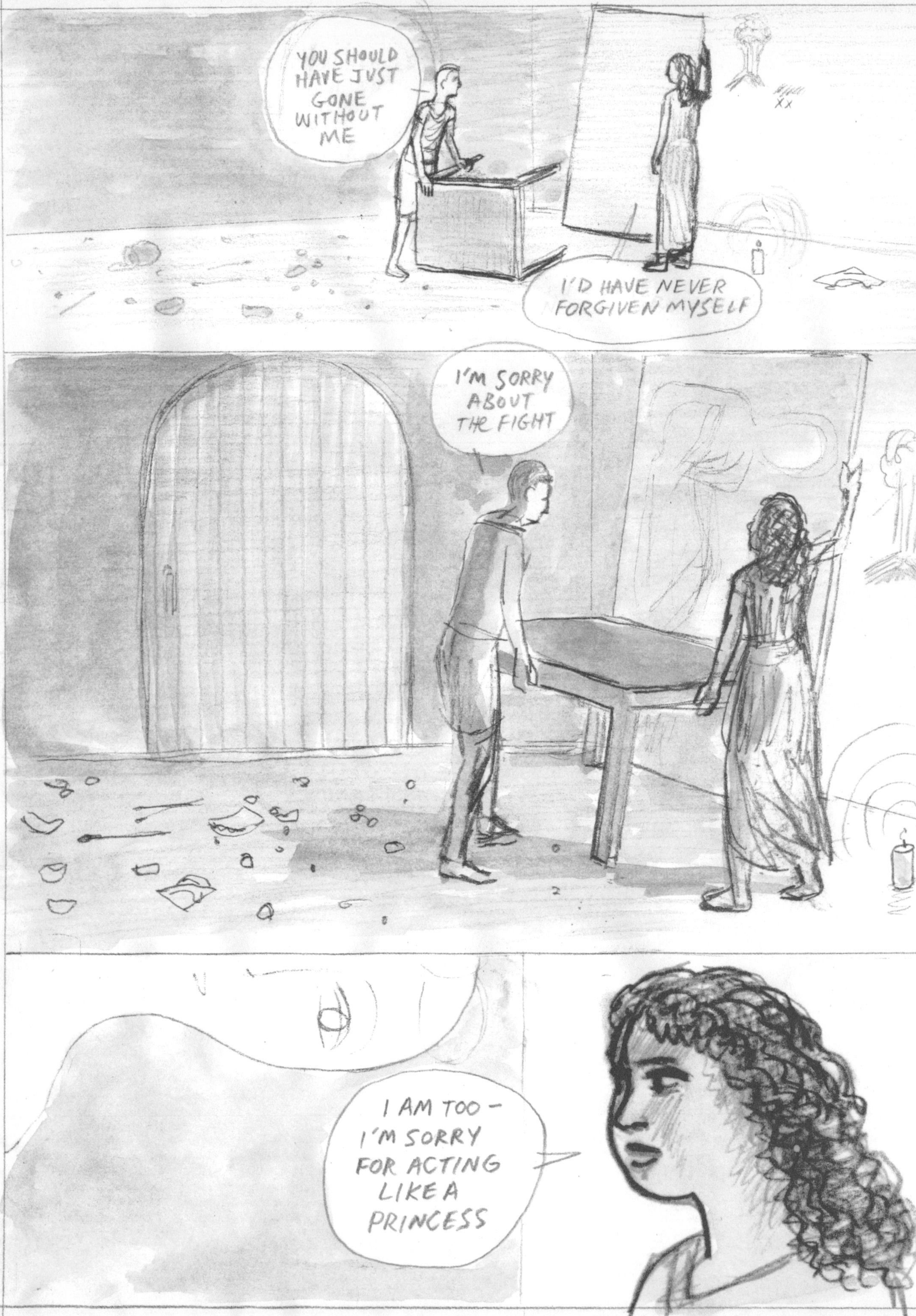
YOU SHOULD HAVE JUST GONE WITHOUT ME
I'D HAVE NEVER FORGIVEN MYSELF
I'M SORRY ABOUT THE FIGHT
I AM TOO - I'M SORRY FOR ACTING LIKE A PRINCESS

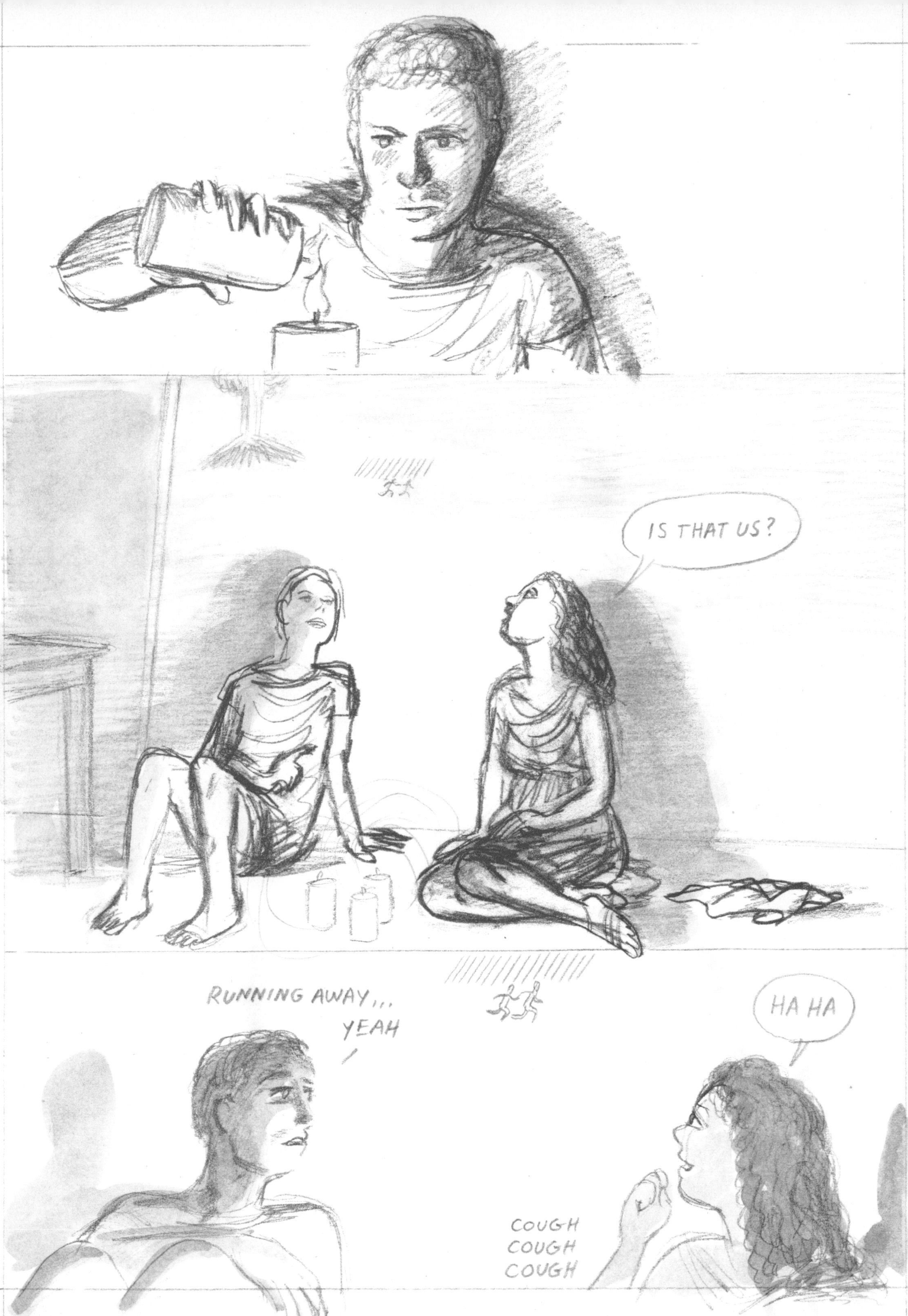
IS THAT US?
RUNNING AWAY... YEAH
HA HA
COUGH
COUGH
COUGH

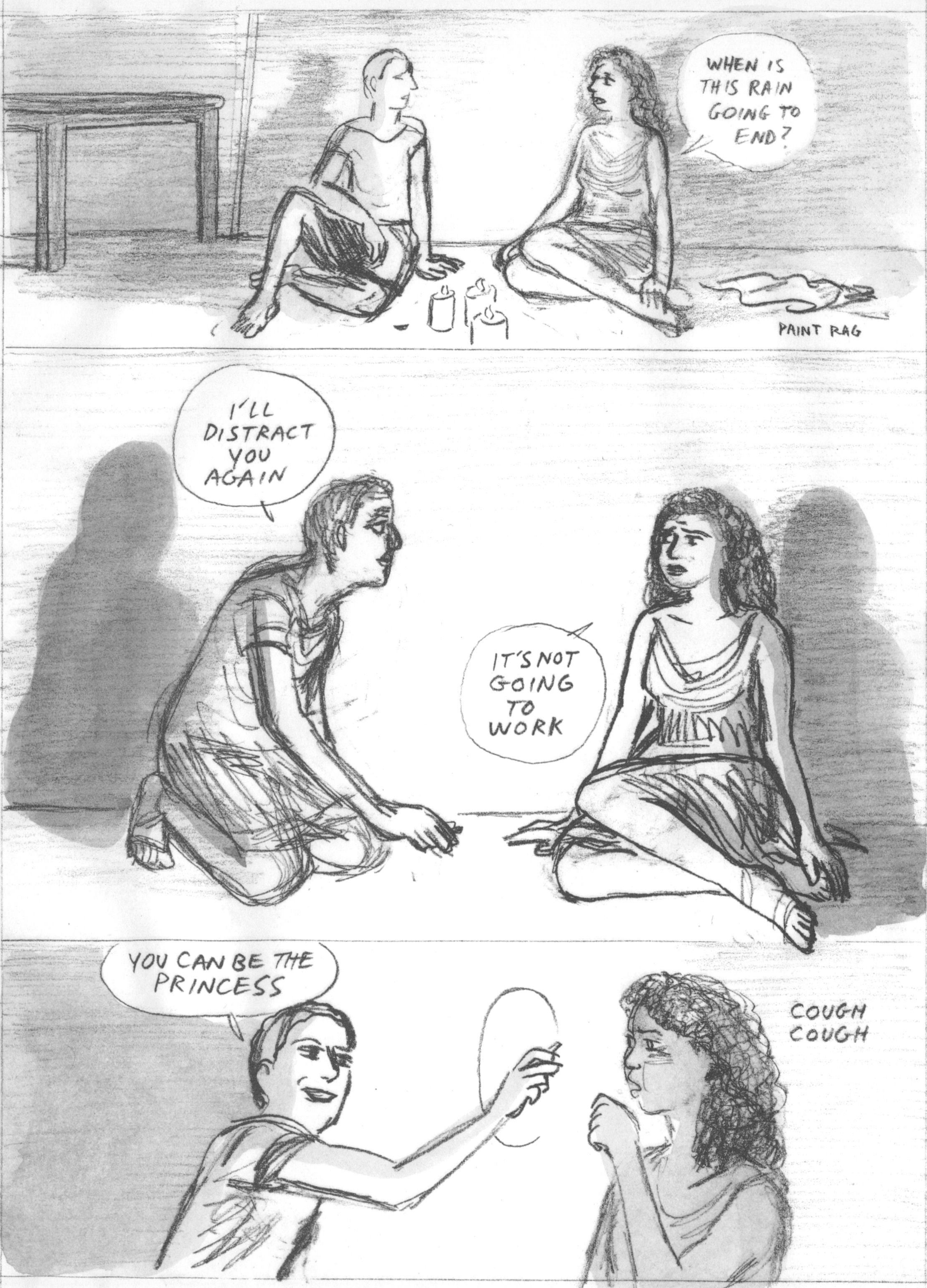
WHEN IS THIS RAIN GOING TO END?
PAINT RAG
I'LL DISTRACT YOU AGAIN
IT'S NOT GOING TO WORK
YOU CAN BE THE PRINCESS
COUGH COUGH

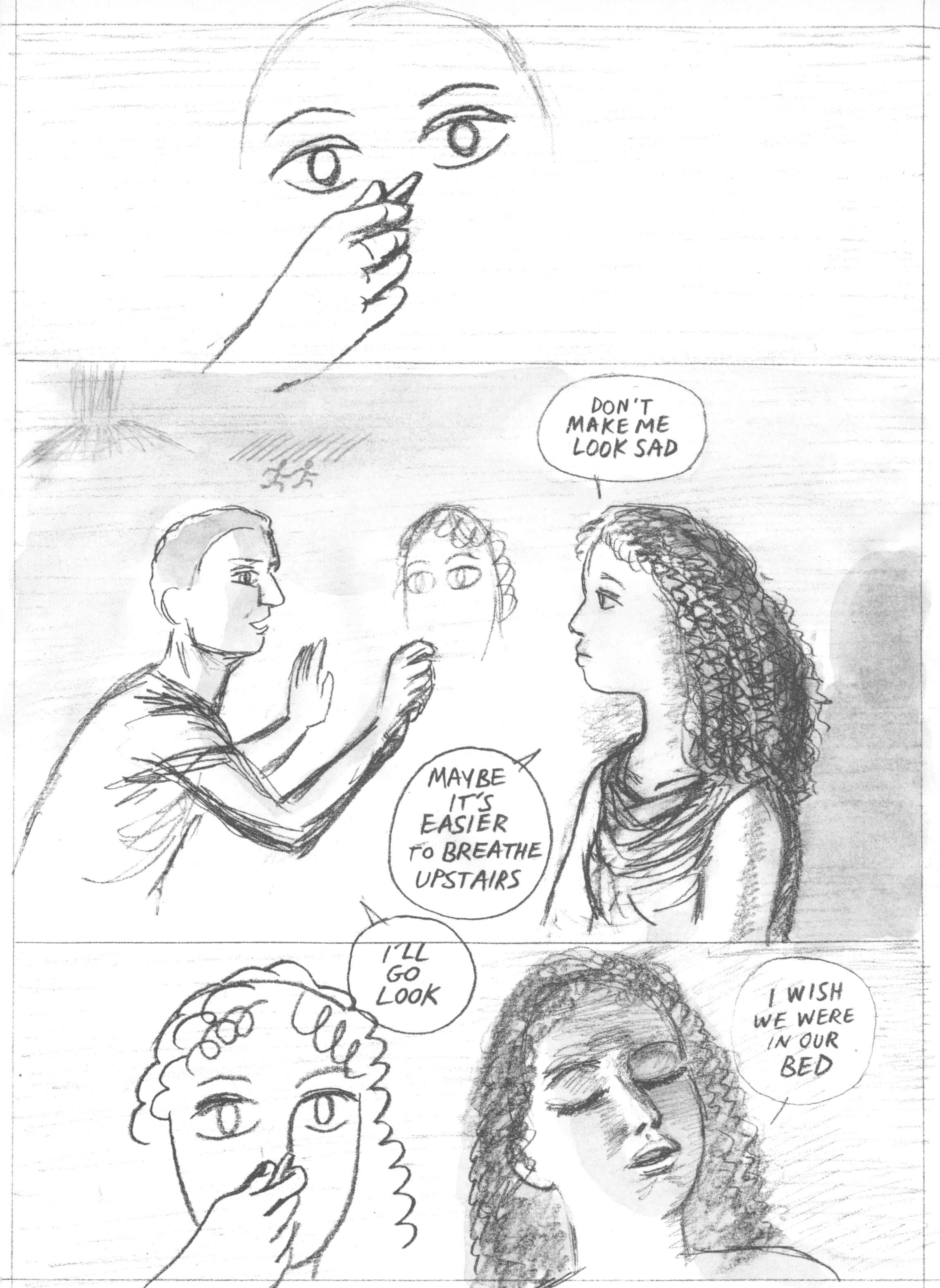
DON'T MAKE ME LOOK SAD
MAYBE IT'S EASIER TO BREATHE UPSTAIRS
I'LL GO LOOK
I WISH WE WERE IN OUR BED

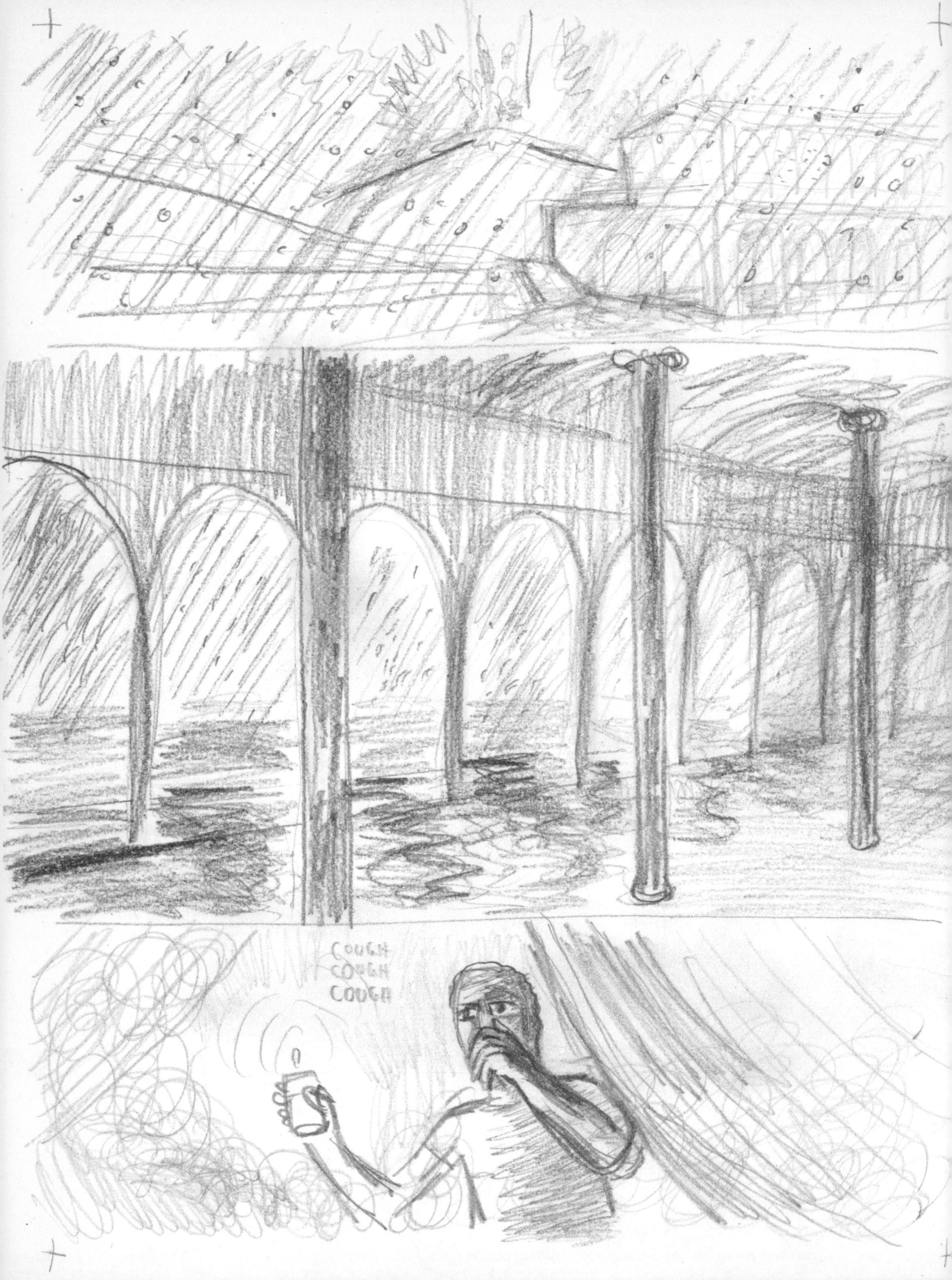
COUGH
COUGH
COUGH

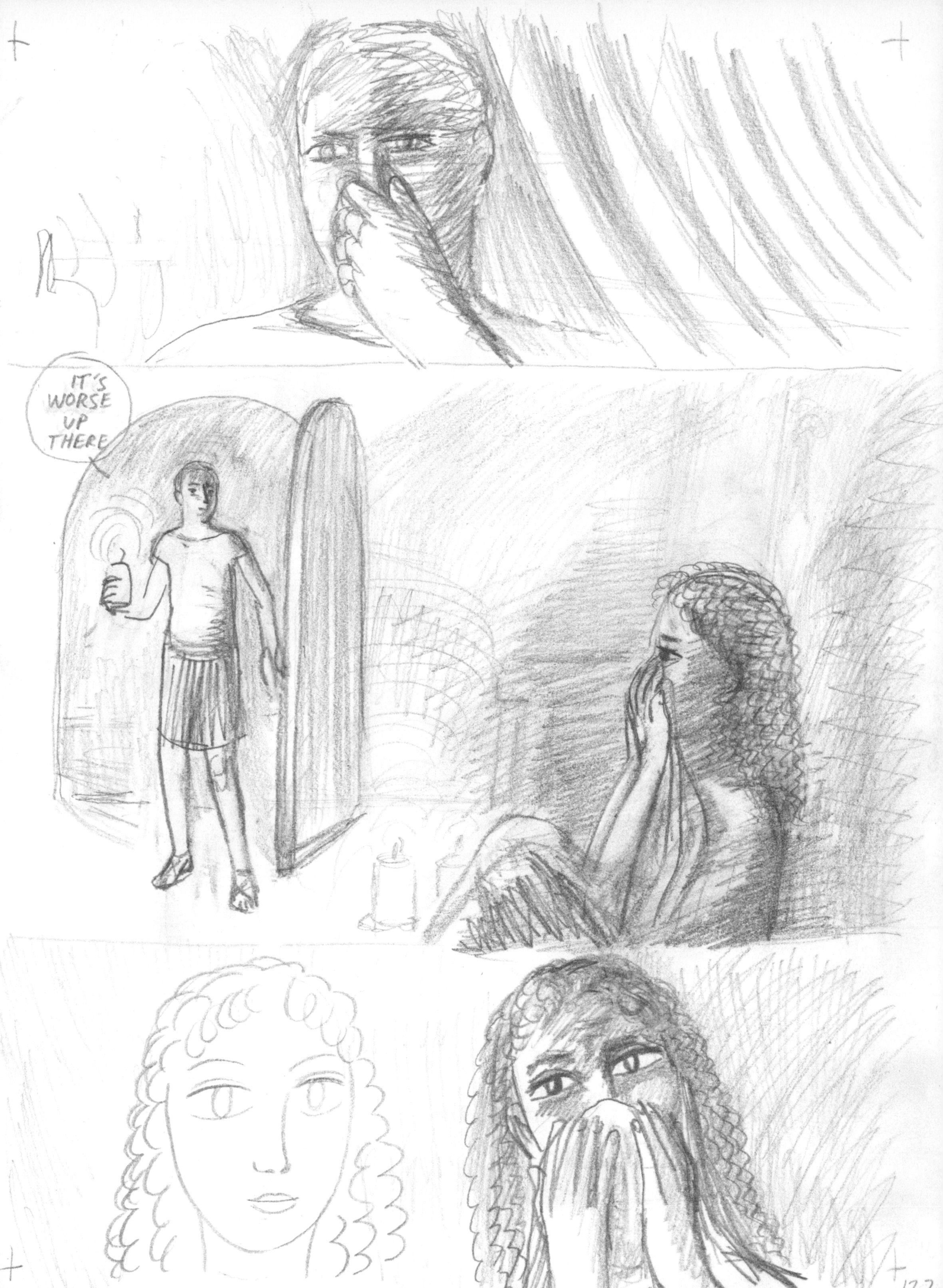
IT'S WORSE UP THERE

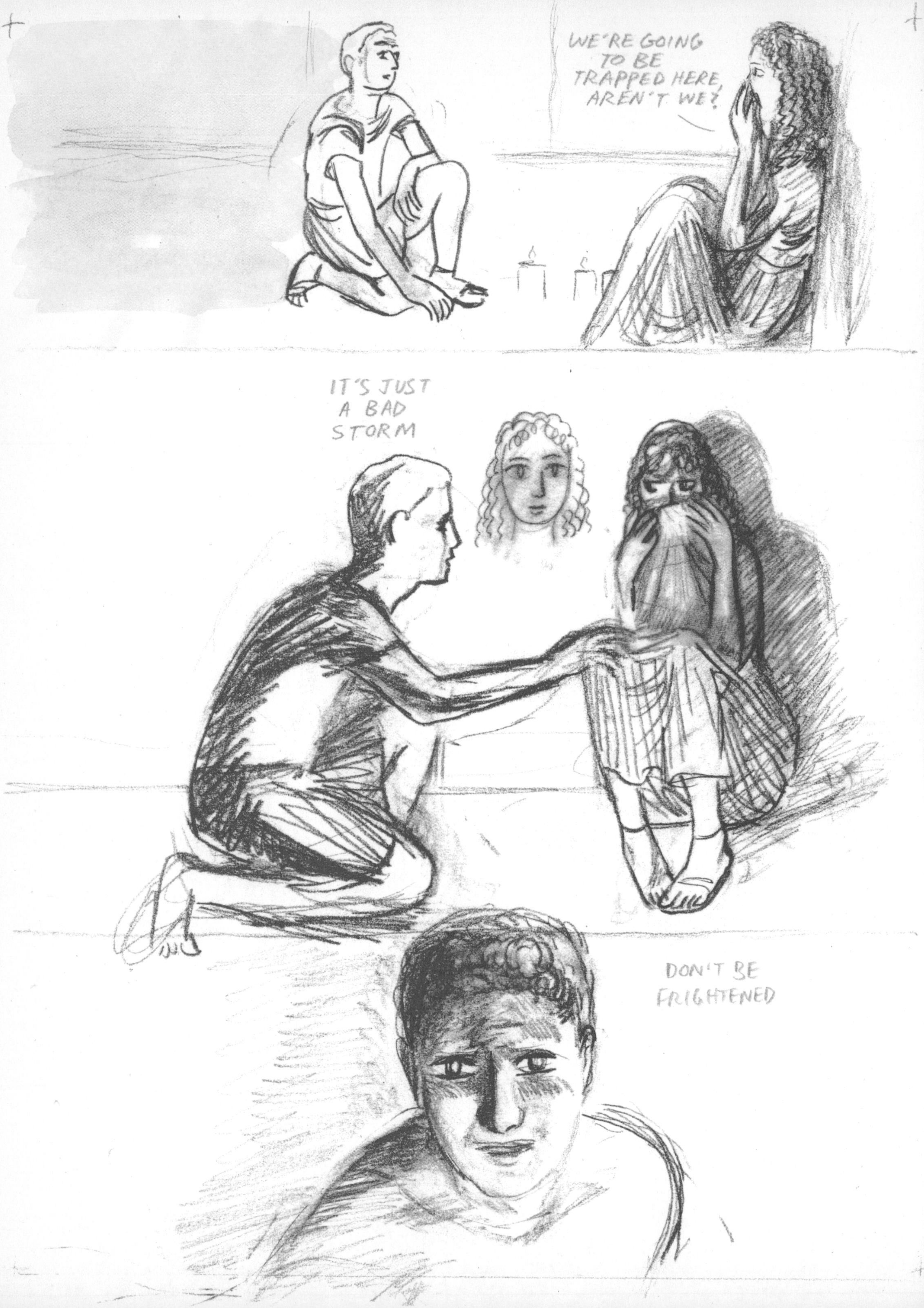
WE'RE GOING TO BE TRAPPED HERE, AREN'T WE?
IT'S JUST A BAD STORM
DON'T BE FRIGHTENED

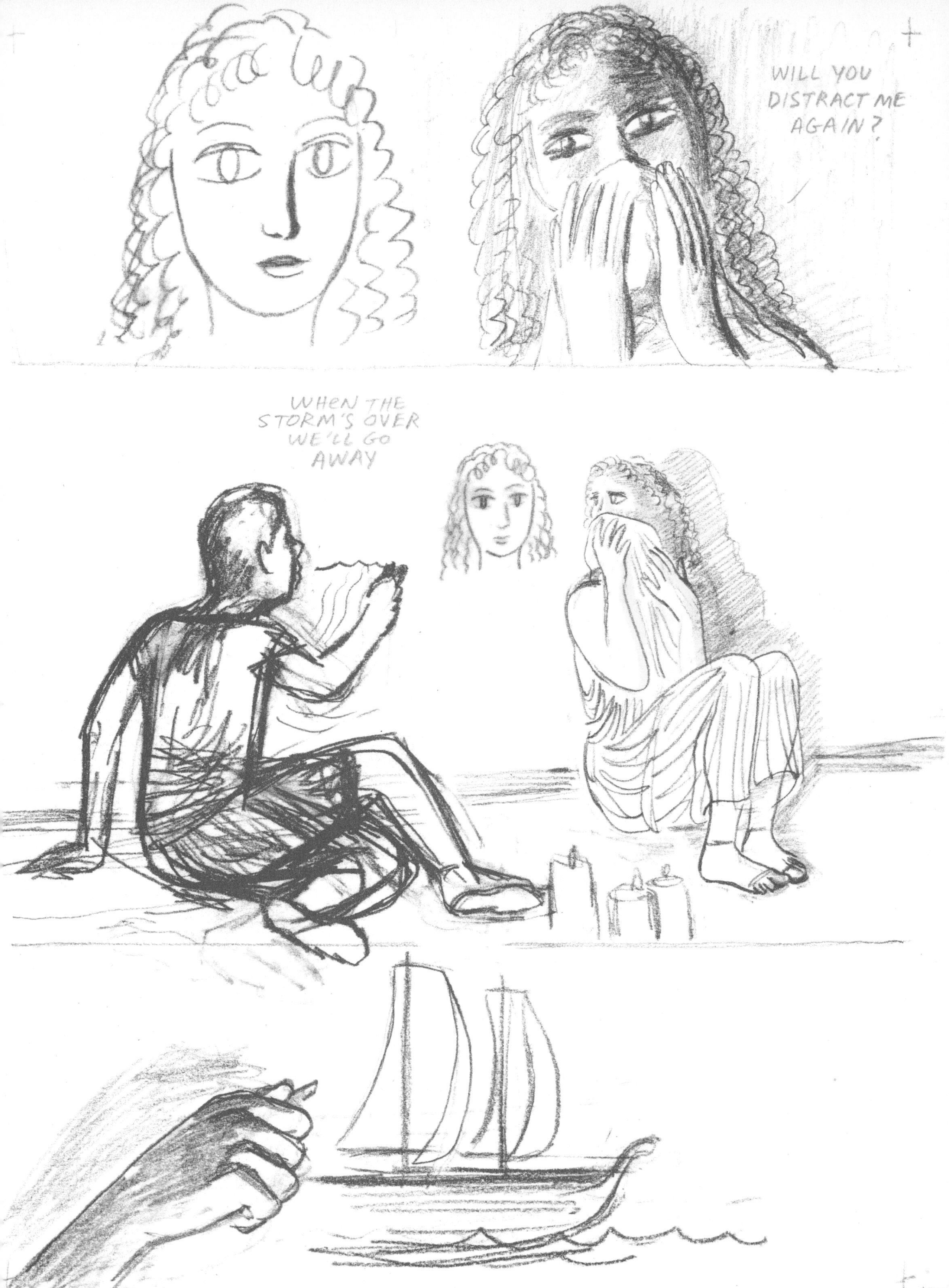
WILL YOU DISTRACT ME AGAIN?
WHEN THE STORM'S OVER WE'LL GO AWAY

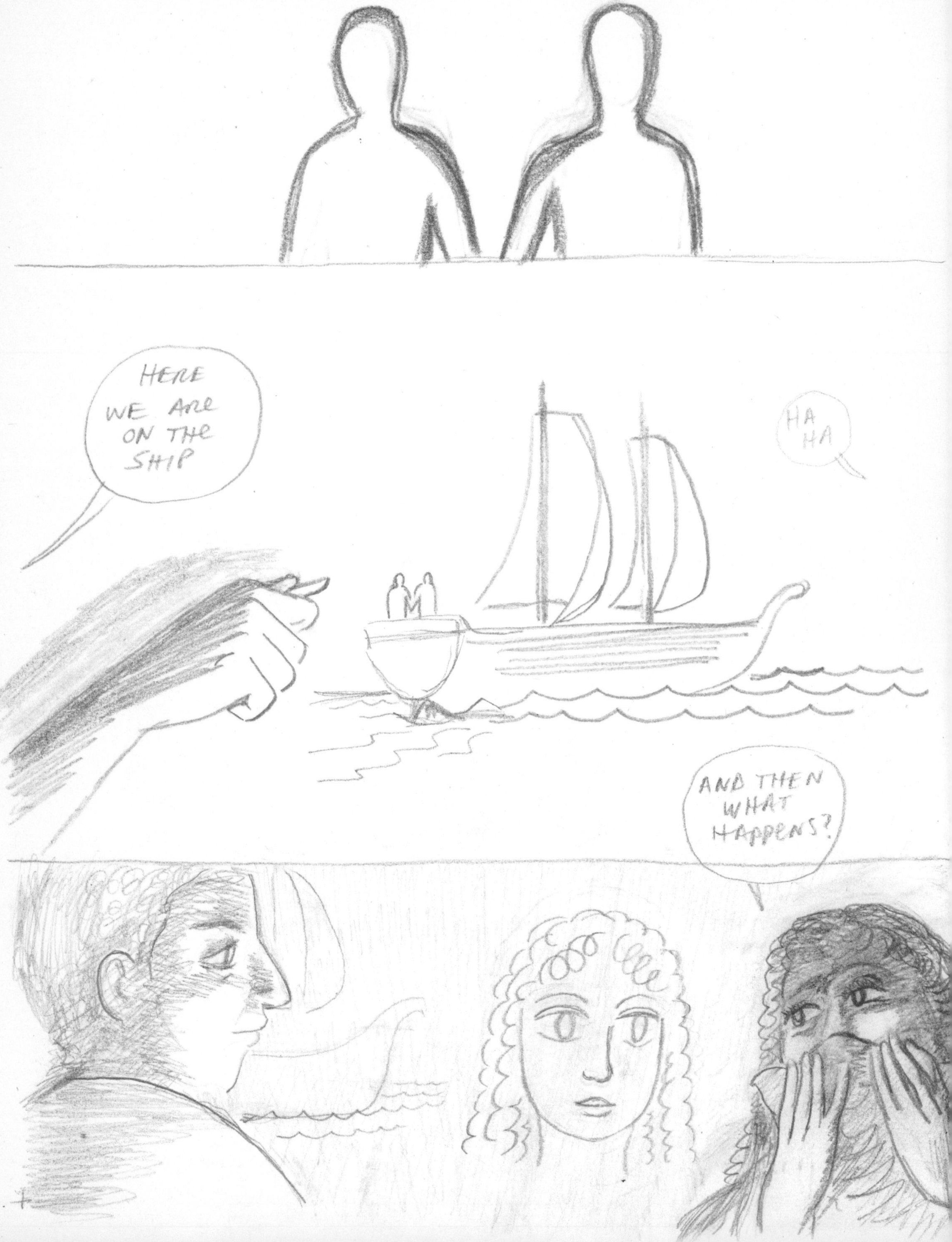
HERE WE ARE ON THE SHIP
HA HA
AND THEN WHAT HAPPENS?

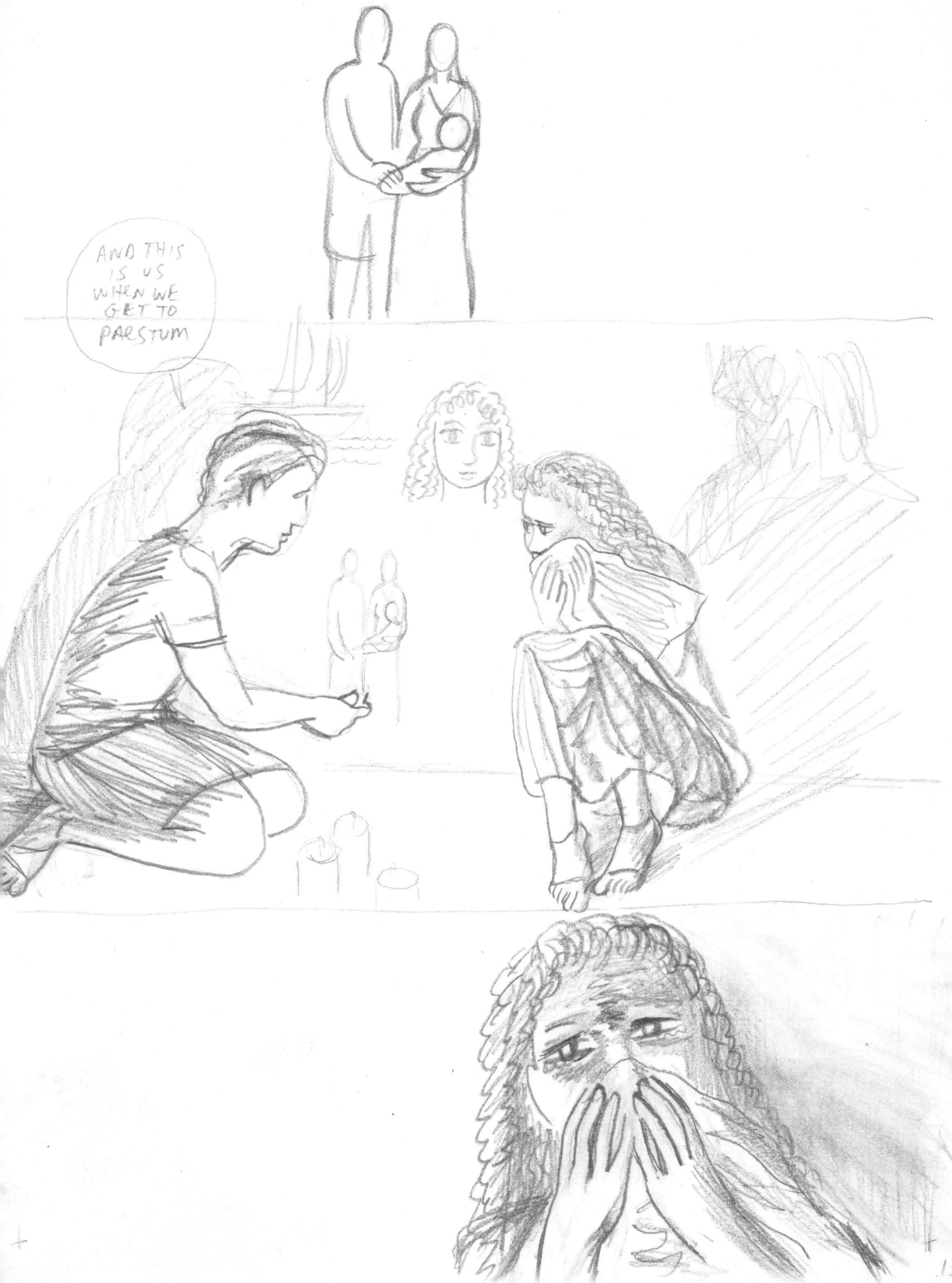
AND THIS IS US WHEN WE GET TO PAESTUM

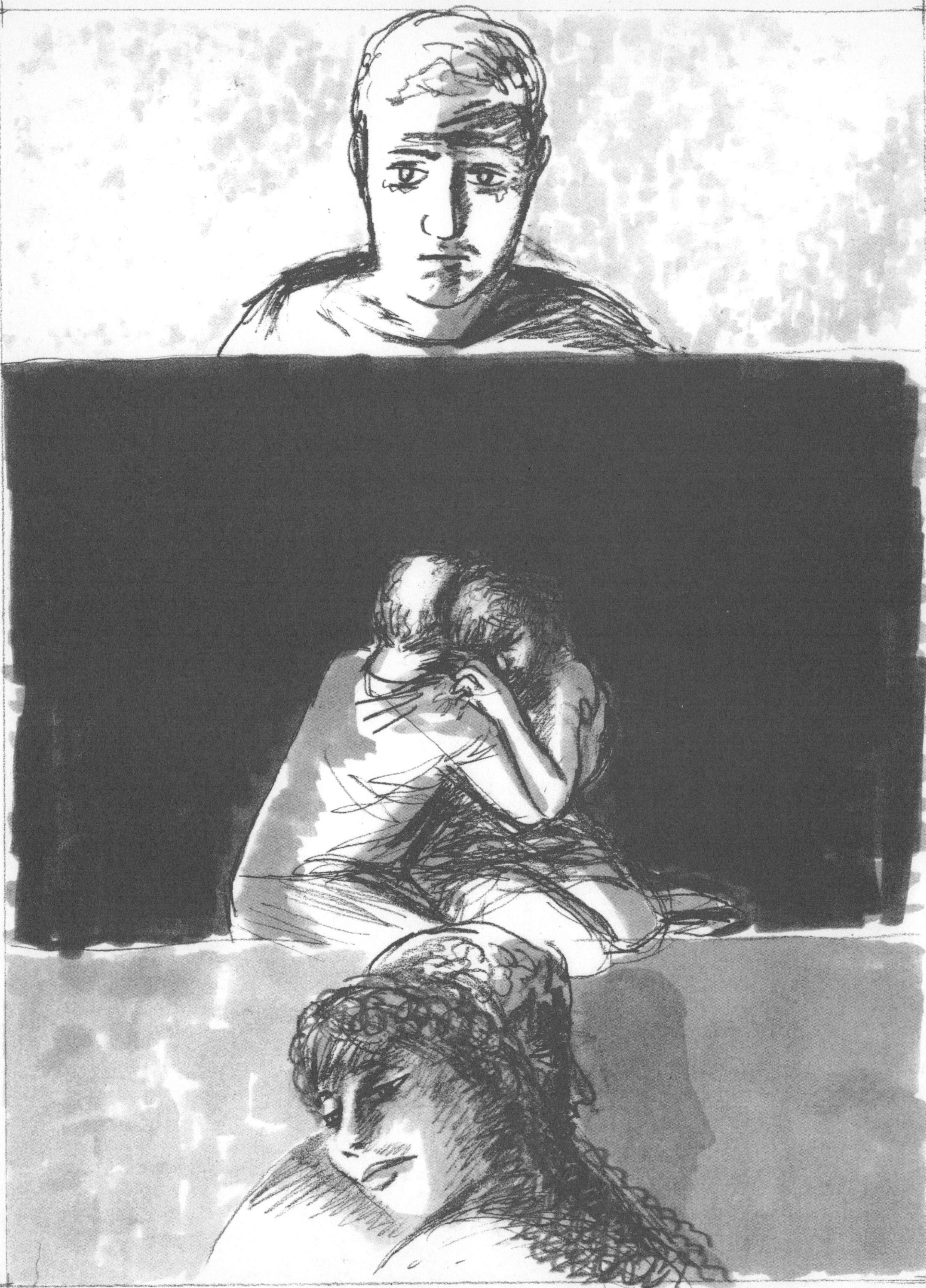

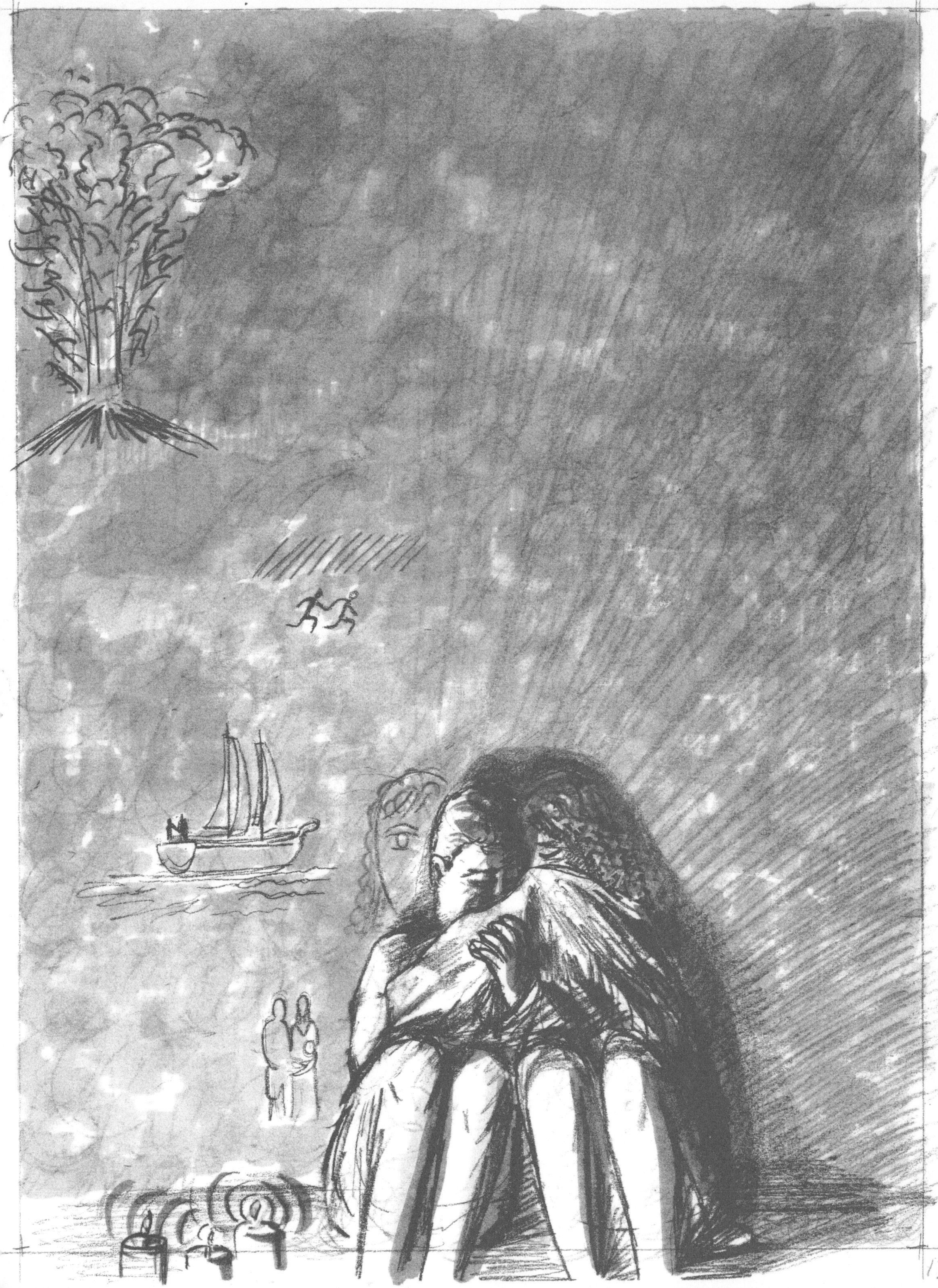

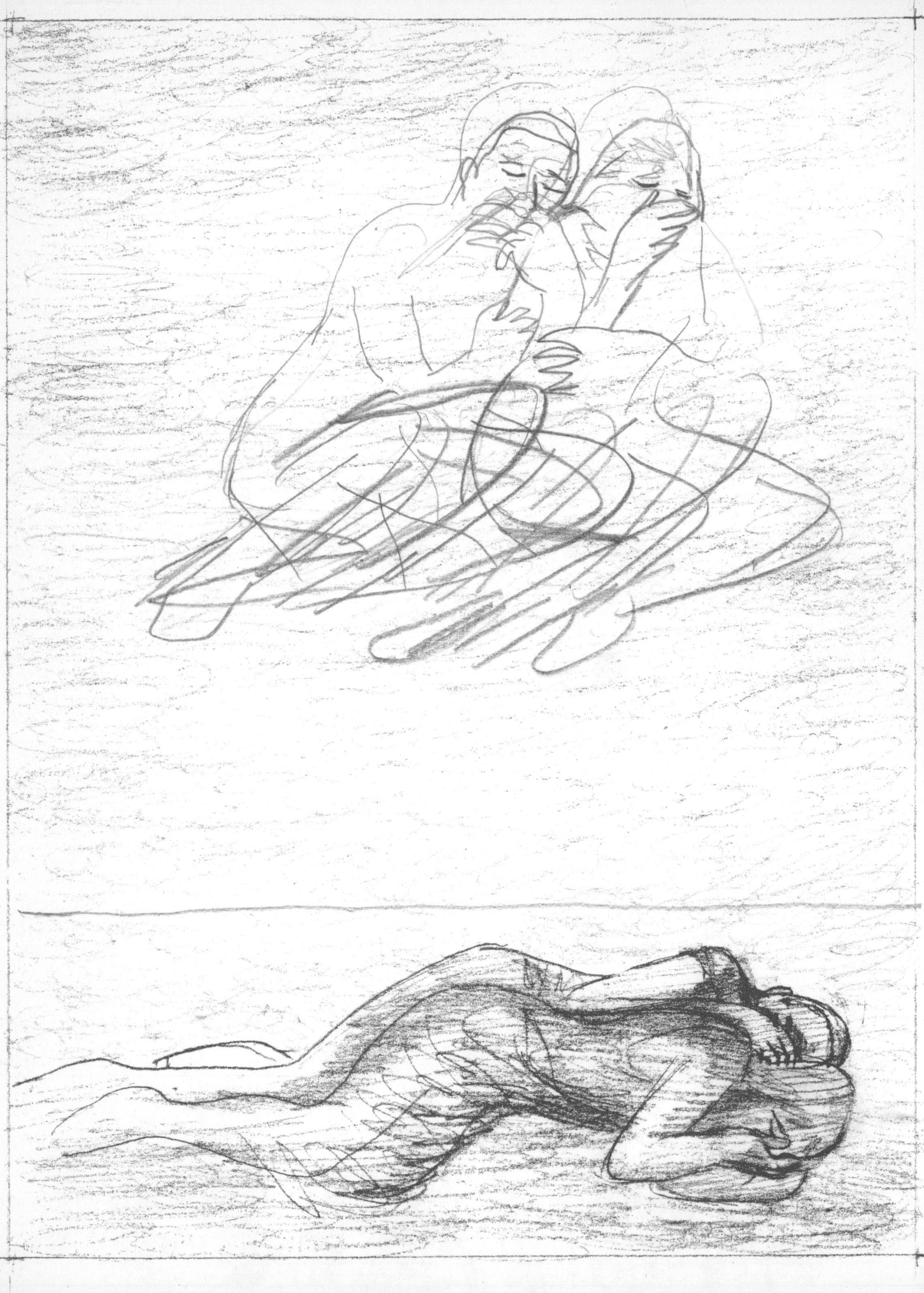

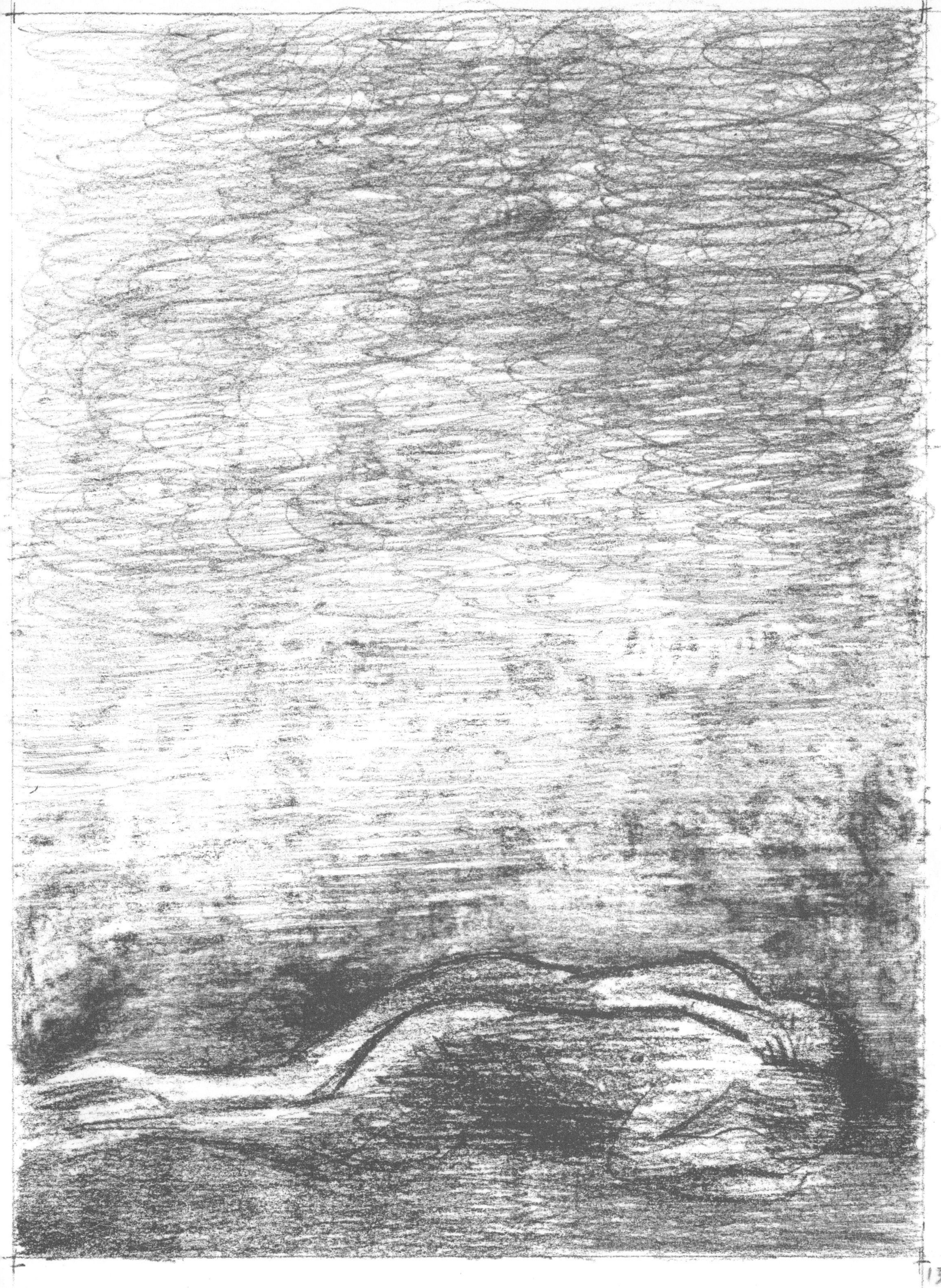

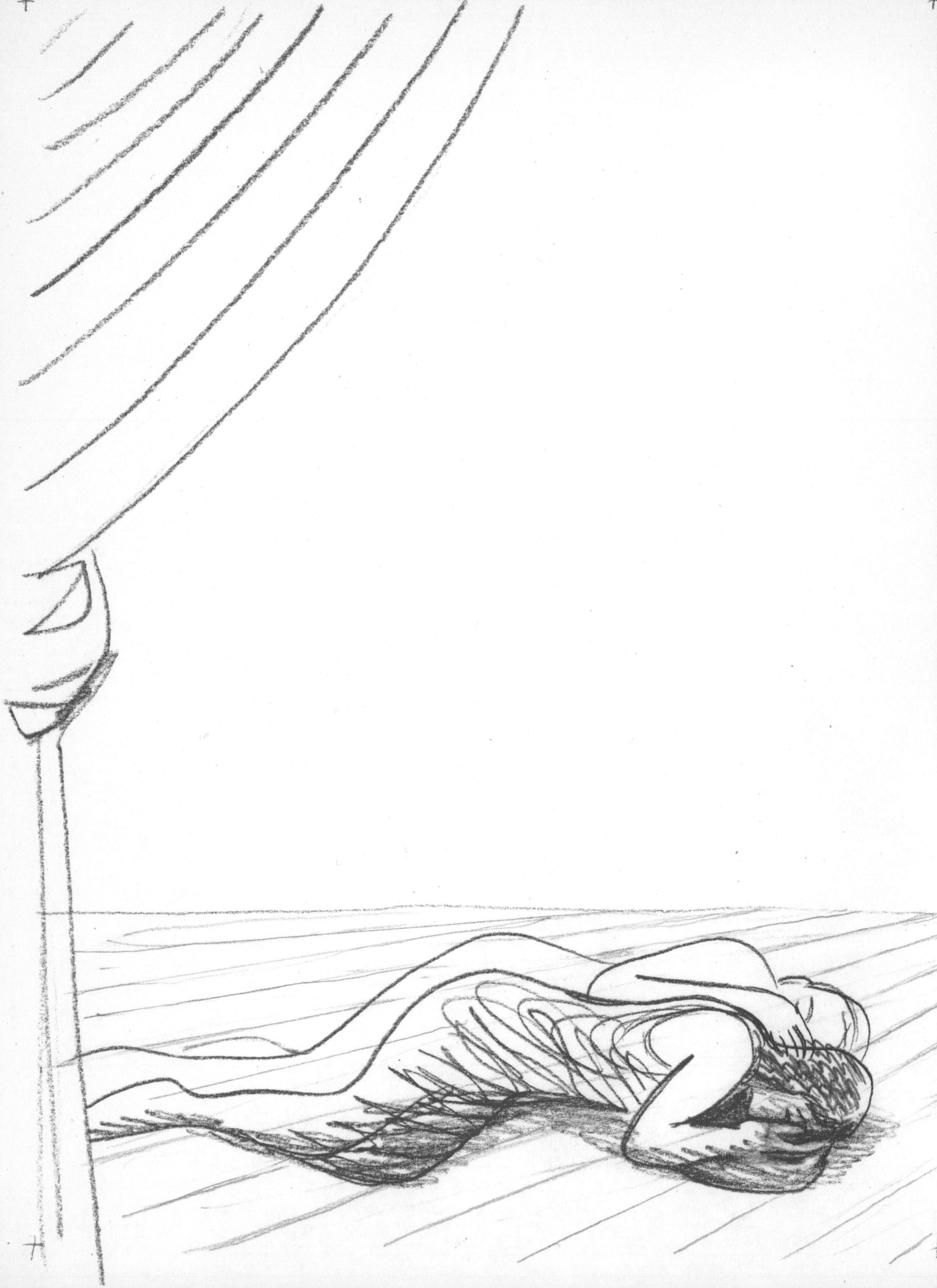

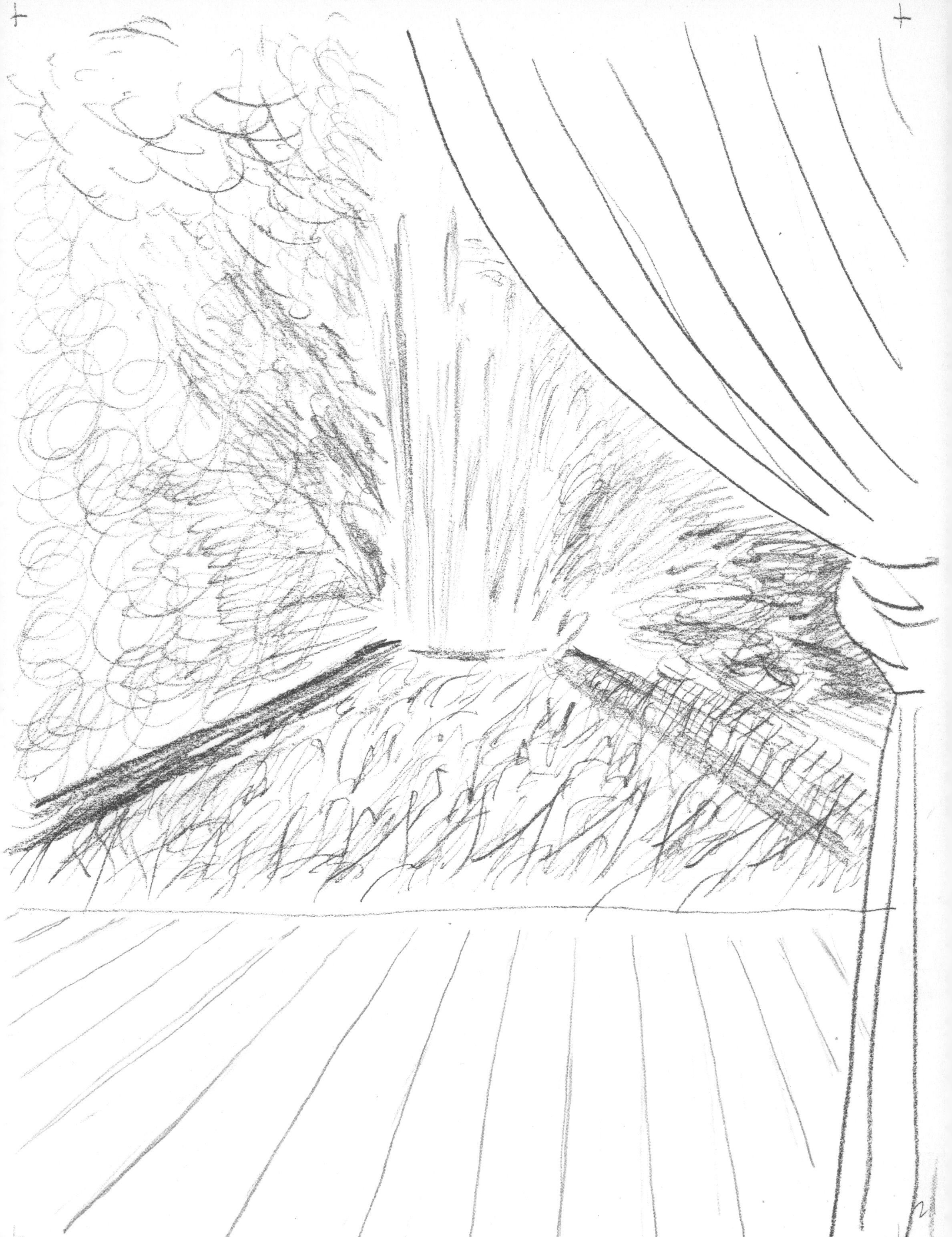

Pompeii was an ancient Roman city that was built at the base of Mount Vesuvius, a volcano near the Bay of Naples. Late in the year 79 AD, Vesuvius erupted and smothered the city under a thick covering of volcanic ash and noxious fumes. Many inhabitants tried to flee and attempts were made to assist in the evacuation by both land and sea, but most were thwarted by the relentless hail of pumice. As a result, those unable to escape were forced to try to wait out the eruption indoors. They were temporarily protected from the falling pebbles, but as the eruption continued, buildings gave way under the weight of the volcanic debris. The buildings still standing were eventually buried by the ash and the people were asphyxiated by the fumes.

At the time of the eruption, Pompeii was a harbor town of perhaps 20,000 inhabitants, that over looked the Sarno river, which was then broad and navigable. It enjoyed economic prosperity, and was considered to be a resort for the wealthy Romans of the era. This can be difficult to visualize today because the 79 AD eruption irrevocably altered the geography of the area. Prior to the eruption, the Sarno river plain was composed of a network of tributaries that served to irrigate fertile farmland dotted with *villae rusticae*. All was buried to a depth of 4-6 meters as a result of the eruption, causing the river to effectively vanish and completely wiping out an entire way of life. Pompeii was abandoned, and its name and very existence were forgotten.

Many centuries, and historical eras, passed before discoveries made at nearby Herculaneum (which was also destroyed by the 79 AD eruption) led the King of Naples to initiate the excavation of Pompeii in 1748. It was not long before it was realized that the city had been fully preserved, frozen in time by the volcanic material that had buried the area. Pompeii is now considered to be the most famous archaeological site in the Western world.

Pompeii
Frank Santoro

Publication design by FS
Production by Dash Shaw,
Jim Rugg, Family Sohn.

PictureBox
PO Box 24744
Brooklyn NY 11231
www.pictureboxinc.com

Pompeii by Frank Santoro.
Published by PictureBox.

ISBN 978-1-939799-10-4.
First Edition: September 2013.

Printed in China
Available through ARTBOOK | D.A.P.

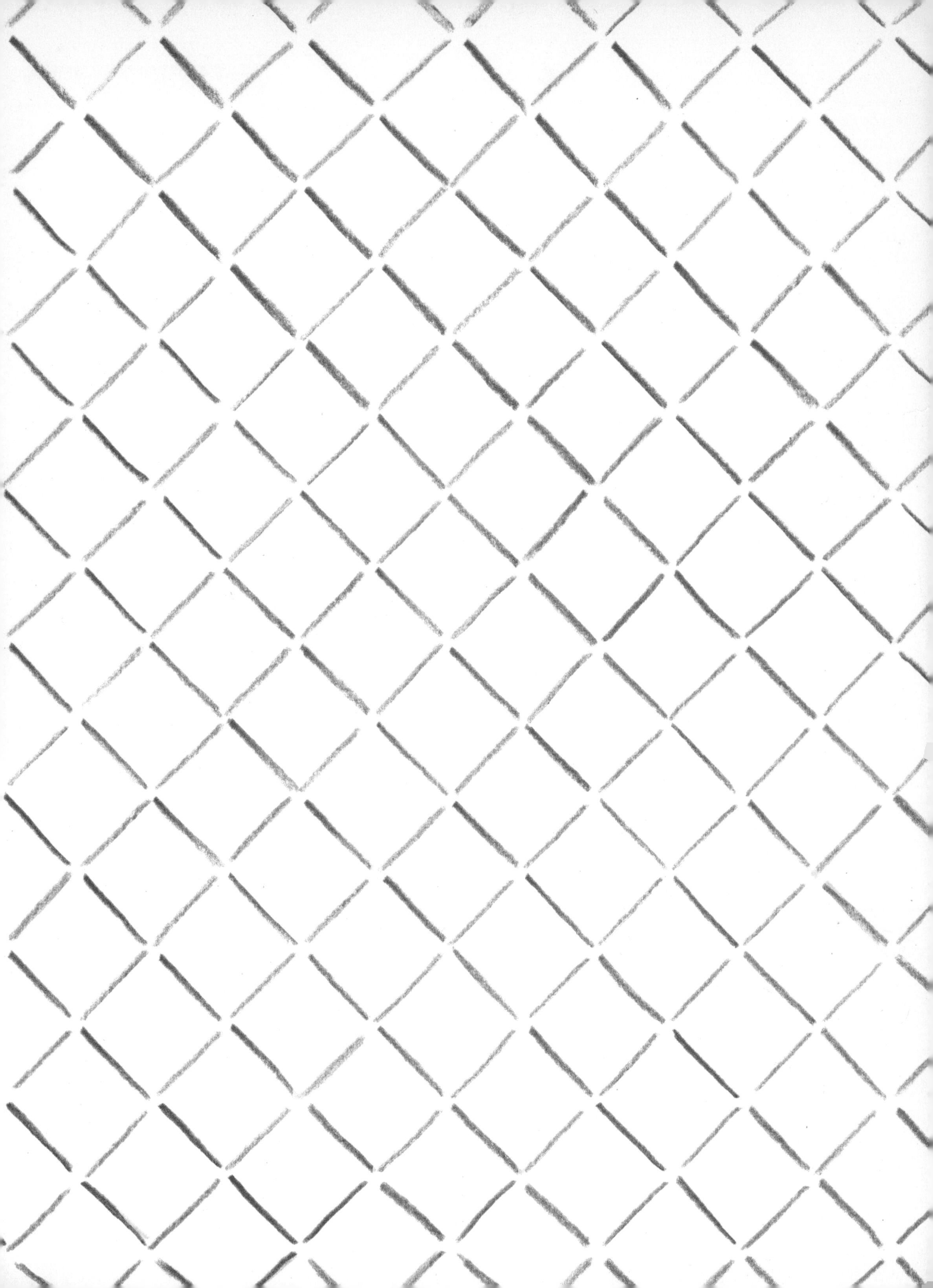

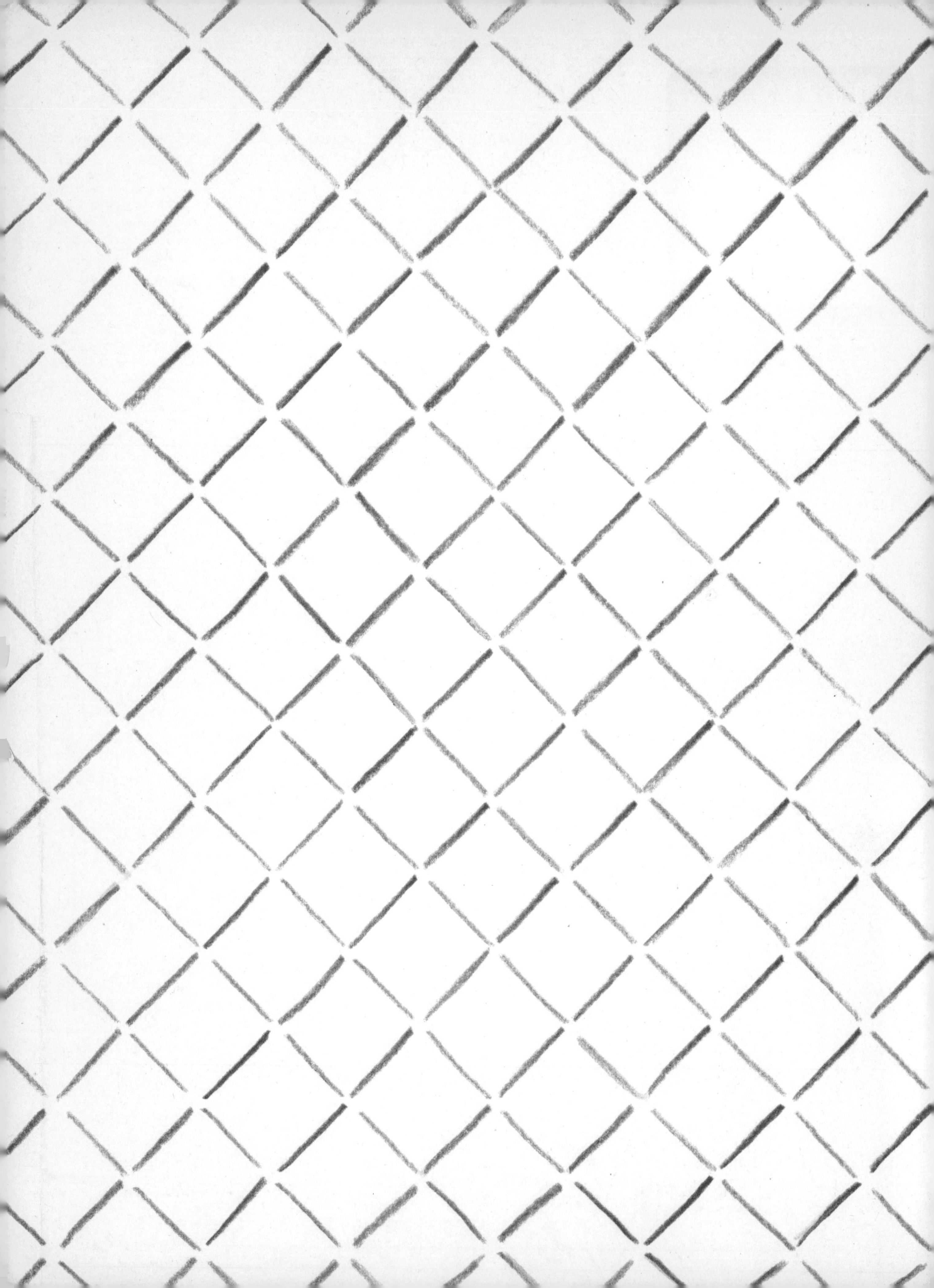